The

Garden
Journal, Planner
& Log Book

by

Joy L. Kieffer

The Garden Journal, Planner & Log Book: Repeat successes & learn from mistakes with complete personal garden records. 28 adaptable year-round forms, logs, garden plot graphs, diary pages, etc. Track weather, pests, diseases & treatments. Add drawings, seed packets & photos. Checkbox easy.

Published by Hidden Cache Media
Copyright 2015 Joy L. Kieffer, Wallingford, Pa
Artwork and cover design by Joy L. Kieffer
Author photos by HR Kelley

ISBN-13: 978-0692573983
ISBN-10: 0692573984

Available from Amazon.com, and other retail outlets.
Available in other formats and in bulk quantities. Visit www.gardenkitch.com to see other available formats, other books in the series or other garden-related items. Email contact@gardenkitch.com for bulk orders for garden clubs, fundraisers or reseller pricing.

Kudos

To you for choosing to take control of your garden! As we both know, there are enough things that can go wrong out there in the land of insects, weeds, and weather.

~

"This is the journal for everyone who desires to grow something or share the love of cultivating. Joy has put together all the ingredients to create the perfect garden in this publication because it allows the grower to be the author. Any book that has the USDA hardiness zone is going to be used by me daily in my creative growing journey because I live by that in my 18 acres and when I help others with their growing adventure. This is the perfect book to keep out on a coffee table for everyone to enjoy and be inspired to garden."

Bren Haas of Creative Living and Growing : http://www.brenhaas.com
Ranked among P. Allen Smiths's 10 Great Garden Blogs (BG Garden Blog)
http://www.pallensmith.com/articles/10-great-garden-blogs

~ Dedication ~

To all the intrepid gardeners out there who continue to be optimistic in the face of weather, pestilence and self-sabotage.

~ Acknowledgements ~

None of this would be possible without the One who designed and created the first garden, with its unlimited potential, and then turned it over to us in the greatest display of faith imaginable.

I want to thank my husband and daughters, interns and volunteers who have all put up with my delusions of grandeur as I dream of perfection in our various gardens.

A special thanks to Sarah Badaracco without whom the Lifewerks Giving Garden would not be possible (not only is she a wiz in the garden, she comes up with dishes this creative author would never be able to imagine in my wildest dreams.) The garden may never have started without John Speckhals, a friend and gardener extraordinaire who made and donated our first bed and has given invaluable advice and help along the way. Thank you both from the bottom of my heart!

And last, I want to thank all the various supporters of the Lifewerks Giving Garden. A portion of the proceeds of every Garden Journal, Planner & Log Book will go to support the Lifewerks Giving Garden.

~ HOW TO USE THIS BOOK ~

Fill out as much or as little information as you like. If you're like me, you don't always have time to do everything you have planned in a day, a week or even a year. So feel free to do the minimal amount of paperwork when the garden madness is upon you, and fill in the missing information later—with a beverage, after your shower—when you have time to relax in your easy chair.

Save those seed packets and plant markers so that you can transfer the information into your forms after your planting sessions! At the bare minimum, as soon as you plant, fill out the plant name, location and planting date on the individual plant page, the plant category page or the garden graph. Then you have an easy reference point to use when the day is done and you've already forgotten what you planted where. My memory is such that I have to take my garden journal into the garden with me when I know I'll be planting a variety of plants. It's a faulty memory that started this whole idea of making a garden journal.

You will notice a place for codes on some of the forms. Use this however you wish; make up your own codes using abbreviations, acronyms, color, symbols, etc.

A note: This is your book. Use it or abuse it as your needs dictate. Cover it with waterproof film, take it to your local printer and have the spine cut off and the pages hole-punched or put into a spiral binding. Just don't copy the book and sell it, or give copies away—that's all I ask. I wouldn't give away your services for free, so I hope you will understand that I want to make a profit to provide for my families' needs and to support great causes like the Lifewerks Giving Garden.

Several of the forms are available in booklet form singly or combined for those of you who want more room than this journal provides. Look for these on Amazon or at gardenkitch.com.

It would be terrific if you would leave a review on Amazon if you find that you like your Garden Journal, Planner & Log Book, and it would be great if you buy more for friends!

Contents

Zone Map ....

Supplier Contact List ....

Purchase Record ....

Weather Guidelines ....

Weather Log ....

Bloom & Harvest Times ....

Garden Layouts ....

Individual Plant Info ....

Annual Logs ....

Biennial Logs ....

Perennial Logs ....

Flower Logs ....

Bulb, Rhizome & Tuber Log ....

Fruit Logs ....

Vegetable Logs ....

Herb Log ....

Vine Log ....

Shrub Logs ....

Tree Log ....

Hardscaping Log ....

Wildlife Sightings ....

Garden Diary ....

One-Year Plan ....

Pruning Guidelines ....

Prune, Trim & Tidy Schedule ....

Plant Propagation ....

Cultivation & Propagation Logs ....

Pest & Disease Prevention ....

Pest & Disease Treatment Logs ....

Soil Testing & Amendments ....

Formulas & Recipes ....

Conversion Charts &Tables ....

(Page numbers intentionally left blank for those who want to cut off the spine of the book and place the pages in a binder in the order of their choice.)

U. S. Plant Zone Map

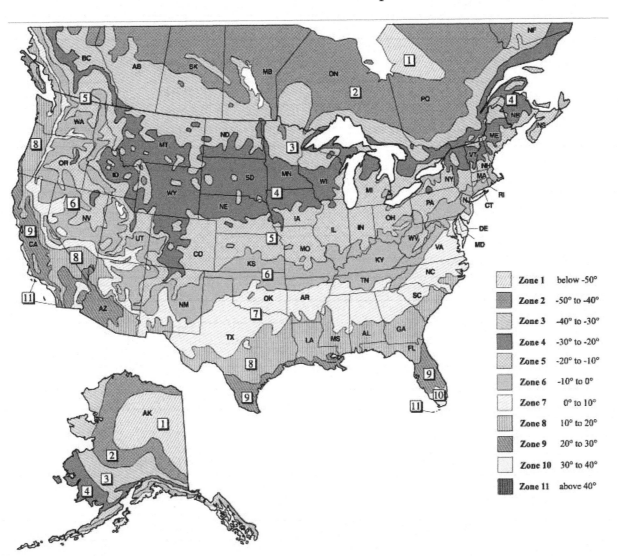

	Zone 1	below -50°
	Zone 2	-50° to -40°
	Zone 3	-40° to -30°
	Zone 4	-30° to -20°
	Zone 5	-20° to -10°
	Zone 6	-10° to 0°
	Zone 7	0° to 10°
	Zone 8	10° to 20°
	Zone 9	20° to 30°
	Zone 10	30° to 40°
	Zone 11	above 40°

Supplier Contact List

Page:

Company Name: _____
Website: _____
E-mail: _____
Contact Name: _____
Office Phone: _____
Cell Phone: _____

Street: _____
City: _____
State: _____ Zip: _____
Products: _____

Notes: _____
_____
_____
_____
_____

Company Name: _____
Website: _____
E-mail: _____
Contact Name: _____
Office Phone: _____
Cell Phone: _____

Street: _____
City: _____
State: _____ Zip: _____
Products: _____

Notes: _____
_____
_____
_____
_____

Company Name: _____
Website: _____
E-mail: _____
Contact Name: _____
Office Phone: _____
Cell Phone: _____

Street: _____
City: _____
State: _____ Zip: _____
Products: _____

Notes: _____
_____
_____
_____
_____

Company Name: _____
Website: _____
E-mail: _____
Contact Name: _____
Office Phone: _____
Cell Phone: _____

Street: _____
City: _____
State: _____ Zip: _____
Products: _____

Notes: _____
_____
_____
_____
_____

Company Name: _____
Website: _____
E-mail: _____
Contact Name: _____
Office Phone: _____
Cell Phone: _____

Street: _____
City: _____
State: _____ Zip: _____
Products: _____

Notes: _____
_____
_____
_____
_____

Supplier Contact List

Page: _____

Company Name: _____ **Street:** _____ **Notes:** _____
Website: _____ **City:** _____ _____
E-mail: _____ **State:** _____ **Zip:** _____ _____
Contact Name: _____ **Products:** _____ _____
Office Phone: _____ _____ _____
Cell Phone: _____

Company Name: _____ **Street:** _____ **Notes:** _____
Website: _____ **City:** _____ _____
E-mail: _____ **State:** _____ **Zip:** _____ _____
Contact Name: _____ **Products:** _____ _____
Office Phone: _____ _____ _____
Cell Phone: _____

Company Name: _____ **Street:** _____ **Notes:** _____
Website: _____ **City:** _____ _____
E-mail: _____ **State:** _____ **Zip:** _____ _____
Contact Name: _____ **Products:** _____ _____
Office Phone: _____ _____ _____
Cell Phone: _____

Company Name: _____ **Street:** _____ **Notes:** _____
Website: _____ **City:** _____ _____
E-mail: _____ **State:** _____ **Zip:** _____ _____
Contact Name: _____ **Products:** _____ _____
Office Phone: _____ _____ _____
Cell Phone: _____

Company Name: _____ **Street:** _____ **Notes:** _____
Website: _____ **City:** _____ _____
E-mail: _____ **State:** _____ **Zip:** _____ _____
Contact Name: _____ **Products:** _____ _____
Office Phone: _____ _____ _____
Cell Phone: _____

Supplier Contact List

Page: _____

Company Name : _____
Website : _____
E-mail : _____
Contact Name : _____
Office Phone : _____
Cell Phone : _____

Street : _____
City : _____
State : _____ Zip : _____
Products : _____

Notes : _____
_____
_____
_____
_____

Company Name : _____
Website : _____
E-mail : _____
Contact Name : _____
Office Phone : _____
Cell Phone : _____

Street : _____
City : _____
State : _____ Zip : _____
Products : _____

Notes : _____
_____
_____
_____
_____

Company Name : _____
Website : _____
E-mail : _____
Contact Name : _____
Office Phone : _____
Cell Phone : _____

Street : _____
City : _____
State : _____ Zip : _____
Products : _____

Notes : _____
_____
_____
_____
_____

Company Name : _____
Website : _____
E-mail : _____
Contact Name : _____
Office Phone : _____
Cell Phone : _____

Street : _____
City : _____
State : _____ Zip : _____
Products : _____

Notes : _____
_____
_____
_____
_____

Company Name : _____
Website : _____
E-mail : _____
Contact Name : _____
Office Phone : _____
Cell Phone : _____

Street : _____
City : _____
State : _____ Zip : _____
Products : _____

Notes : _____
_____
_____
_____
_____

Supplier Contact List

Company Name : _____ Street : _____ Notes : _____

Website : _____ City : _____ _____

E-mail : _____ State : _____ Zip : _____ _____

Contact Name : _____ Products : _____ _____

Office Phone : _____ _____ _____

Cell Phone : _____

Company Name : _____ Street : _____ Notes : _____

Website : _____ City : _____ _____

E-mail : _____ State : _____ Zip : _____ _____

Contact Name : _____ Products : _____ _____

Office Phone : _____ _____ _____

Cell Phone : _____

Company Name : _____ Street : _____ Notes : _____

Website : _____ City : _____ _____

E-mail : _____ State : _____ Zip : _____ _____

Contact Name : _____ Products : _____ _____

Office Phone : _____ _____ _____

Cell Phone : _____

Company Name : _____ Street : _____ Notes : _____

Website : _____ City : _____ _____

E-mail : _____ State : _____ Zip : _____ _____

Contact Name : _____ Products : _____ _____

Office Phone : _____ _____ _____

Cell Phone : _____

Company Name : _____ Street : _____ Notes : _____

Website : _____ City : _____ _____

E-mail : _____ State : _____ Zip : _____ _____

Contact Name : _____ Products : _____ _____

Office Phone : _____ _____ _____

Cell Phone : _____

Purchase Record   Page

Company Name: _____	Contact Name: _____	Products: _____	Notes: _____
Website: _____	Office Phone: _____	_____	_____
Email: _____	Cell Phone: _____	_____	_____
Warranty Period: _____		_____	_____

Company Name: _____	Contact Name: _____	Products: _____	Notes: _____
Website: _____	Office Phone: _____	_____	_____
Email: _____	Cell Phone: _____	_____	_____
Warranty Period: _____		_____	_____

Company Name: _____	Contact Name: _____	Products: _____	Notes: _____
Website: _____	Office Phone: _____	_____	_____
Email: _____	Cell Phone: _____	_____	_____
Warranty Period: _____		_____	_____

Company Name: _____	Contact Name: _____	Products: _____	Notes: _____
Website: _____	Office Phone: _____	_____	_____
Email: _____	Cell Phone: _____	_____	_____
Warranty Period: _____		_____	_____

Company Name: _____	Contact Name: _____	Products: _____	Notes: _____
Website: _____	Office Phone: _____	_____	_____
Email: _____	Cell Phone: _____	_____	_____
Warranty Period: _____		_____	_____

Company Name: _____	Contact Name: _____	Products: _____	Notes: _____
Website: _____	Office Phone: _____	_____	_____
Email: _____	Cell Phone: _____	_____	_____
Warranty Period: _____		_____	_____

Company Name: _____	Contact Name: _____	Products: _____	Notes: _____
Website: _____	Office Phone: _____	_____	_____
Email: _____	Cell Phone: _____	_____	_____
Warranty Period: _____		_____	_____

Purchase Record

Page

Company Name: _____ Contact Name: _____ Products: _____ Notes: _____
Website: _____ Office Phone: _____ _____ _____
Email: _____ Cell Phone: _____ _____ _____
Warranty Period: _____ _____ _____ _____

Company Name: _____ Contact Name: _____ Products: _____ Notes: _____
Website: _____ Office Phone: _____ _____ _____
Email: _____ Cell Phone: _____ _____ _____
Warranty Period: _____ _____ _____ _____

Company Name: _____ Contact Name: _____ Products: _____ Notes: _____
Website: _____ Office Phone: _____ _____ _____
Email: _____ Cell Phone: _____ _____ _____
Warranty Period: _____ _____ _____ _____

Company Name: _____ Contact Name: _____ Products: _____ Notes: _____
Website: _____ Office Phone: _____ _____ _____
Email: _____ Cell Phone: _____ _____ _____
Warranty Period: _____ _____ _____ _____

Company Name: _____ Contact Name: _____ Products: _____ Notes: _____
Website: _____ Office Phone: _____ _____ _____
Email: _____ Cell Phone: _____ _____ _____
Warranty Period: _____ _____ _____ _____

Company Name: _____ Contact Name: _____ Products: _____ Notes: _____
Website: _____ Office Phone: _____ _____ _____
Email: _____ Cell Phone: _____ _____ _____
Warranty Period: _____ _____ _____ _____

Company Name: _____ Contact Name: _____ Products: _____ Notes: _____
Website: _____ Office Phone: _____ _____ _____
Email: _____ Cell Phone: _____ _____ _____
Warranty Period: _____ _____ _____ _____

Purchase Record

Page ____

Company Name: _____   Contact Name: _____   Products: _____   Notes: _____
Website: _____   Office Phone: _____   _____   _____
Email: _____   Cell Phone: _____   _____   _____
Warranty Period: _____   _____   _____

Company Name: _____   Contact Name: _____   Products: _____   Notes: _____
Website: _____   Office Phone: _____   _____   _____
Email: _____   Cell Phone: _____   _____   _____
Warranty Period: _____   _____   _____

Company Name: _____   Contact Name: _____   Products: _____   Notes: _____
Website: _____   Office Phone: _____   _____   _____
Email: _____   Cell Phone: _____   _____   _____
Warranty Period: _____   _____   _____

Company Name: _____   Contact Name: _____   Products: _____   Notes: _____
Website: _____   Office Phone: _____   _____   _____
Email: _____   Cell Phone: _____   _____   _____
Warranty Period: _____   _____   _____

Company Name: _____   Contact Name: _____   Products: _____   Notes: _____
Website: _____   Office Phone: _____   _____   _____
Email: _____   Cell Phone: _____   _____   _____
Warranty Period: _____   _____   _____

Company Name: _____   Contact Name: _____   Products: _____   Notes: _____
Website: _____   Office Phone: _____   _____   _____
Email: _____   Cell Phone: _____   _____   _____
Warranty Period: _____   _____   _____

Company Name: _____   Contact Name: _____   Products: _____   Notes: _____
Website: _____   Office Phone: _____   _____   _____
Email: _____   Cell Phone: _____   _____   _____
Warranty Period: _____   _____   _____

Purchase Record

Company Name: _____   Contact Name: _____   Products: _____   Notes: _____
Website: _____   Office Phone: _____   _____   _____
Email: _____   Cell Phone: _____   _____   _____
Warranty Period: _____   _____   _____

Company Name: _____   Contact Name: _____   Products: _____   Notes: _____
Website: _____   Office Phone: _____   _____   _____
Email: _____   Cell Phone: _____   _____   _____
Warranty Period: _____   _____   _____

Company Name: _____   Contact Name: _____   Products: _____   Notes: _____
Website: _____   Office Phone: _____   _____   _____
Email: _____   Cell Phone: _____   _____   _____
Warranty Period: _____   _____   _____

Company Name: _____   Contact Name: _____   Products: _____   Notes: _____
Website: _____   Office Phone: _____   _____   _____
Email: _____   Cell Phone: _____   _____   _____
Warranty Period: _____   _____   _____

Company Name: _____   Contact Name: _____   Products: _____   Notes: _____
Website: _____   Office Phone: _____   _____   _____
Email: _____   Cell Phone: _____   _____   _____
Warranty Period: _____   _____   _____

Company Name: _____   Contact Name: _____   Products: _____   Notes: _____
Website: _____   Office Phone: _____   _____   _____
Email: _____   Cell Phone: _____   _____   _____
Warranty Period: _____   _____   _____

Company Name: _____   Contact Name: _____   Products: _____   Notes: _____
Website: _____   Office Phone: _____   _____   _____
Email: _____   Cell Phone: _____   _____   _____
Warranty Period: _____   _____   _____

Purchase Record

Company Name: _____
Website: _____
Email: _____
Warranty Period: _____

Contact Name: _____
Office Phone: _____
Cell Phone: _____
_____

Products: _____
_____
_____
_____

Notes: _____
_____
_____
_____

Company Name: _____
Website: _____
Email: _____
Warranty Period: _____

Contact Name: _____
Office Phone: _____
Cell Phone: _____
_____

Products: _____
_____
_____
_____

Notes: _____
_____
_____
_____

Company Name: _____
Website: _____
Email: _____
Warranty Period: _____

Contact Name: _____
Office Phone: _____
Cell Phone: _____
_____

Products: _____
_____
_____
_____

Notes: _____
_____
_____
_____

Company Name: _____
Website: _____
Email: _____
Warranty Period: _____

Contact Name: _____
Office Phone: _____
Cell Phone: _____
_____

Products: _____
_____
_____
_____

Notes: _____
_____
_____
_____

Company Name: _____
Website: _____
Email: _____
Warranty Period: _____

Contact Name: _____
Office Phone: _____
Cell Phone: _____
_____

Products: _____
_____
_____
_____

Notes: _____
_____
_____
_____

Company Name: _____
Website: _____
Email: _____
Warranty Period: _____

Contact Name: _____
Office Phone: _____
Cell Phone: _____
_____

Products: _____
_____
_____
_____

Notes: _____
_____
_____
_____

Company Name: _____
Website: _____
Email: _____
Warranty Period: _____

Contact Name: _____
Office Phone: _____
Cell Phone: _____
_____

Products: _____
_____
_____
_____

Notes: _____
_____
_____
_____

Purchase Record

Page

Company Name: _____ Contact Name: _____ Products: _____ Notes: _____
Website: _____ Office Phone: _____ _____ _____
Email: _____ Cell Phone: _____ _____ _____
Warranty Period: _____ _____ _____ _____

Company Name: _____ Contact Name: _____ Products: _____ Notes: _____
Website: _____ Office Phone: _____ _____ _____
Email: _____ Cell Phone: _____ _____ _____
Warranty Period: _____ _____ _____ _____

Company Name: _____ Contact Name: _____ Products: _____ Notes: _____
Website: _____ Office Phone: _____ _____ _____
Email: _____ Cell Phone: _____ _____ _____
Warranty Period: _____ _____ _____ _____

Company Name: _____ Contact Name: _____ Products: _____ Notes: _____
Website: _____ Office Phone: _____ _____ _____
Email: _____ Cell Phone: _____ _____ _____
Warranty Period: _____ _____ _____ _____

Company Name: _____ Contact Name: _____ Products: _____ Notes: _____
Website: _____ Office Phone: _____ _____ _____
Email: _____ Cell Phone: _____ _____ _____
Warranty Period: _____ _____ _____ _____

Company Name: _____ Contact Name: _____ Products: _____ Notes: _____
Website: _____ Office Phone: _____ _____ _____
Email: _____ Cell Phone: _____ _____ _____
Warranty Period: _____ _____ _____ _____

Company Name: _____ Contact Name: _____ Products: _____ Notes: _____
Website: _____ Office Phone: _____ _____ _____
Email: _____ Cell Phone: _____ _____ _____
Warranty Period: _____ _____ _____ _____

~ Weather Guidelines ~

  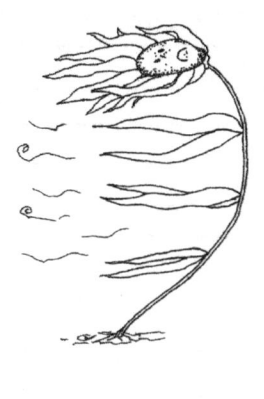  

Water Concerns ~

Balance is the key in both the amount of water and the timing for each plant. Most plants absorb almost all their water through their roots. The more roots they have, the better they absorb moisture. A plant grown in proper moisture conditions will develop a root system with a healthy amount of sponge-like root hairs.

For a good root system, the roots need to be able to push out into the soil. This means they need a loose, moist soil with sufficient organic matter. On the converse, overwatering can rot or discourage the roots to push farther out into the soil to seek water. When moisture conditions alternate drastically between wet and dry, the root hairs get stressed and damaged. Covering the soil surface with a layer of mulch reduces water loss, and helps maintain a consistent moisture level in the soil to keep delicate root hairs healthy.

Sun and Wind Concerns ~

Plants lose water through their leaves. In a process called transpiration, 98% of the water absorbed by a plant goes out through microscopic pores (stomates) on the plant's leaves. Transpiration moves the nutrients into the plant cells and also cools the plant during hot weather. Droopy leaves on a hot day are not always cause for concern. Some plants are able to close their stomata and reduce transpiration to protect themselves from moisture loss. When the air temperature begins to cool as the sun goes down, these plants will perk up.

For sun protection, make use of the trees in your yard, put up a lattice, landscape fabric or screen roof over plants, or plant so that tall plants provide shade for shorter plants.

For wind protection use manmade windbreaks such as picket fences and garden fabric, or natural wind breaks such as shrubs, trees and larger, more sturdy plants.

Freezing and Frost Concerns ~

In the north, and occasionally in the south, damage can be significant from extreme winter conditions.

For frost protection, use natural or man-made covers to protect plants that aren't ready or able to withstand sudden or early cold temperatures.

For freezing protection, and to prevent heaving of plants, use of covers is recommended as well as heavy mulching over properly prepared soil to provide good drainage balanced with moisture retention. This is often needed for a fragile or first year planting.

For ice and heavy snow it may be advisable to brace delicate shrubs and young trees with poles stuck into the ground with rope intertwined between the poles and the branches, and perhaps burlap over it all. Extremely fragile trees like Birch may be supported over winter with guy wires with pieces of hose covering the wires where they wrap around the trunk.

Weather Log

Code	Date	Temperature	Humidity	Dew Point	Wind Speed	Wind Direction	Barometric Pressure	Rain Fall	Frost	Snow	General Observations

Weather Log

Code	Date	Temperature	Humidity	Dew Point	Wind Speed	Wind Direction	Barometric Pressure	Rain Fall	Frost	Snow	General Observations

Weather Log

Code	Date	Temperature	Humidity	Dew Point	Wind Speed	Wind Direction	Barometric Pressure	Rain Fall	Frost	Snow	General Observations

Page:

Weather Log

Weather Log

Code	Date	Temperature	Humidity	Dew Point	Wind Speed	Wind Direction	Barometric Pressure	Rain Fall	Frost	Snow	General Observations

Page:

Weather Log

Weather Log

Code	Date	Temperature	Humidity	Dew Point	Wind Speed	Wind Direction	Barometric Pressure	Rain Fall	Frost	Snow	General Observations

Page:

Weather Log

Code	Date	Temperature	Humidity	Dew Point	Wind Speed	Wind Direction	Barometric Pressure	Rain Fall	Frost	Snow	General Observations

Page:

Weather Log

Weather Log

Code	Date	Temperature	Humidity	Dew Point	Wind Speed	Wind Direction	Barometric Pressure	Rain Fall	Frost	Snow	General Observations

Weather Log

Page:

Code	Date	Temperature	Humidity	Dew Point	Wind Speed	Wind Direction	Barometric Pressure	Rain Fall	Frost	Snow	General Observations

Weather Log

Code	Date	Temperature	Humidity	Dew Point	Wind Speed	Wind Direction	Barometric Pressure	Rain Fall	Frost	Snow	General Observations

Weather Log

Code	Date	Temperature	Humidity	Dew Point	Wind Speed	Wind Direction	Barometric Pressure	Rain Fall	Frost	Snow	General Observations

Weather Log

Code	Date	Temperature	Humidity	Dew Point	Wind Speed	Wind Direction	Barometric Pressure	Rain Fall	Frost	Snow	General Observations

Weather Log

Code	Date	Temperature	Humidity	Dew Point	Wind Speed	Wind Direction	Barometric Pressure	Rain Fall	Frost	Snow	General Observations

Weather Log

Code	Date	Temperature	Humidity	Dew Point	Wind Speed	Wind Direction	Barometric Pressure	Rain Fall	Frost	Snow	General Observations

Weather Log

Code	Date	Temperature	Humidity	Dew Point	Wind Speed	Wind Direction	Barometric Pressure	Rain Fall	Frost	Snow	General Observations

Weather Log

Code	Date	Temperature	Humidity	Dew Point	Wind Speed	Wind Direction	Barometric Pressure	Rain Fall	Frost	Snow	General Observations

Weather Log

Code	Date	Temperature	Humidity	Dew Point	Wind Speed	Wind Direction	Barometric Pressure	Rain Fall	Frost	Snow	General Observations

Code	Date	Temperature	Humidity	Dew Point	Wind Speed	Wind Direction	Barometric Pressure	Rain Fall	Frost	Snow	General Observations

Weather Log

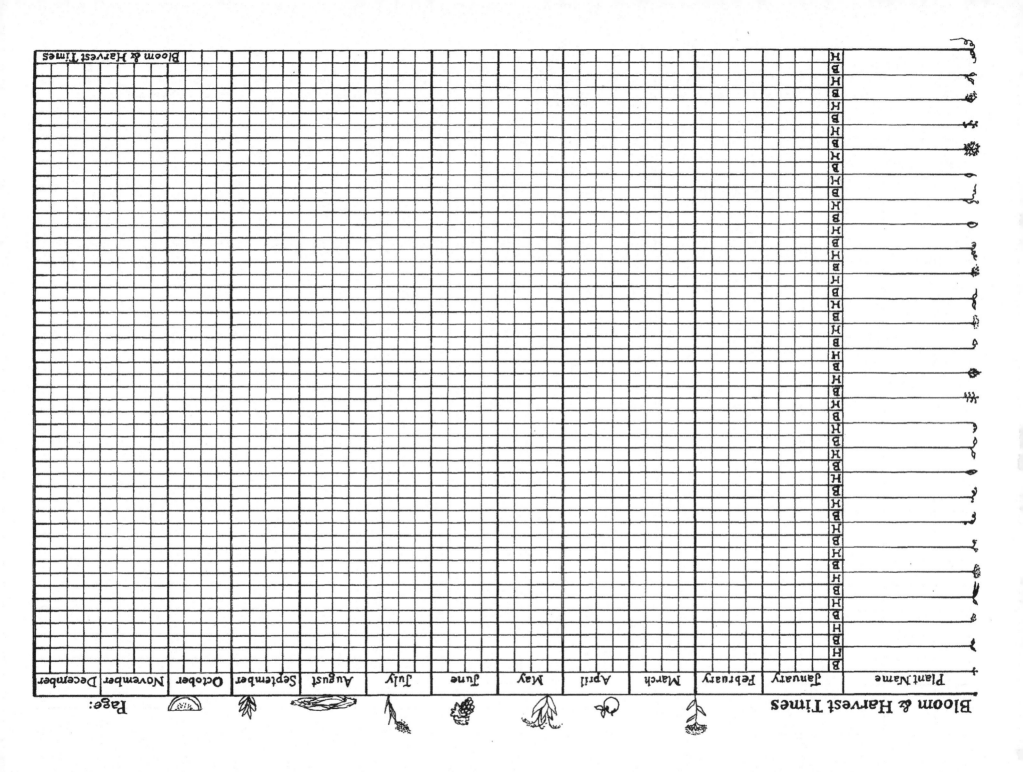

Bloom & Harvest Times

Plant Name	January	February	March	April	May	June	July	August	September	October	November	December

Page:

Bloom & Harvest Times

Page:

Plant Name		January	February	March	April	May	June	July	August	September	October	November	December
	B												
	H												
	B												
	H												
	B												
	H												
	B												
	H												
	B												
	H												
	B												
	H												
	B												
	H												
	B												
	H												
	B												
	H												
	B												
	H												
	B												
	H												
	B												
	H												
	B												
	H												
	B												
	H												
	B												
	H												

Bloom & Harvest Times

Bloom & Harvest Times

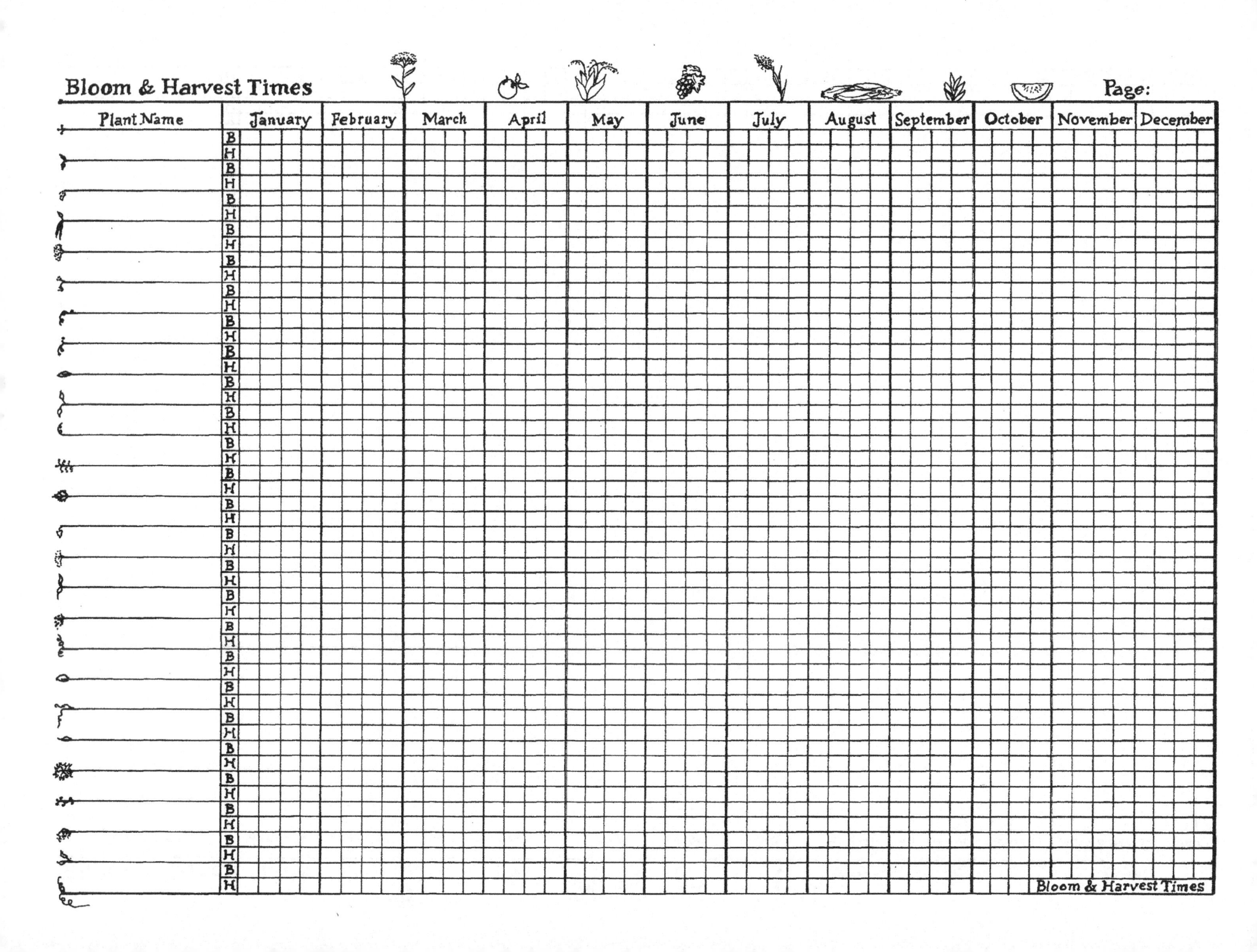

Page:

Plant Name		January	February	March	April	May	June	July	August	September	October	November	December
	B												
	H												
	B												
	H												
	B												
	H												
	B												
	H												
	B												
	H												
	B												
	H												
	B												
	H												
	B												
	H												
	B												
	H												
	B												
	H												
	B												
	H												
	B												
	H												
	B												
	H												
	B												
	H												
	B												
	H												
	B												
	H												
	B												
	H												
	B												
	H												
	B												
	H												

Bloom & Harvest Times

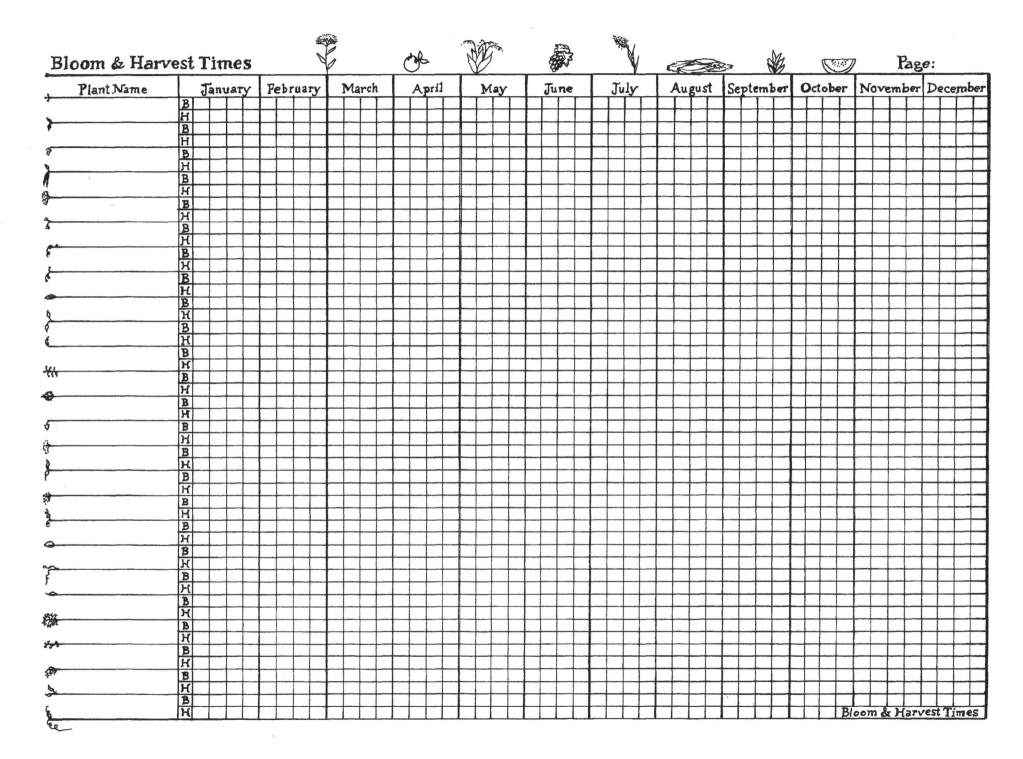

Bloom & Harvest Times

Page:

Plant Name		January	February	March	April	May	June	July	August	September	October	November	December
	B												
	H												
	B												
	H												
	B												
	H												
	B												
	H												
	B												
	H												
	B												
	H												
	B												
	H												
	B												
	H												
	B												
	H												
	B												
	H												
	B												
	H												
	B												
	H												
	B												
	H												
	B												
	H												
	B												
	H												
	B												
	H												
	B												
	H												
	B												
	H												

Bloom & Harvest Times

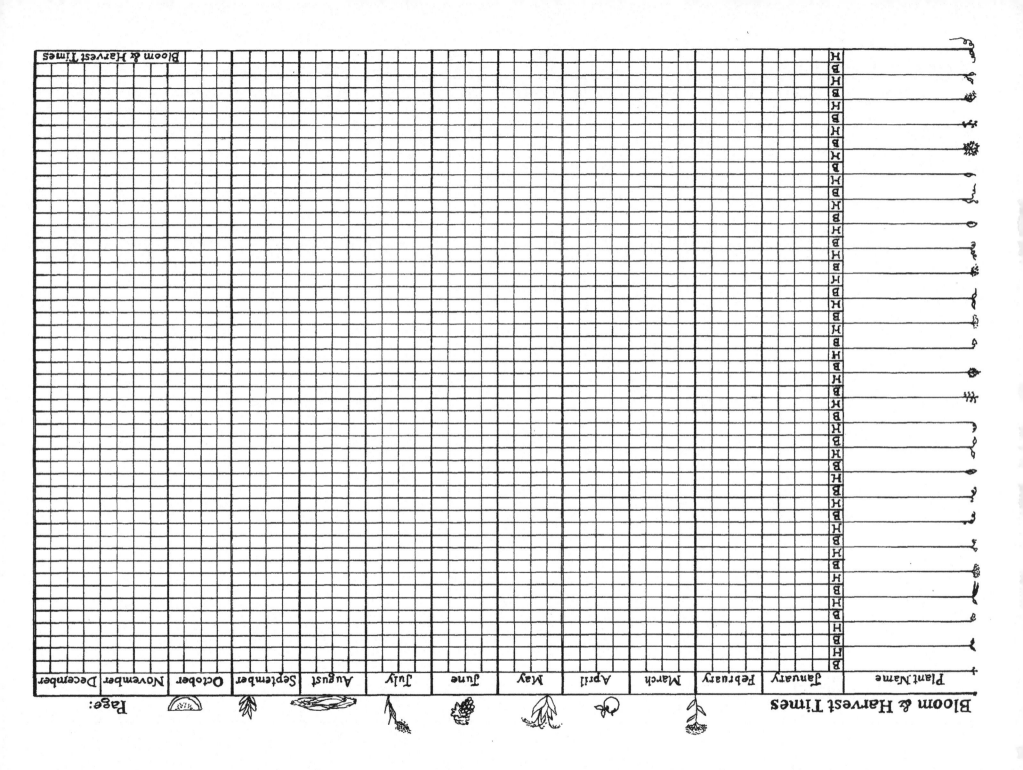

Bloom & Harvest Times

Plant Name	January	February	March	April	May	June	July	August	September	October	November	December	

Page:

Bloom & Harvest Times

Bloom & Harvest Times

Page:

Plant Name		January	February	March	April	May	June	July	August	September	October	November	December
	B												
	H												
	B												
	H												
	B												
	H												
	B												
	H												
	B												
	H												
	B												
	H												
	B												
	H												
	B												
	H												
	B												
	H												
	B												
	H												
	B												
	H												
	B												
	H												
	B												
	H												
	B												
	H												
	B												
	H												
	B												
	H												
	B												
	H												
	B												
	H												
	B												
	H												
	B												
	H												

Bloom & Harvest Times

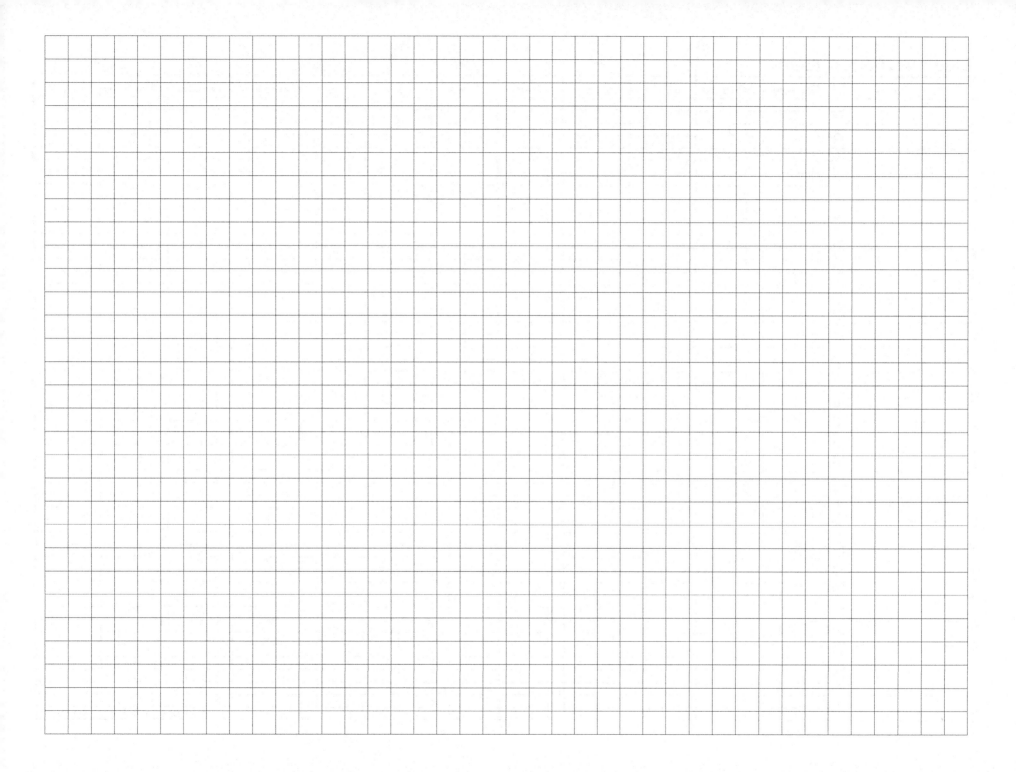

Garden Plot:

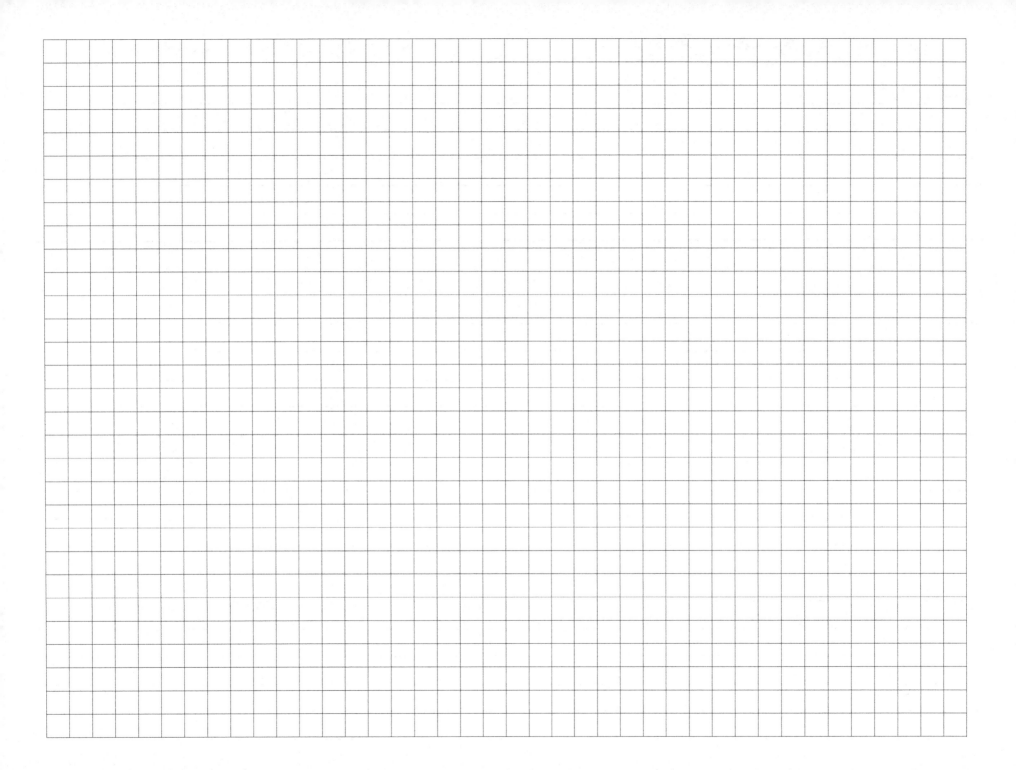

Garden Plot:

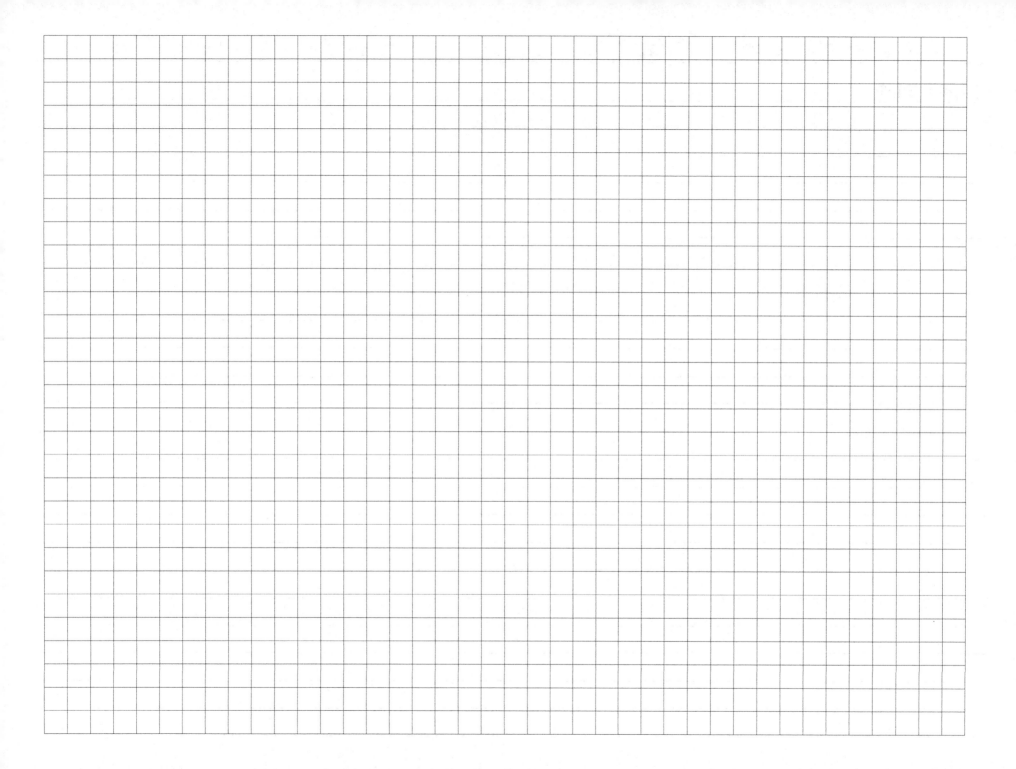

Garden Plot: _____

_____

_____

_____

_____

_____

_____

_____

_____

_____

_____

_____

_____

_____

_____

_____

_____

_____

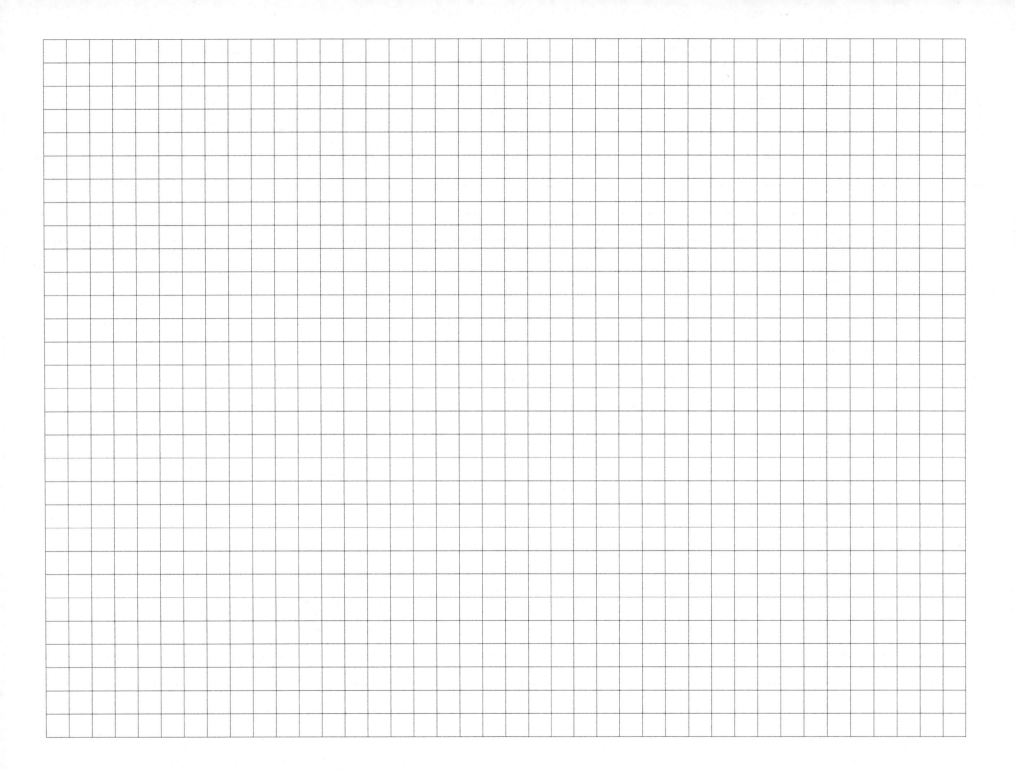

Garden Plot:

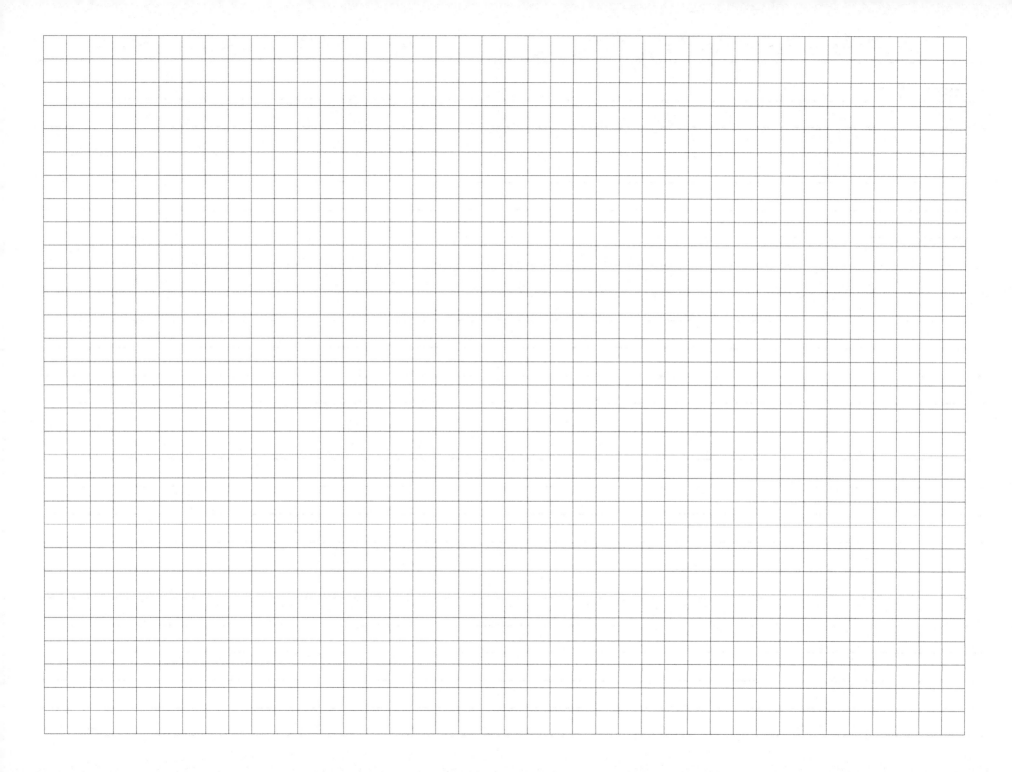

Garden Plot:

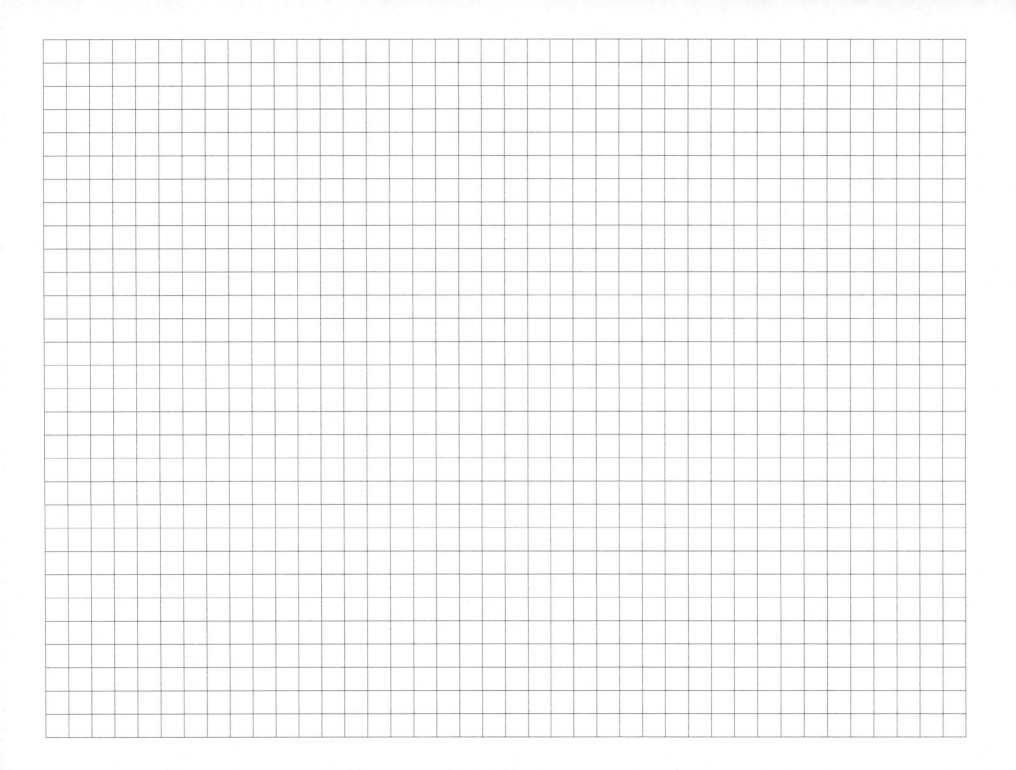

Garden Plot:

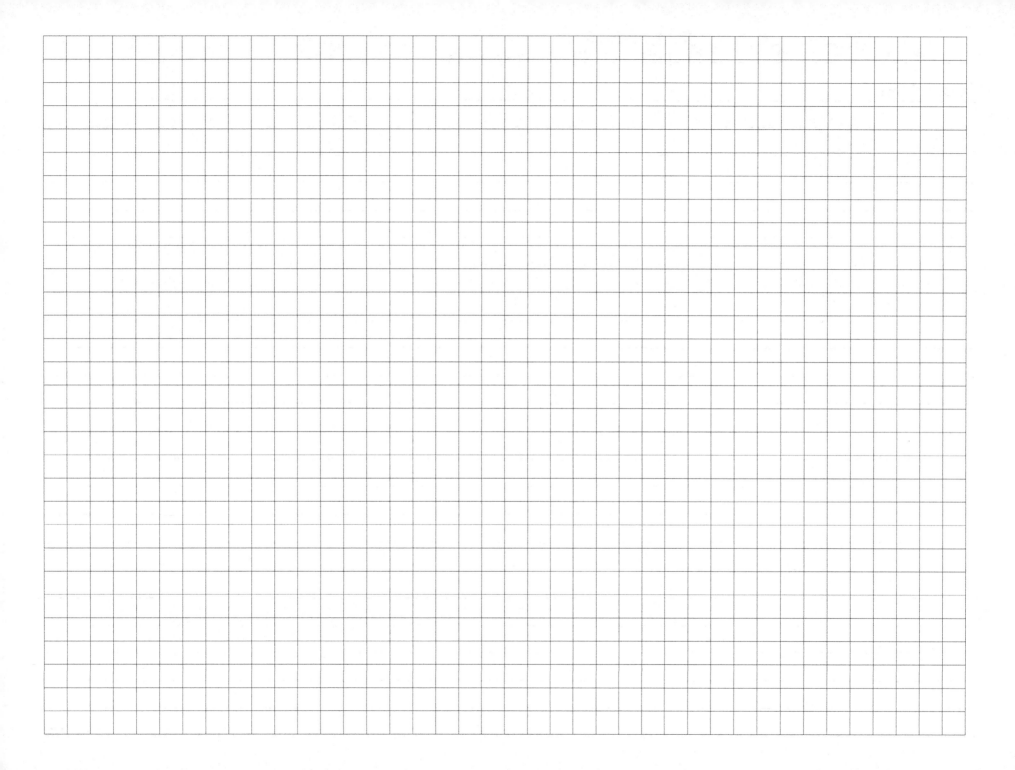

Garden Plot:

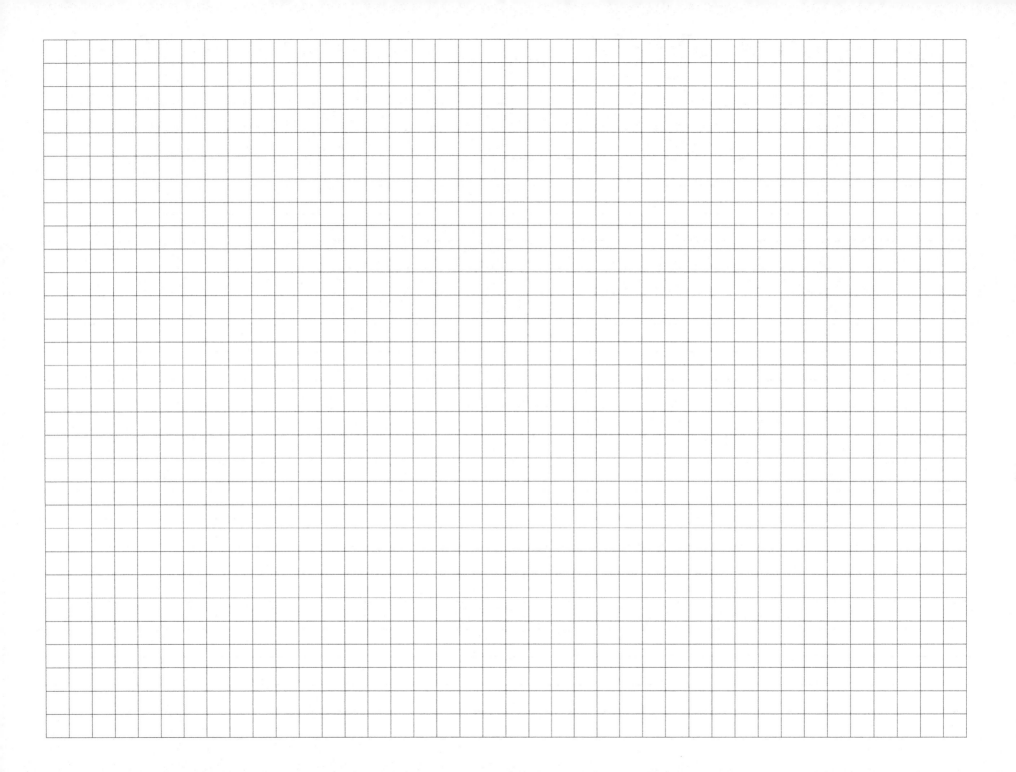

Garden Plot:

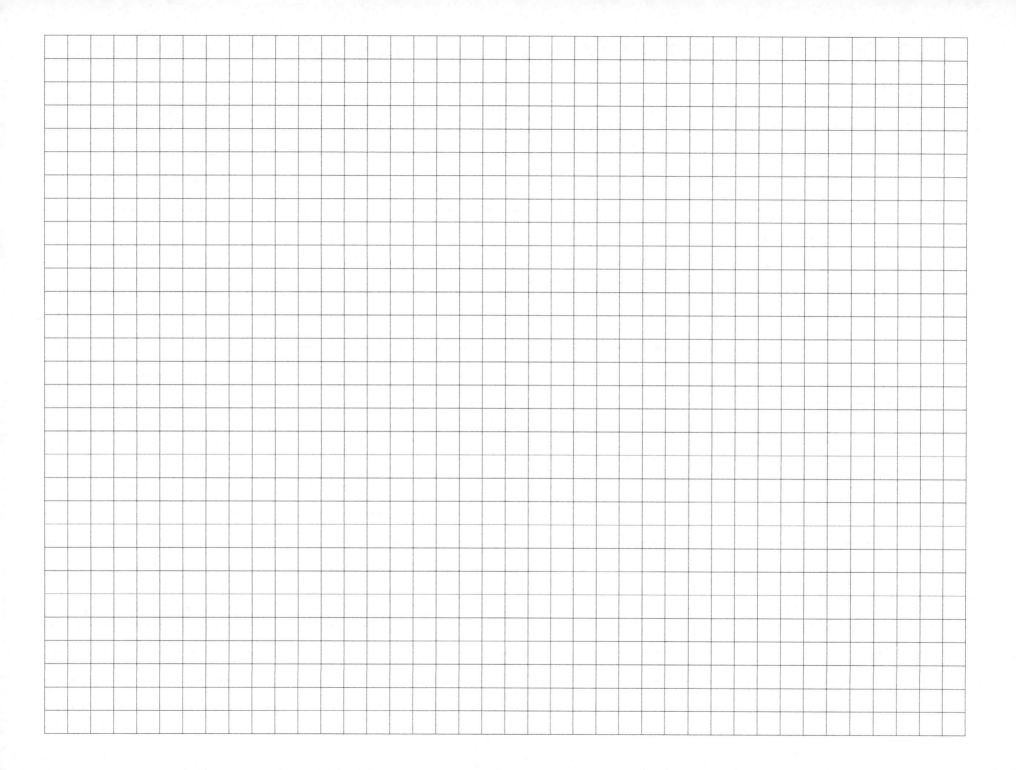

Garden Plot:

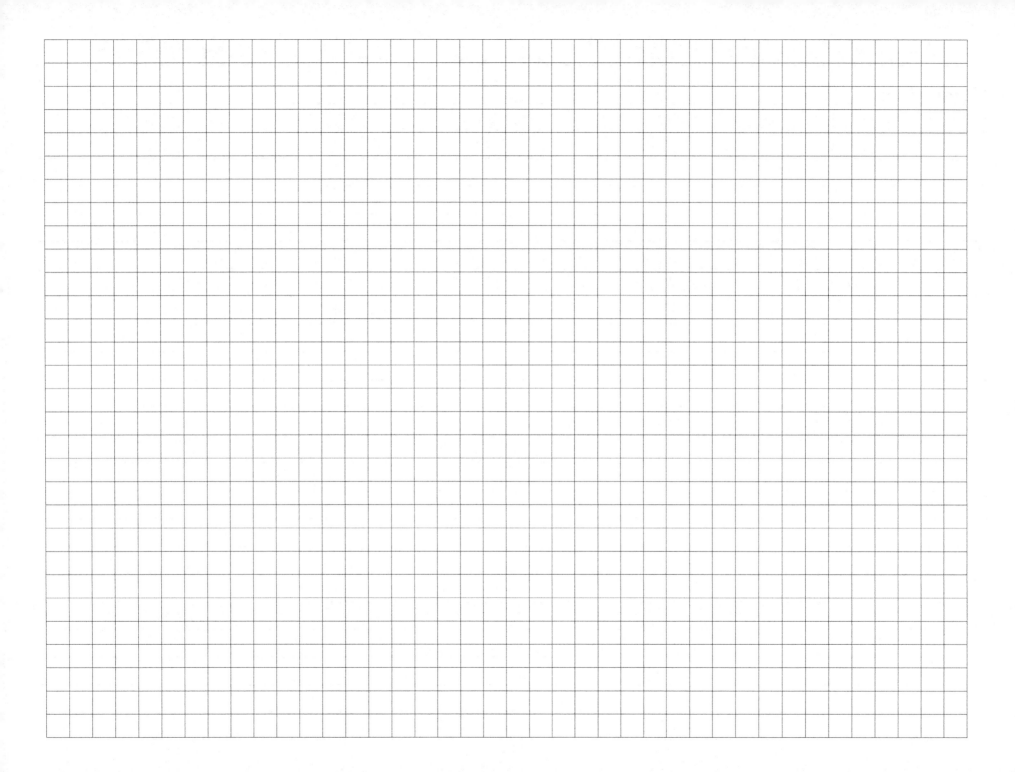

Garden Plot:

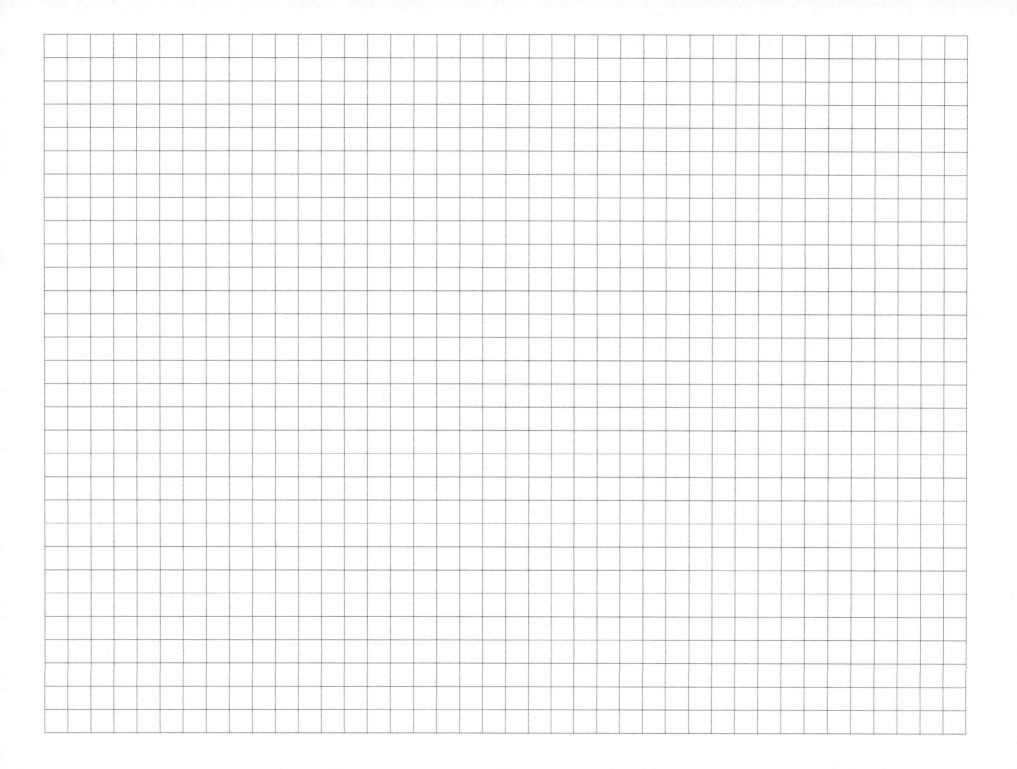

Garden Plot:

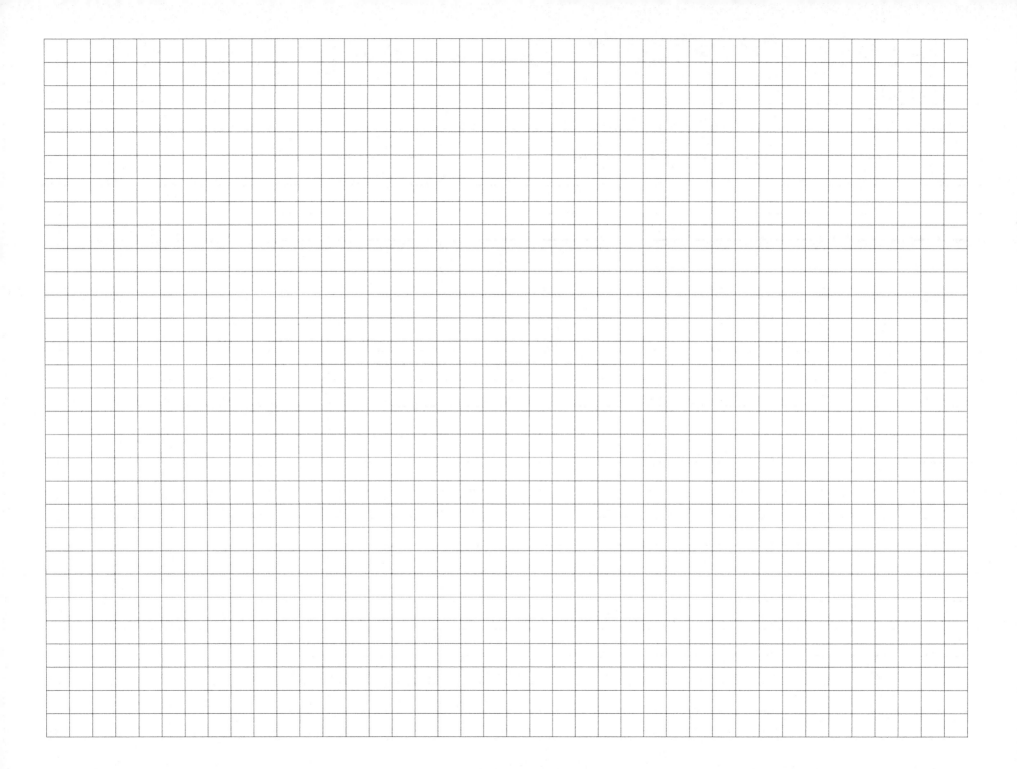

Garden Plot:

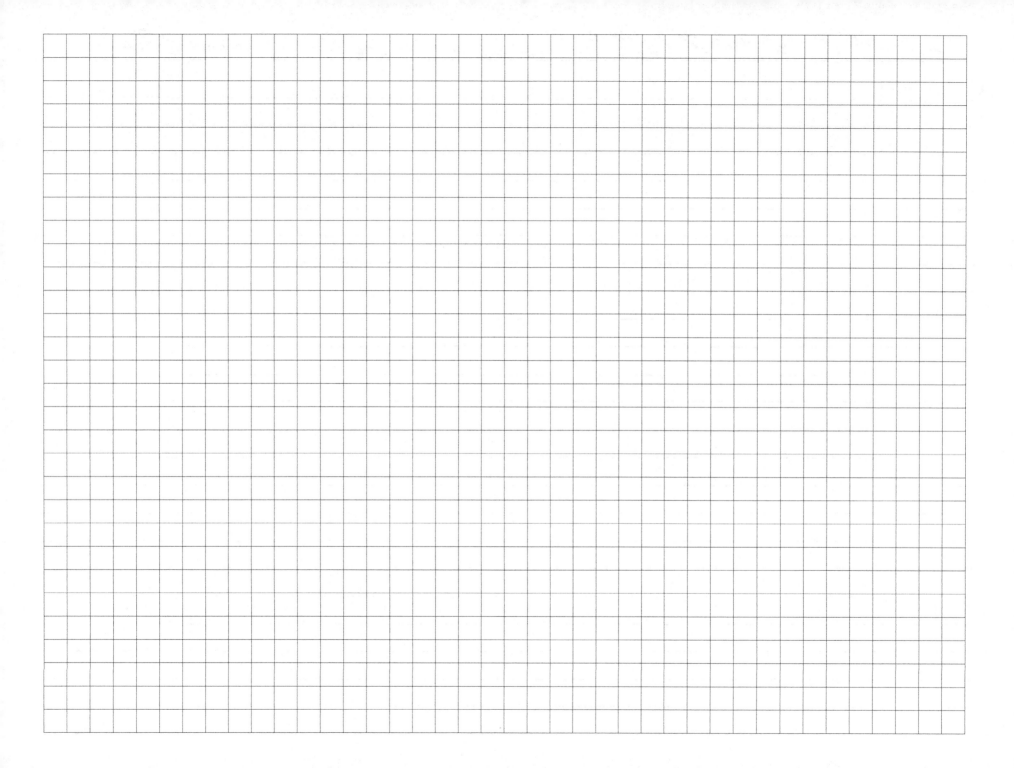

Garden Plot:

Garden Plot

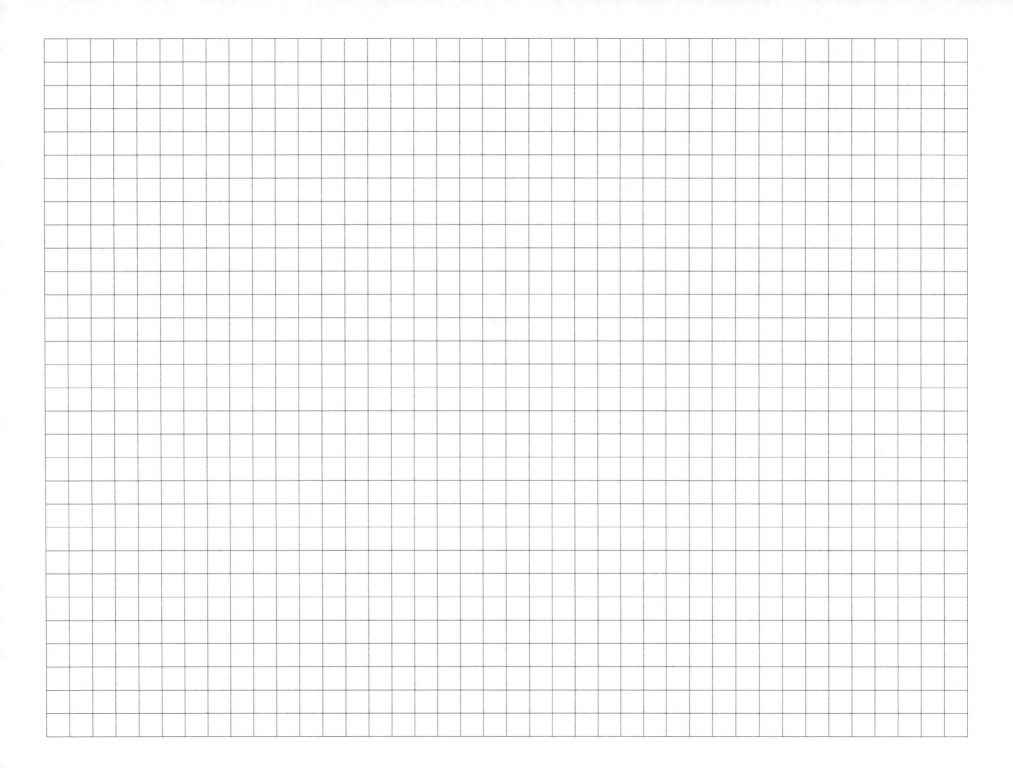

Garden Plot:

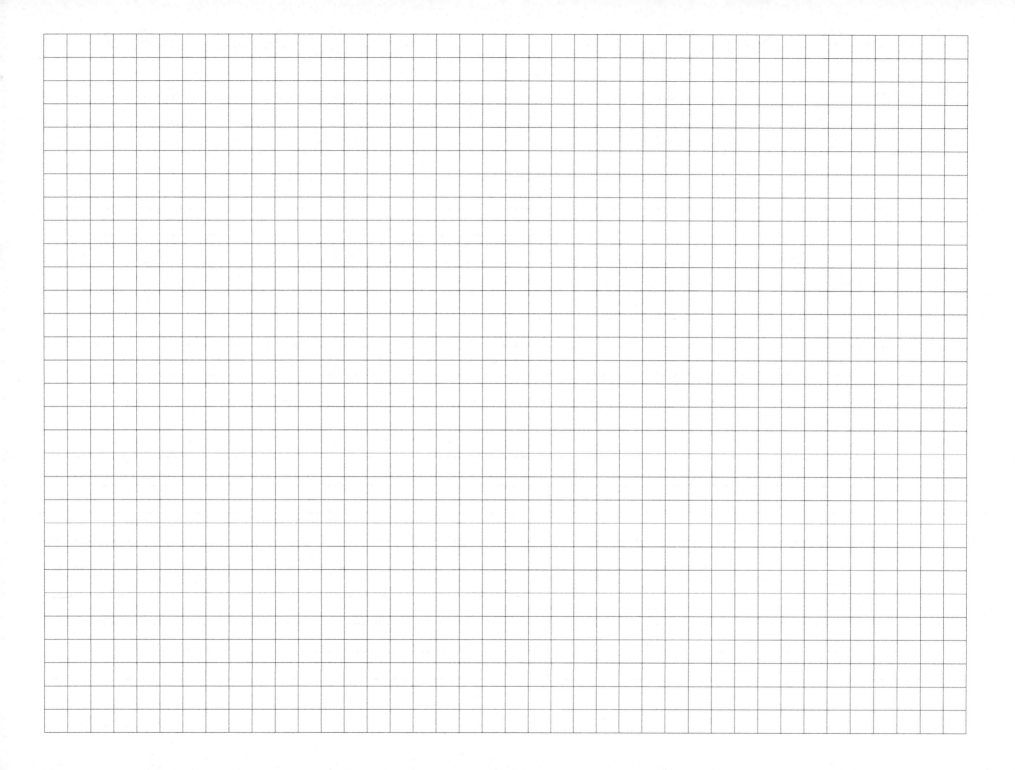

Garden Plot:

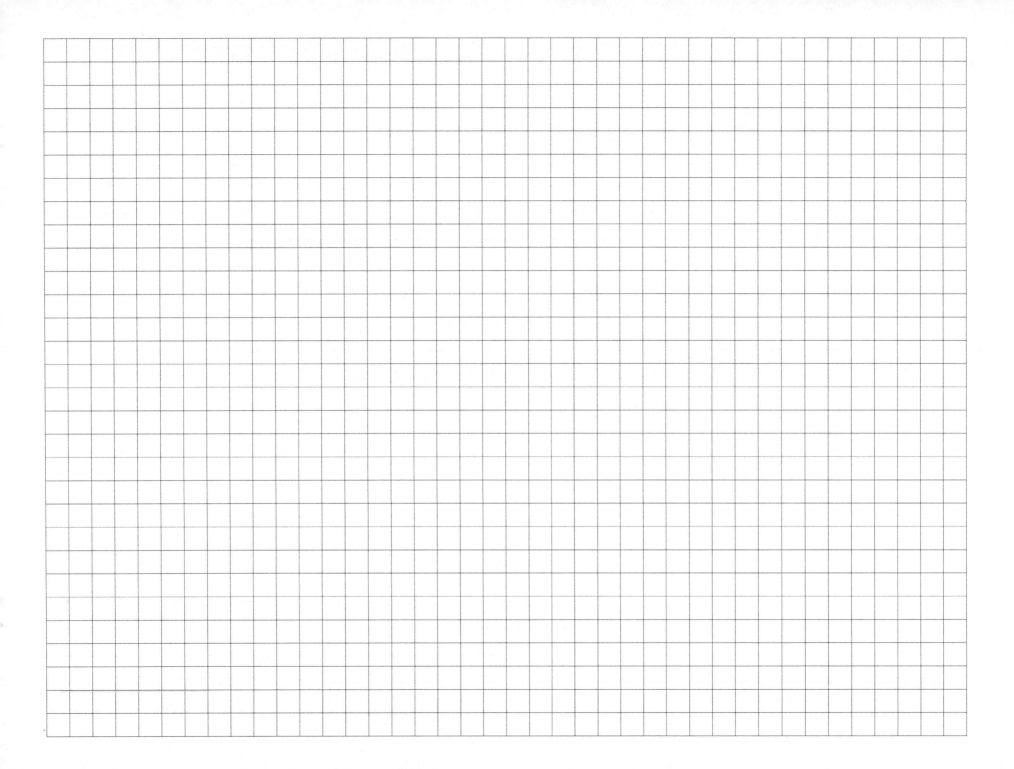

Garden Plot:

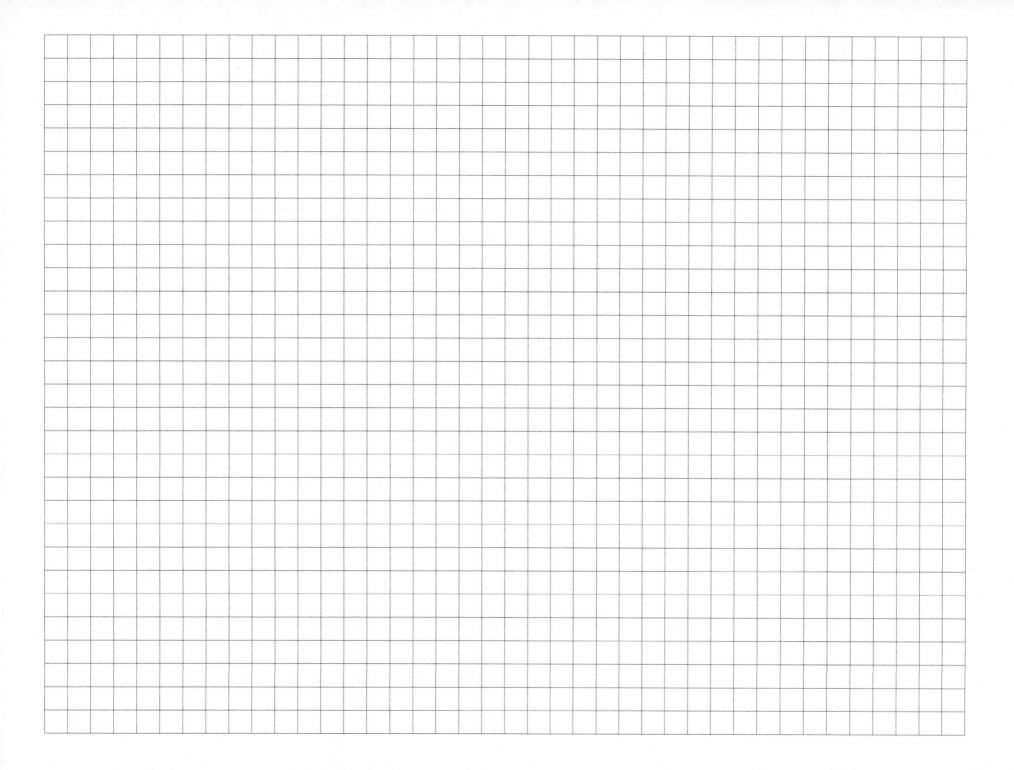

Garden Plot:

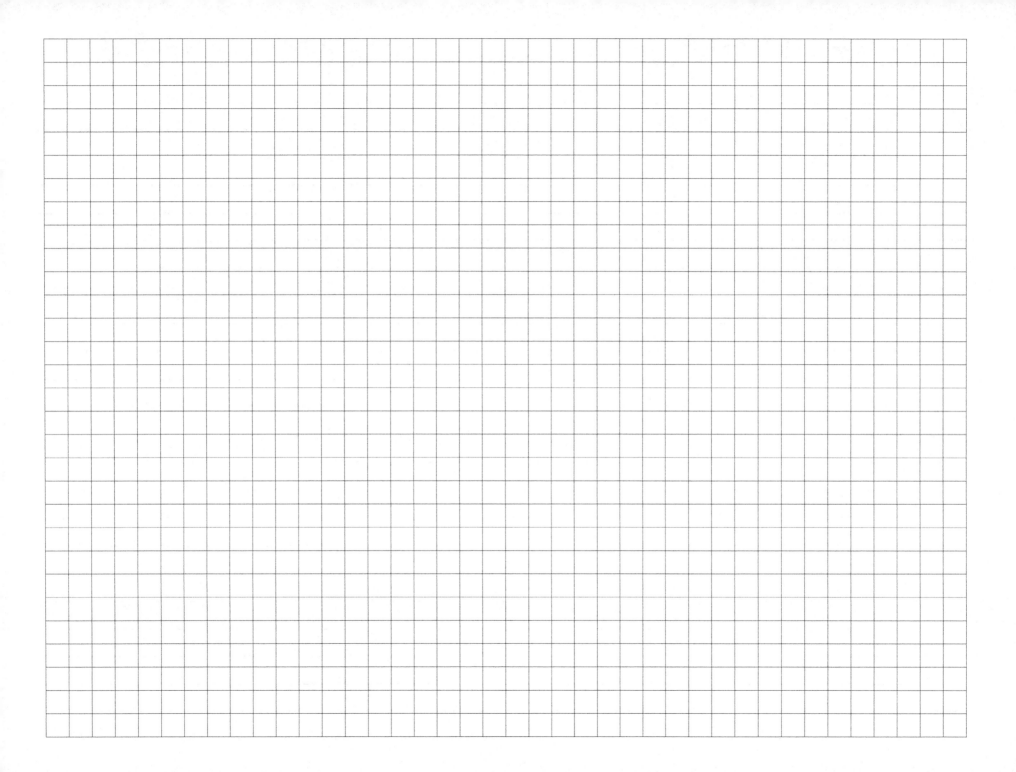

Garden Plot:

Individual Plant Info

Soil Requirements:
- ◯ Rich
- ◯ Average
- ◯ Poor
- ◯ Moist
- ◯ Dry
- ◯ Sandy
- ◯ Rocky
- ◯ Sandy
- ◯ Well-Drained
- ◯ Alkaline
- ◯ Acid
- ◯ PH

Notes:

Sowing and Planting Dates:

Treatment and Dates:

- ◯ Fertilize with: _____   Dates: _____
- ◯ Spray with: _____   _____
- ◯ Treat with:

Prune:
- ◯ Spring
- ◯ Fall
- ◯ Summer
- ◯ Anytime
- ◯ After Bloom
- ◯ Other

Tidy:
- ◯ Deadhead
- ◯ Pinch
- ◯ Shear
- ◯ Thin

Protect:
- ◯ in Winter
- ◯ from Wind
- ◯ from Frost
- ◯ Store indoors for Winter
- ◯ Other
- ◯ Stake
- ◯ Mulch
- ◯ Wrap trunk

Cultivation Notes:

Poisonous To:
- ◯ People
- ◯ Pets
- ◯ Livestock

Part Poisonous:
- ◯ Leaves
- ◯ Flower
- ◯ Stem
- ◯ Roots

Problems:

Notes:

Botanical Name:

Common Name:

Photo, Drawing, Seed Packet or Plant Marker:

Plant Type:
- ◯ Annual
- ◯ Biennial
- ◯ Perennial
- ◯ Fruit
- ◯ Vegetable
- ◯ Herb
- ◯ Tree
- ◯ Shrub
- ◯ Vine
- ◯ Bulb

Size at Maturity:
Height   Width   Root Depth

Attributes:
- ◯ Disease Resistant
- ◯ Pest Resistant
- ◯ Deer Resistant
- ◯ Invasive
- ◯ Deciduous
- ◯ Self-Propagating

Attracts
- ◯ Butterflies
- ◯ Hummingbirds
- ◯ Birds:

☆ ☆ ☆ ☆ ☆

Sun Exposure:

Water Requirements:

Hardiness Zone:

Propagation:
- ◯ Layering
- ◯ Cutting:
  - ◯ in Soil
  - ◯ in Water
- ◯ Seed
- ◯ Dividing:
  - ◯ Spring
  - ◯ Fall
  - ◯ Other

Uses:

Companion Plants:

Characteristics

Individual Plant Info

Soil Requirements:
- ○ Rich
- ○ Average
- ○ Poor
- ○ Moist
- ○ Dry
- ○ Sandy
- ○ Rocky
- ○ Sandy
- ○ Well-Drained
- ○ Alkaline
- ○ Acid
- ○ PH

Notes:

Sowing and Planting Dates:

Treatment and Dates:

Dates:

- ○ Fertilize with: _____ _____
- ○ Spray with: _____ _____
- ○ Treat with:

Prune:	Tidy:	Protect:	
○ Spring	○ Deadhead	○ in Winter	○ Stake
○ Fall	○ Pinch	○ from Wind	○ Mulch
○ Summer	○ Shear	○ from Frost	○ Wrap trunk
○ Anytime	○ Thin	○ Store indoors for Winter	
○ After Bloom		○ Other	
○ Other			

Cultivation Notes:

Poisonous To:
- ○ People
- ○ Pets
- ○ Livestock

Part Poisonous:
- ○ Leaves
- ○ Flower
- ○ Stem
- ○ Roots

Problems:

Notes:

Botanical Name:

Common Name:

Photo, Drawing, Seed Packet or Plant Marker:

Plant Type:
- ○ Annual
- ○ Biennial
- ○ Perennial
- ○ Fruit
- ○ Vegetable
- ○ Herb
- ○ Tree
- ○ Shrub
- ○ Vine
- ○ Bulb

Size at Maturity:
Height   Width   Root Depth

Attributes:
- ○ Disease Resistant
- ○ Pest Resistant
- ○ Deer Resistant
- ○ Invasive
- ○ Deciduous
- ○ Self-Propagating

Attracts
- ○ Butterflies
- ○ Hummingbirds
- ○ Birds:

☆ ☆ ☆ ☆ ☆

Sun Exposure:

Water Requirements:

Hardiness Zone:

Propagation:
- ○ Layering
- ○ Cutting:
  - ○ in Soil
  - ○ in Water
- ○ Seed
- ○ Dividing:
  - ○ Spring
  - ○ Fall
  - ○ Other

Uses:

Companion Plants:

Characteristics

Individual Plant Info

Soil Requirements:
- ○ Rich
- ○ Average
- ○ Poor
- ▢ Moist
- ▢ Dry
- ▢ Sandy
- ▢ Rocky
- ▢ Sandy
- ▢ Well-Drained
- ▢ Alkaline
- ▢ Acid
- ▢ PH

Notes:

Sowing and Planting Dates:

Treatment and Dates:

Dates:
- ○ Fertilize with: _____ _____
- ○ Spray with: _____ _____
- ○ Treat with:

Prune:
- ○ Spring
- ○ Fall
- ○ Summer
- ○ Anytime
- ○ After Bloom
- ○ Other

Tidy:
- ▢ Deadhead
- ▢ Pinch
- ▢ Shear
- ▢ Thin

Protect:
- ○ in Winter
- ○ from Wind
- ○ from Frost
- ○ Store indoors for Winter
- ○ Other
- ○ Stake
- ○ Mulch
- ○ Wrap trunk

Cultivation Notes:

Poisonous To: ○ People ○ Pets ○ Livestock

Part Poisonous: ○ Leaves ○ Flower ○ Stem ○ Roots

Problems:

Notes:

Botanical Name:

Common Name:

Photo, Drawing, Seed Packet or Plant Marker:

Plant Type:
- ○ Annual
- ○ Biennial
- ○ Perennial
- ▢ Fruit
- ▢ Vegetable
- ○ Herb
- ○ Tree
- ○ Shrub
- ○ Vine
- ○ Bulb

Size at Maturity:
Height   Width   Root Depth

Attributes:
- ○ Disease Resistant
- ○ Pest Resistant
- ○ Deer Resistant
- ○ Invasive
- ○ Deciduous
- ○ Self-Propagating

Attracts
- ○ Butterflies
- ○ Hummingbirds
- ○ Birds:

☆ ☆ ☆ ☆ ☆

Sun Exposure:

Water Requirements:

Hardiness Zone:

Propagation:
- ○ Layering
- ○ Cutting:
  - ▢ in Soil
  - ▢ in Water
- ○ Seed
- ○ Dividing:
  - ○ Spring
  - ○ Fall
  - ○ Other

Uses:

Companion Plants:

Characteristics

Individual Plant Info

Soil Requirements:
- ○ Rich
- ○ Average
- ○ Poor
- ○ Moist
- ○ Dry
- ○ Sandy
- ■ Rocky
- ■ Sandy
- ■ Well-Drained
- ○ Alkaline
- ○ Acid
- ○ PH

Notes:

Sowing and Planting Dates:

Treatment and Dates:

Dates:

- ○ Fertilize with: _____ _____
- ○ Spray with: _____ _____
- ○ Treat with:

Prune:
- ○ Spring
- ○ Fall
- ○ Summer
- ○ Anytime
- ○ After Bloom
- ○ Other

Tidy:
- ■ Deadhead
- ○ Pinch
- ○ Shear
- ○ Thin

Protect:
- ■ in Winter
- ■ from Wind
- ■ from Frost
- ○ Store indoors for Winter
- ○ Other

- ■ Stake
- ■ Mulch
- ○ Wrap trunk

Cultivation Notes:

Poisonous To:
○ People	○ Pets	○ Livestock

Part Poisonous:
○ Leaves	○ Flower	○ Stem	○ Roots

Problems:

Notes:

Botanical Name:

Common Name:

Photo, Drawing, Seed Packet or Plant Marker:

Plant Type:
- ○ Annual
- ○ Biennial
- ○ Perennial
- ■ Fruit
- ○ Vegetable
- ○ Herb
- ■ Tree
- ○ Shrub
- ○ Vine
- ○ Bulb

Size at Maturity:
Height   Width   Root Depth

Attributes:
- ○ Disease Resistant
- ○ Pest Resistant
- ○ Deer Resistant
- ○ Invasive
- ○ Deciduous
- ○ Self-Propagating

Attracts
- ○ Butterflies
- ○ Hummingbirds
- ○ Birds:

☆ ☆☆ ☆ ☆

Sun Exposure:

Water Requirements:

Hardiness Zone:

Propagation:
- ○ Layering
- ○ Cutting:
  - ■ in Soil
  - ■ in Water
- ○ Seed
- ○ Dividing:
  - ■ Spring
  - ■ Fall
  - ■ Other

Uses:

Companion Plants:

Characteristics

Individual Plant Info

Soil Requirements:
○ Rich   ○ Moist   ○ Rocky   ○ Alkaline
○ Average ○ Dry   ○ Sandy   ○ Acid
○ Poor   ○ Sandy   ○ Well-Drained   ○ PH

Notes:

Sowing and Planting Dates:

Treatment and Dates:

Dates:

○ Fertilize with: _____   _____
○ Spray with: _____   _____
○ Treat with:

Prune: **Tidy:**   **Protect:**
○ Spring   ○ Deadhead   ○ in Winter   ○ Stake
○ Fall   ○ Pinch   ○ from Wind   ○ Mulch
○ Summer   ○ Shear   ○ from Frost   ○ Wrap trunk
○ Anytime   ○ Thin   ○ Store indoors for Winter
○ After Bloom   ○ Other
○ Other

Cultivation Notes:

Poisonous To: ○ People   ○ Pets   ○ Livestock
Part Poisonous: ○ Leaves   ○ Flower   ○ Stem   ○ Roots
Problems:

Notes:

Botanical Name:

Common Name:

Photo, Drawing, Seed Packet or Plant Marker:

Plant Type:
○ Annual   ○ Fruit   ○ Tree
○ Biennial   ○ Vegetable   ○ Shrub
○ Perennial ○ Herb   ○ Vine
                           ○ Bulb

Size at Maturity:
Height   Width   Root Depth

Attributes: **Attracts**
○ Disease Resistant   ○ Invasive   ○ Butterflies
○ Pest Resistant   ○ Deciduous   ○ Hummingbirds
○ Deer Resistant   ○ Self-Propagating ○ Birds:

☆ ☆ ☆ ☆ ☆

Sun Exposure:

Water Requirements:

Hardiness Zone:

Propagation:
○ Layering
○ Cutting:
  ○ in Soil
  ○ in Water
○ Seed
○ Dividing:
  ○ Spring
  ○ Fall
  ○ Other

Uses:

Companion Plants:

Characteristics

Individual Plant Info

Soil Requirements:
- ◯ Rich
- ◯ Average
- ◯ Poor
- ◯ Moist
- ◯ Dry
- ◯ Sandy
- ◉ Rocky
- ◯ Sandy
- ◉ Well-Drained
- ◯ Alkaline
- ◯ Acid
- ◯ PH

Notes:

Sowing and Planting Dates:

Treatment and Dates:

Dates:

- ◯ Fertilize with: _____ _____
- ◯ Spray with: _____ _____
- ◯ Treat with:

Prune:
- ◯ Spring
- ◯ Fall
- ◯ Summer
- ◯ Anytime
- ◯ After Bloom
- ◯ Other

Tidy:
- ◯ Deadhead
- ◯ Pinch
- ◯ Shear
- ◯ Thin

Protect:
- ◯ in Winter
- ◯ from Wind
- ◯ from Frost
- ◯ Store indoors for Winter
- ◯ Other
- ◯ Stake
- ◯ Mulch
- ◯ Wrap trunk

Cultivation Notes:

Poisonous To:
- ◯ People
- ◯ Pets
- ◯ Livestock

Part Poisonous:
- ◯ Leaves
- ◯ Flower
- ◯ Stem
- ◯ Roots

Problems:

Notes:

Botanical Name:

Common Name:

Photo, Drawing, Seed Packet or Plant Marker:

Plant Type:
- ◯ Annual
- ◯ Biennial
- ◯ Perennial
- ◯ Fruit
- ◯ Vegetable
- ◯ Herb
- ◯ Tree
- ◯ Shrub
- ◯ Vine
- ◯ Bulb

Size at Maturity:
Height   Width   Root Depth

Attributes:
- ◯ Disease Resistant
- ◯ Pest Resistant
- ◯ Deer Resistant
- ◯ Invasive
- ◯ Deciduous
- ◯ Self-Propagating

Attracts
- ◯ Butterflies
- ◯ Hummingbirds
- ◯ Birds:

☆ ☆ ★ ★ ☆

Sun Exposure:

Water Requirements:

Hardiness Zone:

Propagation:
- ◯ Layering
- ◯ Cutting:
  - ◯ in Soil
  - ◯ in Water
- ◯ Seed
- ◯ Dividing:
  - ◯ Spring
  - ◯ Fall
  - ◯ Other

Uses:

Companion Plants:

Characteristics

Individual Plant Info

Soil Requirements:
- ◯ Rich
- ◯ Average
- ◯ Poor

- ◯ Moist
- ◯ Dry
- ◯ Sandy

- ◼ Rocky
- ◼ Sandy
- ◼ Well-Drained

- ◼ Alkaline
- ◼ Acid
- ◼ PH

Notes:

Sowing and Planting Dates:

Treatment and Dates:

Dates:

- ◯ Fertilize with: _____ _____
- ◯ Spray with: _____ _____
- ◯ Treat with:

Prune:
- ◯ Spring
- ◯ Fall
- ◯ Summer
- ◯ Anytime
- ◯ After Bloom
- ◯ Other

Tidy:
- ◼ Deadhead
- ◼ Pinch
- ◼ Shear
- ◼ Thin

Protect:
- ◯ in Winter
- ◯ from Wind
- ◯ from Frost
- ◯ Store indoors for Winter
- ◯ Other

- ◯ Stake
- ◯ Mulch
- ◯ Wrap trunk

Cultivation Notes:

Poisonous To:
- ◯ People
- ◯ Pets
- ◯ Livestock

Part Poisonous:
- ◯ Leaves
- ◯ Flower
- ◯ Stem
- ◯ Roots

Problems:

Notes:

Botanical Name:

Common Name:

Photo, Drawing, Seed Packet or Plant Marker:

Plant Type:
- ◯ Annual
- ◯ Biennial
- ◯ Perennial

- ◯ Fruit
- ◼ Vegetable
- ◯ Herb

- ◯ Tree
- ◯ Shrub
- ◯ Vine
- ◯ Bulb

Size at Maturity:

Height   Width   Root Depth

Attributes:
- ◯ Disease Resistant
- ◯ Pest Resistant
- ◯ Deer Resistant

- ◯ Invasive
- ◯ Deciduous
- ◯ Self-Propagating

Attracts
- ◯ Butterflies
- ◯ Hummingbirds
- ◯ Birds:

☆ ☆ ☆ ☆ ☆

Sun Exposure:

Water Requirements:

Hardiness Zone:

Propagation:
- ◯ Layering
- ◯ Cutting:
  - ◼ in Soil
  - ◼ in Water
- ◯ Seed
- ◯ Dividing:
  - ◯ Spring
  - ◯ Fall
  - ◯ Other

Uses:

Companion Plants:

Characteristics

Individual Plant Info

Soil Requirements:

- ( ) Rich
- ( ) Average
- ( ) Poor
- ( ) Moist
- ( ) Dry
- ( ) Sandy
- ( ) Rocky
- ( ) Sandy
- ( ) Well-Drained
- ( ) Alkaline
- ( ) Acid
- ( ) PH

Notes:

Sowing and Planting Dates:

Treatment and Dates:

Dates:

- ( ) Fertilize with: _____ _____
- ( ) Spray with: _____ _____
- ( ) Treat with:

Prune:
- ( ) Spring
- ( ) Fall
- ( ) Summer
- ( ) Anytime
- ( ) After Bloom
- ( ) Other

Tidy:
- ( ) Deadhead
- ( ) Pinch
- ( ) Shear
- ( ) Thin

Protect:
- ( ) in Winter
- ( ) from Wind
- ( ) from Frost
- ( ) Store indoors for Winter
- ( ) Other
- ( ) Stake
- ( ) Mulch
- ( ) Wrap trunk

Cultivation Notes:

Poisonous To: ( ) People ( ) Pets ( ) Livestock

Part Poisonous: ( ) Leaves ( ) Flower ( ) Stem ( ) Roots

Problems:

Notes:

Botanical Name:

Common Name:

Photo, Drawing, Seed Packet or Plant Marker:

Plant Type:
- ( ) Annual
- ( ) Biennial
- ( ) Perennial
- ( ) Fruit
- ( ) Vegetable
- ( ) Herb
- ( ) Tree
- ( ) Shrub
- ( ) Vine
- ( ) Bulb

Size at Maturity:

Height   Width   Root Depth

Attributes:
- ( ) Disease Resistant
- ( ) Pest Resistant
- ( ) Deer Resistant
- ( ) Invasive
- ( ) Deciduous
- ( ) Self-Propagating

Attracts
- ( ) Butterflies
- ( ) Hummingbirds
- ( ) Birds:

☆ ☆ ☆ ☆ ☆

Sun Exposure:

Water Requirements:

Hardiness Zone:

Propagation:
- ( ) Layering
- ( ) Cutting:
  - ( ) in Soil
  - ( ) in Water
- ( ) Seed
- ( ) Dividing:
  - ( ) Spring
  - ( ) Fall
  - ( ) Other

Uses:

Companion Plants:

Characteristics

Individual Plant Info

Soil Requirements:
- ○ Rich
- ○ Average
- ○ Poor
- ● Moist
- ● Dry
- ● Sandy
- ○ Rocky
- ○ Sandy
- ○ Well-Drained
- ○ Alkaline
- ○ Acid
- ○ PH

Notes:

Sowing and Planting Dates:

Treatment and Dates:

Dates:

- ● Fertilize with: _____ _____
- ● Spray with: _____ _____
- ● Treat with:

Prune:
- ○ Spring
- ○ Fall
- ○ Summer
- ○ Anytime
- ○ After Bloom
- ○ Other

Tidy:
- ● Deadhead
- ● Pinch
- ● Shear
- ● Thin

Protect:
- ● in Winter
- ● from Wind
- ● from Frost
- ● Store indoors for Winter
- ● Other
- ● Stake
- ● Mulch
- ● Wrap trunk

Cultivation Notes:

Poisonous To: ● People ● Pets ● Livestock

Part Poisonous: ● Leaves ● Flower ● Stem ● Roots

Problems:

Notes:

Botanical Name:

Common Name:

Photo, Drawing, Seed Packet or Plant Marker:

Plant Type:
- ○ Annual
- ○ Biennial
- ○ Perennial
- ○ Fruit
- ○ Vegetable
- ○ Herb
- ○ Tree
- ○ Shrub
- ○ Vine
- ○ Bulb

Size at Maturity:

Height   Width   Root Depth

Attributes:
- ○ Disease Resistant
- ○ Pest Resistant
- ○ Deer Resistant

- ○ Invasive
- ○ Deciduous
- ○ Self-Propagating

Attracts
- ○ Butterflies
- ○ Hummingbirds
- ○ Birds:

☆ ☆ ☆ ☆ ☆

Sun Exposure:

Water Requirements:

Hardiness Zone:

Propagation:
- ○ Layering
- ○ Cutting:
  - ○ in Soil
  - ○ in Water
- ○ Seed
- ○ Dividing:
  - ○ Spring
  - ○ Fall
  - ○ Other

Uses:

Companion Plants:

Characteristics

Individual Plant Info

Soil Requirements:
- ○ Rich
- ○ Average
- ○ Poor
- ○ Moist
- ○ Dry
- ○ Sandy
- ○ Rocky
- ○ Sandy
- ○ Well-Drained
- ○ Alkaline
- ○ Acid
- ○ PH

Notes:

Sowing and Planting Dates:

Treatment and Dates:

Dates:
- ○ Fertilize with: _____ _____
- ○ Spray with: _____ _____
- ○ Treat with:

Prune:
- ○ Spring
- ○ Fall
- ○ Summer
- ○ Anytime
- ○ After Bloom
- ○ Other

Tidy:
- ○ Deadhead
- ○ Pinch
- ○ Shear
- ○ Thin

Protect:
- ○ in Winter
- ○ from Wind
- ○ from Frost
- ○ Store indoors for Winter
- ○ Other
- ○ Stake
- ○ Mulch
- ○ Wrap trunk

Cultivation Notes:

Poisonous To:
- ○ People
- ○ Pets
- ○ Livestock

Part Poisonous:
- ○ Leaves
- ○ Flower
- ○ Stem
- ○ Roots

Problems:

Notes:

Botanical Name:

Common Name:

Photo, Drawing, Seed Packet or Plant Marker:

Plant Type:
- ○ Annual
- ○ Biennial
- ○ Perennial
- ○ Fruit
- ○ Vegetable
- ○ Herb
- ○ Tree
- ○ Shrub
- ○ Vine
- ○ Bulb

Size at Maturity:
Height   Width   Root Depth

Attributes:
- ○ Disease Resistant
- ○ Pest Resistant
- ○ Deer Resistant
- ○ Invasive
- ○ Deciduous
- ○ Self-Propagating

Attracts
- ○ Butterflies
- ○ Hummingbirds
- ○ Birds:

☆ ★ ★ ★ ☆

Sun Exposure:

Water Requirements:

Hardiness Zone:

Propagation:
- ○ Layering
- ○ Cutting:
  - ○ in Soil
  - ○ in Water
- ○ Seed
- ○ Dividing:
  - ○ Spring
  - ○ Fall
  - ○ Other

Uses:

Companion Plants:

Characteristics

Individual Plant Info

Soil Requirements:
- ◯ Rich
- ◯ Average
- ◯ Poor
- ◯ Moist
- ◉ Dry
- ◯ Sandy
- ◉ Rocky
- ◉ Sandy
- ◯ Well-Drained
- ◯ Alkaline
- ◯ Acid
- ◯ PH

Notes:

Sowing and Planting Dates:

Treatment and Dates:

Dates:

- ◯ Fertilize with: _____ _____
- ◯ Spray with: _____ _____
- ◯ Treat with:

Prune:
- ◯ Spring
- ◯ Fall
- ◯ Summer
- ◯ Anytime
- ◯ After Bloom
- ◯ Other

Tidy:
- ◯ Deadhead
- ◯ Pinch
- ◯ Shear
- ◯ Thin

Protect:
- ◯ in Winter
- ◯ from Wind
- ◯ from Frost
- ◯ Store indoors for Winter
- ◯ Other
- ◯ Stake
- ◯ Mulch
- ◯ Wrap trunk

Cultivation Notes:

Poisonous To: ◯ People ◯ Pets ◯ Livestock

Part Poisonous: ◯ Leaves ◯ Flower ◯ Stem ◯ Roots

Problems:

Notes:

Botanical Name:

Common Name:

Photo, Drawing, Seed Packet or Plant Marker:

Plant Type:
- ◯ Annual
- ◯ Biennial
- ◯ Perennial
- ◯ Fruit
- ◉ Vegetable
- ◯ Herb
- ◯ Tree
- ◯ Shrub
- ◯ Vine
- ◯ Bulb

Size at Maturity:
Height   Width   Root Depth

Attributes:
- ◯ Disease Resistant
- ◯ Pest Resistant
- ◯ Deer Resistant
- ◯ Invasive
- ◯ Deciduous
- ◯ Self-Propagating

Attracts
- ◯ Butterflies
- ◯ Hummingbirds
- ◯ Birds:

☆ ☆ ☆ ☆ ☆

Sun Exposure:

Water Requirements:

Hardiness Zone:

Propagation:
- ◯ Layering
- ◯ Cutting:
  - ◯ in Soil
  - ◯ in Water
- ◯ Seed
- ◯ Dividing:
  - ◯ Spring
  - ◯ Fall
  - ◯ Other

Uses:

Companion Plants:

Characteristics

Individual Plant Info

Soil Requirements:
- ◯ Rich
- ◯ Average
- ◯ Poor
- ● Moist
- ● Dry
- ◯ Sandy
- ● Rocky
- ● Sandy
- ● Well-Drained
- ● Alkaline
- ● Acid
- ◯ PH

Notes:

Sowing and Planting Dates:

Treatment and Dates:

Dates:
- ◯ Fertilize with: _____ _____
- ◯ Spray with: _____ _____
- ◯ Treat with:

Prune:
- ◯ Spring
- ◯ Fall
- ◯ Summer
- ◯ Anytime
- ◯ After Bloom
- ◯ Other

Tidy:
- ● Deadhead
- ◯ Pinch
- ◯ Shear
- ◯ Thin

Protect:
- ● in Winter
- ● from Wind
- ● from Frost
- ● Store indoors for Winter
- ● Other
- ● Stake
- ● Mulch
- ● Wrap trunk

Cultivation Notes:

Poisonous To: ◯ People ◯ Pets ◯ Livestock

Part Poisonous: ◯ Leaves ◯ Flower ◯ Stem ◯ Roots

Problems:

Notes:

Botanical Name:

Common Name:

Photo, Drawing, Seed Packet or Plant Marker:

Plant Type:
- ◯ Annual
- ◯ Biennial
- ◯ Perennial
- ● Fruit
- ● Vegetable
- ● Herb
- ● Tree
- ● Shrub
- ● Vine
- ● Bulb

Size at Maturity:
Height   Width   Root Depth

Attributes:
- ◯ Disease Resistant
- ◯ Pest Resistant
- ◯ Deer Resistant
- ◯ Invasive
- ◯ Deciduous
- ◯ Self-Propagating

Attracts
- ◯ Butterflies
- ◯ Hummingbirds
- ◯ Birds:

☆ ☆ ☆ ☆ ☆

Sun Exposure:

Water Requirements:

Hardiness Zone:

Propagation:
- ◯ Layering
- ◯ Cutting:
  - ◯ in Soil
  - ◯ in Water
- ◯ Seed
- ◯ Dividing:
  - ◯ Spring
  - ◯ Fall
  - ◯ Other

Uses:

Companion Plants:

Characteristics

Individual Plant Info

Soil Requirements:
- ○ Rich
- ● Average
- ● Poor
- ○ Moist
- ○ Dry
- ○ Sandy
- ○ Rocky
- ○ Sandy
- ○ Well-Drained
- ○ Alkaline
- ○ Acid
- ○ PH

Notes:

Sowing and Planting Dates:

Treatment and Dates:

Dates:

- ○ Fertilize with: _____ _____
- ○ Spray with: _____ _____
- ○ Treat with:

Prune:
- ○ Spring
- ○ Fall
- ○ Summer
- ○ Anytime
- ○ After Bloom
- ○ Other

Tidy:
- ○ Deadhead
- ○ Pinch
- ○ Shear
- ○ Thin

Protect:
- ○ in Winter
- ○ from Wind
- ○ from Frost
- ○ Store indoors for Winter
- ○ Other
- ○ Stake
- ○ Mulch
- ○ Wrap trunk

Cultivation Notes:

Poisonous To:
- ○ People
- ○ Pets
- ○ Livestock

Part Poisonous:
- ○ Leaves
- ○ Flower
- ○ Stem
- ○ Roots

Problems:

Notes:

Botanical Name:

Common Name:

Photo, Drawing, Seed Packet or Plant Marker:

Plant Type:
- ○ Annual
- ○ Biennial
- ○ Perennial
- ○ Fruit
- ○ Vegetable
- ○ Herb
- ○ Tree
- ○ Shrub
- ○ Vine
- ○ Bulb

Size at Maturity:

Height   Width   Root Depth

Attributes:
- ● Disease Resistant
- ● Pest Resistant
- ○ Deer Resistant
- ○ Invasive
- ○ Deciduous
- ○ Self-Propagating

Attracts
- ○ Butterflies
- ○ Hummingbirds
- ○ Birds:

☆ ☆ ☆ ☆ ☆

Sun Exposure:

Water Requirements:

Hardiness Zone:

Propagation:
- ○ Layering
- ○ Cutting:
  - ○ in Soil
  - ○ in Water
- ○ Seed
- ○ Dividing:
  - ○ Spring
  - ○ Fall
  - ○ Other

Uses:

Companion Plants:

Characteristics

Individual Plant Info

Soil Requirements:
- ◯ Rich
- ◯ Average
- ◯ Poor
- ◯ Moist
- ◯ Dry
- ◯ Sandy
- ◯ Rocky
- ◯ Sandy
- ◯ Well-Drained
- ◯ Alkaline
- ◯ Acid
- ◯ PH

Notes:

Sowing and Planting Dates:

Treatment and Dates:

Dates:
- ◯ Fertilize with: _____ _____
- ◯ Spray with: _____ _____
- ◯ Treat with:

Prune:
- ◯ Spring
- ◯ Fall
- ◯ Summer
- ◯ Anytime
- ◯ After Bloom
- ◯ Other

Tidy:
- ◯ Deadhead
- ◯ Pinch
- ◯ Shear
- ◯ Thin

Protect:
- ◯ in Winter
- ◯ from Wind
- ◯ from Frost
- ◯ Store indoors for Winter
- ◯ Other
- ◯ Stake
- ◯ Mulch
- ◯ Wrap trunk

Cultivation Notes:

Poisonous To: ◯ People   ◯ Pets   ◯ Livestock
Part Poisonous: ◯ Leaves   ◯ Flower   ◯ Stem   ◯ Roots

Problems:

Notes:

Botanical Name:

Common Name:

Photo, Drawing, Seed Packet or Plant Marker:

Plant Type:
- ◯ Annual
- ◯ Biennial
- ◯ Perennial
- ◯ Fruit
- ◯ Vegetable
- ◯ Herb
- ◯ Tree
- ◯ Shrub
- ◯ Vine
- ◯ Bulb

Size at Maturity:
Height   Width   Root Depth

Attributes:
- ◯ Disease Resistant
- ◯ Pest Resistant
- ◯ Deer Resistant
- ◯ Invasive
- ◯ Deciduous
- ◯ Self-Propagating

Attracts
- ◯ Butterflies
- ◯ Hummingbirds
- ◯ Birds:

☆ ☆☆ ☆☆ ☆☆ ☆

Sun Exposure:

Water Requirements:

Hardiness Zone:

Propagation:
- ◯ Layering
- ◯ Cutting:
  - ◯ in Soil
  - ◯ in Water
- ◯ Seed
- ◯ Dividing:
  - ◯ Spring
  - ◯ Fall
  - ◯ Other

Uses:

Companion Plants:

Characteristics

Individual Plant Info

Soil Requirements:

- Rich
- Average
- Poor
- Moist
- Dry
- Sandy
- Rocky
- Sandy
- Well-Drained
- Alkaline
- Acid
- PH

Notes:

Sowing and Planting Dates:

Treatment and Dates:

- Fertilize with: _____ Dates: _____
- Spray with: _____ _____
- Treat with:

Prune:
- Spring
- Fall
- Summer
- Anytime
- After Bloom
- Other

Tidy:
- Deadhead
- Pinch
- Shear
- Thin

Protect:
- in Winter
- from Wind
- from Frost
- Store indoors for Winter
- Other
- Stake
- Mulch
- Wrap trunk

Cultivation Notes:

Poisonous To:
- People
- Pets
- Livestock

Part Poisonous:
- Leaves
- Flower
- Stem
- Roots

Problems:

Notes:

Botanical Name:

Common Name:

Photo, Drawing, Seed Packet or Plant Marker:

Plant Type:
- Annual
- Biennial
- Perennial
- Fruit
- Vegetable
- Herb
- Tree
- Shrub
- Vine
- Bulb

Size at Maturity:

Height	Width	Root Depth

Attributes:
- Disease Resistant
- Pest Resistant
- Deer Resistant
- Invasive
- Deciduous
- Self-Propagating

Attracts
- Butterflies
- Hummingbirds
- Birds:

☆ ☆ ☆ ☆ ☆

Sun Exposure:

Water Requirements:

Hardiness Zone:

Propagation:
- Layering
- Cutting:
  - in Soil
  - in Water
- Seed
- Dividing:
  - Spring
  - Fall
  - Other

Uses:

Companion Plants:

Characteristics

Individual Plant Info

Soil Requirements:
- ○ Rich
- ○ Average
- ○ Poor
- ○ Moist
- ○ Dry
- ○ Sandy
- ○ Rocky
- ○ Sandy
- ○ Well-Drained
- ○ Alkaline
- ○ Acid
- ○ PH

Notes:

Sowing and Planting Dates:

Treatment and Dates:

- ○ Fertilize with: _____   Dates: _____
- ○ Spray with: _____   _____
- ○ Treat with:

Prune:
- ○ Spring
- ○ Fall
- ○ Summer
- ○ Anytime
- ○ After Bloom
- ○ Other

Tidy:
- ○ Deadhead
- ○ Pinch
- ○ Shear
- ○ Thin

Protect:
- ○ in Winter
- ○ from Wind
- ○ from Frost
- ○ Store indoors for Winter
- ○ Other
- ○ Stake
- ○ Mulch
- ○ Wrap trunk

Cultivation Notes:

Poisonous To: ○ People ○ Pets ○ Livestock

Part Poisonous: ○ Leaves ○ Flower ○ Stem ○ Roots

Problems:

Notes:

Botanical Name:

Common Name:

Photo, Drawing, Seed Packet or Plant Marker:

Plant Type:
- ○ Annual
- ○ Biennial
- ○ Perennial
- ○ Fruit
- ○ Vegetable
- ○ Herb
- ○ Tree
- ○ Shrub
- ○ Vine
- ○ Bulb

Size at Maturity:

Height   Width   Root Depth

Attributes:
- ○ Disease Resistant
- ○ Pest Resistant
- ○ Deer Resistant
- ○ Invasive
- ○ Deciduous
- ○ Self-Propagating

Attracts
- ○ Butterflies
- ○ Hummingbirds
- ○ Birds:

☆ ☆☆ ☆ ☆

Sun Exposure:

Water Requirements:

Hardiness Zone:

Propagation:
- ○ Layering
- ○ Cutting:
  - ○ in Soil
  - ○ in Water
- ○ Seed
- ○ Dividing:
  - ○ Spring
  - ○ Fall
  - ○ Other

Uses:

Companion Plants:

Characteristics

Individual Plant Info

Soil Requirements:
- ○ Rich
- ○ Average
- ○ Poor
- ○ Moist
- ○ Dry
- ○ Sandy
- ○ Rocky
- ○ Sandy
- ○ Well-Drained
- ○ Alkaline
- ○ Acid
- ○ PH

Notes:

Sowing and Planting Dates:

Treatment and Dates:

Dates:
- ● Fertilize with: _____   _____
- ● Spray with: _____   _____
- ● Treat with:

Prune:
- ○ Spring
- ○ Fall
- ○ Summer
- ○ Anytime
- ○ After Bloom
- ○ Other

Tidy:
- ○ Deadhead
- ○ Pinch
- ○ Shear
- ○ Thin

Protect:
- ○ in Winter
- ○ from Wind
- ○ from Frost
- ○ Store indoors for Winter
- ○ Other
- ○ Stake
- ○ Mulch
- ○ Wrap trunk

Cultivation Notes:

Poisonous To:
- ○ People
- ○ Pets
- ○ Livestock

Part Poisonous:
- ○ Leaves
- ○ Flower
- ○ Stem
- ○ Roots

Problems:

Notes:

Botanical Name:

Common Name:

Photo, Drawing, Seed Packet or Plant Marker:

Plant Type:
- ○ Annual
- ○ Biennial
- ○ Perennial
- ○ Fruit
- ○ Vegetable
- ○ Herb
- ○ Tree
- ○ Shrub
- ○ Vine
- ○ Bulb

Size at Maturity:

Height	Width	Root Depth

Attributes:
- ● Disease Resistant
- ○ Pest Resistant
- ○ Deer Resistant
- ● Invasive
- ● Deciduous
- ○ Self-Propagating

Attracts
- ○ Butterflies
- ○ Hummingbirds
- ○ Birds:

☆ ☆ ☆ ☆ ☆

Sun Exposure:

Water Requirements:

Hardiness Zone:

Propagation:
- ○ Layering
- ○ Cutting:
  - ○ in Soil
  - ○ in Water
- ○ Seed
- ○ Dividing:
  - ○ Spring
  - ○ Fall
  - ○ Other

Uses:

Companion Plants:

Characteristics

Individual Plant Info

Soil Requirements:
- ◯ Rich
- ◯ Average
- ◯ Poor
- ◯ Moist
- ◯ Dry
- ◯ Sandy
- ◯ Rocky
- ◯ Sandy
- ◯ Well-Drained
- ◯ Alkaline
- ◯ Acid
- ◯ PH

Notes:

Sowing and Planting Dates:

Treatment and Dates:

Dates:
- ◯ Fertilize with: _____ _____
- ◯ Spray with: _____ _____
- ◯ Treat with:

Prune:
- ◯ Spring
- ◯ Fall
- ◯ Summer
- ◯ Anytime
- ◯ After Bloom
- ◯ Other

Tidy:
- ◯ Deadhead
- ◯ Pinch
- ◯ Shear
- ◯ Thin

Protect:
- ◯ in Winter
- ◯ from Wind
- ◯ from Frost
- ◯ Store indoors for Winter
- ◯ Other
- ◯ Stake
- ◯ Mulch
- ◯ Wrap trunk

Cultivation Notes:

Poisonous To: ◯ People ◯ Pets ◯ Livestock

Part Poisonous: ◯ Leaves ◯ Flower ◯ Stem ◯ Roots

Problems:

Notes:

Botanical Name:

Common Name:

Photo, Drawing, Seed Packet or Plant Marker:

Plant Type:
- ◯ Annual
- ◯ Biennial
- ◯ Perennial
- ◯ Fruit
- ◯ Vegetable
- ◯ Herb
- ◯ Tree
- ◯ Shrub
- ◯ Vine
- ◯ Bulb

Size at Maturity:
Height   Width   Root Depth

Attributes:
- ◯ Disease Resistant
- ◯ Pest Resistant
- ◯ Deer Resistant
- ◯ Invasive
- ◯ Deciduous
- ◯ Self-Propagating

Attracts
- ◯ Butterflies
- ◯ Hummingbirds
- ◯ Birds:

☆ ☆ ☆ ☆ ☆

Sun Exposure:

Water Requirements:

Hardiness Zone:

Propagation:
- ◯ Layering
- ◯ Cutting:
  - ◯ in Soil
  - ◯ in Water
- ◯ Seed
- ◯ Dividing:
  - ◯ Spring
  - ◯ Fall
  - ◯ Other

Uses:

Companion Plants:

Characteristics

Individual Plant Info

Soil Requirements:
- ⊘ Rich
- ⊘ Average
- ⊘ Poor
- ⊞ Moist
- ⊞ Dry
- ⊞ Sandy
- ⊞ Rocky
- ⊞ Sandy
- ⊞ Well-Drained
- ⊞ Alkaline
- ⊞ Acid
- ⊞ PH

Notes:

Sowing and Planting Dates:

Treatment and Dates:

Dates:

- ⊘ Fertilize with: _____ _____
- ⊘ Spray with: _____ _____
- ⊘ Treat with: _____

Prune:
- ⊘ Spring
- ⊘ Fall
- ⊘ Summer
- ⊘ Anytime
- ⊘ After Bloom
- ⊘ Other

Tidy:
- ⊞ Deadhead
- ⊞ Pinch
- ⊞ Shear
- ⊞ Thin

Protect:
- ⊞ in Winter
- ⊞ from Wind
- ⊞ from Frost
- ⊞ Store indoors for Winter
- ⊞ Other

- ⊞ Stake
- ⊞ Mulch
- ⊞ Wrap trunk

Cultivation Notes:

Botanical Name:

Common Name:

Photo, Drawing, Seed Packet or Plant Marker:

☆ ☆ ☆ ☆ ☆

Sun Exposure:

Water Requirements:

Hardiness Zone:

Propagation:
- ⊘ Layering
- ⊘ Cutting:
  - ⊘ in Soil
  - ⊘ in Water
- ⊘ Seed
- ⊘ Dividing:
  - ⊘ Spring
  - ⊘ Fall
  - ⊘ Other

Uses:

Poisonous To:
- ⊘ People
- ⊘ Pets
- ⊘ Livestock

Part Poisonous:
- ⊞ Leaves
- ⊞ Flower
- ⊞ Stem
- ⊘ Roots

Problems:

Notes:

Plant Type:
- ⊘ Annual
- ⊘ Biennial
- ⊘ Perennial
- ⊞ Fruit
- ⊞ Vegetable
- ⊞ Herb
- ⊘ Tree
- ⊘ Shrub
- ⊘ Vine
- ⊘ Bulb

Size at Maturity:

Height   Width   Root Depth

Attributes:
- ⊘ Disease Resistant
- ⊘ Pest Resistant
- ⊘ Deer Resistant
- ⊘ Invasive
- ⊘ Deciduous
- ⊘ Self-Propagating

Attracts
- ⊘ Butterflies
- ⊘ Hummingbirds
- ⊘ Birds:

Companion Plants:

Characteristics

Individual Plant Info

Soil Requirements:
- ○ Rich
- ○ Average
- ○ Poor
- ○ Moist
- ○ Dry
- ○ Sandy
- ○ Rocky
- ○ Sandy
- ○ Well-Drained
- ○ Alkaline
- ○ Acid
- ○ PH

Notes:

Sowing and Planting Dates:

Treatment and Dates:

Dates:

- ○ Fertilize with: _____ _____
- ○ Spray with: _____ _____
- ○ Treat with:

Prune:
- ○ Spring
- ○ Fall
- ○ Summer
- ○ Anytime
- ○ After Bloom
- ○ Other

Tidy:
- ○ Deadhead
- ○ Pinch
- ○ Shear
- ○ Thin

Protect:
- ○ in Winter
- ○ from Wind
- ○ from Frost
- ○ Store indoors for Winter
- ○ Other
- ○ Stake
- ○ Mulch
- ○ Wrap trunk

Cultivation Notes:

Poisonous To: ○ People ○ Pets ○ Livestock

Part Poisonous: ○ Leaves ○ Flower ○ Stem ○ Roots

Problems:

Notes:

Botanical Name:

Common Name:

Photo, Drawing, Seed Packet or Plant Marker:

Plant Type:
- ○ Annual
- ○ Biennial
- ○ Perennial
- ○ Fruit
- ○ Vegetable
- ○ Herb
- ○ Tree
- ○ Shrub
- ○ Vine
- ○ Bulb

Size at Maturity:
Height   Width   Root Depth

Attributes:
- ○ Disease Resistant
- ○ Pest Resistant
- ○ Deer Resistant
- ○ Invasive
- ○ Deciduous
- ○ Self-Propagating

Attracts
- ○ Butterflies
- ○ Hummingbirds
- ○ Birds:

☆ ☆ ☆ ☆ ☆

Sun Exposure:

Water Requirements:

Hardiness Zone:

Propagation:
- ○ Layering
- ○ Cutting:
  - ○ in Soil
  - ○ in Water
- ○ Seed
- ○ Dividing:
  - ○ Spring
  - ○ Fall
  - ○ Other

Uses:

Companion Plants:

Characteristics

Individual Plant Info

Soil Requirements:
- ○ Rich
- ○ Average
- ○ Poor

- ○ Moist
- ● Dry
- ○ Sandy

- ● Rocky
- ○ Sandy
- ○ Well-Drained

- ○ Alkaline
- ● Acid
- ○ PH

Notes:

Sowing and Planting Dates:

Treatment and Dates:

Dates:

- ● Fertilize with: _____ _____
- ● Spray with: _____ _____
- ○ Treat with:

Prune:
- ○ Spring
- ● Fall
- ● Summer
- ● Anytime
- ● After Bloom
- ○ Other

Tidy:
- ○ Deadhead
- ○ Pinch
- ○ Shear
- ○ Thin

Protect:
- ○ in Winter
- ○ from Wind
- ○ from Frost
- ○ Store indoors for Winter
- ○ Other

- ○ Stake
- ○ Mulch
- ○ Wrap trunk

Cultivation Notes:

Poisonous To:
- ○ People
- ○ Pets
- ○ Livestock

Part Poisonous:
- ○ Leaves
- ○ Flower
- ○ Stem
- ○ Roots

Problems:

Notes:

Botanical Name:

Common Name:

Photo, Drawing, Seed Packet or Plant Marker:

Plant Type:
- ○ Annual
- ○ Biennial
- ○ Perennial

- ○ Fruit
- ○ Vegetable
- ○ Herb

- ○ Tree
- ○ Shrub
- ○ Vine
- ○ Bulb

Size at Maturity:
Height   Width   Root Depth

Attributes:
- ○ Disease Resistant
- ○ Pest Resistant
- ○ Deer Resistant

- ○ Invasive
- ○ Deciduous
- ○ Self-Propagating

Attracts
- ○ Butterflies
- ○ Hummingbirds
- ○ Birds:

☆ ☆ ☆ ☆ ☆

Sun Exposure:

Water Requirements:

Hardiness Zone:

Propagation:
- ○ Layering
- ○ Cutting:
  - ○ in Soil
  - ○ in Water
- ○ Seed
- ○ Dividing:
  - ○ Spring
  - ○ Fall
  - ○ Other

Uses:

Companion Plants:

Characteristics

Individual Plant Info

Soil Requirements:
- ○ Rich
- ○ Average
- ○ Poor

- ○ Moist
- ○ Dry
- ○ Sandy

- ○ Rocky
- ○ Sandy
- ○ Well-Drained

- ○ Alkaline
- ○ Acid
- ○ PH

Notes:

Sowing and Planting Dates:

Treatment and Dates:

Dates:

- ○ Fertilize with: _____   _____
- ○ Spray with: _____   _____
- ○ Treat with:

Prune:
- ○ Spring
- ○ Fall
- ○ Summer
- ○ Anytime
- ○ After Bloom
- ○ Other

Tidy:
- ○ Deadhead
- ○ Pinch
- ○ Shear
- ○ Thin

Protect:
- ○ in Winter
- ○ from Wind
- ○ from Frost
- ○ Store indoors for Winter
- ○ Other

- ○ Stake
- ○ Mulch
- ○ Wrap trunk

Cultivation Notes:

Poisonous To:
- ○ People
- ○ Pets
- ○ Livestock

Part Poisonous:
- ○ Leaves
- ○ Flower
- ○ Stem
- ○ Roots

Problems:

Notes:

Botanical Name:

Common Name:

Photo, Drawing, Seed Packet or Plant Marker:

Plant Type:
- ○ Annual
- ○ Biennial
- ○ Perennial

- ○ Fruit
- ○ Vegetable
- ○ Herb

- ○ Tree
- ○ Shrub
- ○ Vine
- ○ Bulb

Size at Maturity:
Height   Width   Root Depth

Attributes:
- ○ Disease Resistant
- ○ Pest Resistant
- ○ Deer Resistant

- ○ Invasive
- ○ Deciduous
- ○ Self-Propagating

Attracts
- ○ Butterflies
- ○ Hummingbirds
- ○ Birds:

☆ ☆ ☆ ☆ ☆

Sun Exposure:

Water Requirements:

Hardiness Zone:

Propagation:
- ○ Layering
- ○ Cutting:
  - ○ in Soil
  - ○ in Water
- ○ Seed
- ○ Dividing:
  - ○ Spring
  - ○ Fall
  - ○ Other

Uses:

Companion Plants:

Characteristics

Individual Plant Info

Soil Requirements:
- ○ Rich
- ○ Average
- ○ Poor
- ○ Moist
- ○ Dry
- ○ Sandy
- ■ Rocky
- ■ Sandy
- ■ Well-Drained
- ■ Alkaline
- ■ Acid
- ■ PH

Notes:

Sowing and Planting Dates:

Treatment and Dates:

Dates:

- ○ Fertilize with: _____ _____
- ○ Spray with: _____ _____
- ○ Treat with:

Prune:
- ○ Spring
- ○ Fall
- ○ Summer
- ○ Anytime
- ○ After Bloom
- ○ Other

Tidy:
- ○ Deadhead
- ○ Pinch
- ○ Shear
- ○ Thin

Protect:
- ■ in Winter
- ■ from Wind
- ■ from Frost
- ■ Store indoors for Winter
- ■ Other

- ○ Stake
- ○ Mulch
- ○ Wrap trunk

Cultivation Notes:

Poisonous To: ○ People   ○ Pets   ○ Livestock

Part Poisonous: ○ Leaves   ○ Flower   ○ Stem   ○ Roots

Problems:

Notes:

Botanical Name:

Common Name:

Photo, Drawing, Seed Packet or Plant Marker:

Plant Type:
- ○ Annual
- ○ Biennial
- ○ Perennial
- ■ Fruit
- ■ Vegetable
- ○ Herb
- ○ Tree
- ○ Shrub
- ○ Vine
- ○ Bulb

Size at Maturity:

Height   Width   Root Depth

Attributes:
- ○ Disease Resistant
- ○ Pest Resistant
- ○ Deer Resistant
- ○ Invasive
- ○ Deciduous
- ○ Self-Propagating

Attracts
- ○ Butterflies
- ○ Hummingbirds
- ○ Birds:

☆ ☆ ☆ ☆ ☆

Sun Exposure:

Water Requirements:

Hardiness Zone:

Propagation:
- ○ Layering
- ○ Cutting:
  - ■ in Soil
  - ■ in Water
- ○ Seed
- ○ Dividing:
  - ○ Spring
  - ○ Fall
  - ○ Other

Uses:

Companion Plants:

Characteristics

Individual Plant Info

Soil Requirements:
- ( ) Rich
- ( ) Average
- ( ) Poor
- (●) Moist
- (●) Dry
- ( ) Sandy
- ( ) Rocky
- ( ) Sandy
- ( ) Well-Drained
- ( ) Alkaline
- ( ) Acid
- ( ) PH

Notes:

Sowing and Planting Dates:

Treatment and Dates:

Dates:

- ( ) Fertilize with: _____   _____
- ( ) Spray with: _____   _____
- ( ) Treat with:

Prune:
- ( ) Spring
- ( ) Fall
- ( ) Summer
- ( ) Anytime
- ( ) After Bloom
- ( ) Other

Tidy:
- ( ) Deadhead
- ( ) Pinch
- ( ) Shear
- ( ) Thin

Protect:
- ( ) in Winter
- ( ) from Wind
- ( ) from Frost
- ( ) Store indoors for Winter
- ( ) Other
- ( ) Stake
- ( ) Mulch
- ( ) Wrap trunk

Cultivation Notes:

Poisonous To: ( ) People ( ) Pets ( ) Livestock

Part Poisonous: ( ) Leaves ( ) Flower ( ) Stem ( ) Roots

Problems:

Notes:

Botanical Name:

Common Name:

Photo, Drawing, Seed Packet or Plant Marker:

Plant Type:
- ( ) Annual
- ( ) Biennial
- ( ) Perennial
- ( ) Fruit
- ( ) Vegetable
- ( ) Herb
- ( ) Tree
- ( ) Shrub
- ( ) Vine
- ( ) Bulb

Size at Maturity:
Height   Width   Root Depth

Attributes: Attracts
- ( ) Disease Resistant
- ( ) Pest Resistant
- ( ) Deer Resistant
- ( ) Invasive
- ( ) Deciduous
- ( ) Self-Propagating
- ( ) Butterflies
- ( ) Hummingbirds
- ( ) Birds:

☆ ☆ ☆ ☆ ☆

Sun Exposure:

Water Requirements:

Hardiness Zone:

Propagation:
- ( ) Layering
- ( ) Cutting:
  - ( ) in Soil
  - ( ) in Water
- ( ) Seed
- ( ) Dividing:
  - ( ) Spring
  - ( ) Fall
  - ( ) Other

Uses:

Companion Plants:

Characteristics

Individual Plant Info

Soil Requirements:
- ○ Rich
- ○ Average
- ○ Poor
- ○ Moist
- ○ Dry
- ○ Sandy
- ○ Rocky
- ○ Sandy
- ○ Well-Drained
- ○ Alkaline
- ○ Acid
- ○ PH

Notes:

Sowing and Planting Dates:

Treatment and Dates:

- ○ Fertilize with: _____ Dates: _____
- ○ Spray with: _____ _____
- ○ Treat with:

Prune:
- ○ Spring
- ○ Fall
- ○ Summer
- ○ Anytime
- ○ After Bloom
- ○ Other

Tidy:
- ○ Deadhead
- ○ Pinch
- ○ Shear
- ○ Thin

Protect:
- ○ in Winter
- ○ from Wind
- ○ from Frost
- ○ Store indoors for Winter
- ○ Other
- ○ Stake
- ○ Mulch
- ○ Wrap trunk

Cultivation Notes:

Poisonous To:
- ○ People
- ○ Pets
- ○ Livestock

Part Poisonous:
- ○ Leaves
- ○ Flower
- ○ Stem
- ○ Roots

Problems:

Notes:

Botanical Name:

Common Name:

Photo, Drawing, Seed Packet or Plant Marker:

Plant Type:
- ○ Annual
- ○ Biennial
- ○ Perennial
- ○ Fruit
- ○ Vegetable
- ○ Herb
- ○ Tree
- ○ Shrub
- ○ Vine
- ○ Bulb

Size at Maturity:
Height   Width   Root Depth

Attributes:
- ○ Disease Resistant
- ○ Pest Resistant
- ○ Deer Resistant
- ○ Invasive
- ○ Deciduous
- ○ Self-Propagating

Attracts
- ○ Butterflies
- ○ Hummingbirds
- ○ Birds:

☆ ☆ ☆ ☆ ☆

Sun Exposure:

Water Requirements:

Hardiness Zone:

Propagation:
- ○ Layering
- ○ Cutting:
  - ○ in Soil
  - ○ in Water
- ○ Seed
- ○ Dividing:
  - ○ Spring
  - ○ Fall
  - ○ Other

Uses:

Companion Plants:

Characteristics

Individual Plant Info

Soil Requirements:
- ○ Rich
- ○ Average
- ○ Poor

- ○ Moist
- ○ Dry
- ○ Sandy

- ○ Rocky
- ○ Sandy
- ○ Well-Drained

- ○ Alkaline
- ○ Acid
- ○ PH

Notes:

Sowing and Planting Dates:

Treatment and Dates:

Dates:

- ○ Fertilize with: _____ _____
- ○ Spray with: _____ _____
- ○ Treat with:

Prune:
- ○ Spring
- ○ Fall
- ○ Summer
- ○ Anytime
- ○ After Bloom
- ○ Other

Tidy:
- ○ Deadhead
- ○ Pinch
- ○ Shear
- ○ Thin

Protect:
- ○ in Winter
- ○ from Wind
- ○ from Frost
- ○ Store indoors for Winter
- ○ Other

- ○ Stake
- ○ Mulch
- ○ Wrap trunk

Cultivation Notes:

Poisonous To:
- ○ People ○ Pets ○ Livestock

Part Poisonous:
- ○ Leaves ○ Flower ○ Stem ○ Roots

Problems:

Notes:

Botanical Name:

Common Name:

Photo, Drawing, Seed Packet or Plant Marker:

Plant Type:
- ○ Annual
- ○ Biennial
- ○ Perennial

- ○ Fruit
- ○ Vegetable
- ○ Herb

- ○ Tree
- ○ Shrub
- ○ Vine
- ○ Bulb

Size at Maturity:

Height   Width   Root Depth

Attributes:
- ○ Disease Resistant
- ○ Pest Resistant
- ○ Deer Resistant

- ○ Invasive
- ○ Deciduous
- ○ Self-Propagating

Attracts
- ○ Butterflies
- ○ Hummingbirds
- ○ Birds:

☆ ☆ ☆ ☆ ☆

Sun Exposure:

Water Requirements:

Hardiness Zone:

Propagation:
- ○ Layering
- ○ Cutting:
  - ○ in Soil
  - ○ in Water
- ○ Seed
- ○ Dividing:
  - ○ Spring
  - ○ Fall
  - ○ Other

Uses:

Companion Plants:

Characteristics

Individual Plant Info

Soil Requirements:

- ○ Rich
- ○ Average
- ○ Poor

- ○ Moist
- ○ Dry
- ○ Sandy

- ○ Rocky
- ○ Sandy
- ○ Well-Drained

- ○ Alkaline
- ○ Acid
- ○ PH

Notes:

Sowing and Planting Dates:

Treatment and Dates:

Dates:

- ○ Fertilize with: _____ _____
- ○ Spray with: _____ _____
- ○ Treat with:

Prune:
- ○ Spring
- ○ Fall
- ○ Summer
- ○ Anytime
- ○ After Bloom
- ○ Other

Tidy:
- ○ Deadhead
- ○ Pinch
- ○ Shear
- ○ Thin

Protect:
- ○ in Winter
- ○ from Wind
- ○ from Frost
- ○ Store indoors for Winter
- ○ Other

- ○ Stake
- ○ Mulch
- ○ Wrap trunk

Cultivation Notes:

| Poisonous To: | ○ People | ○ Pets | ○ Livestock | |
| Part Poisonous: | ○ Leaves | ○ Flower | ○ Stem | ○ Roots |

Problems:

Notes:

Botanical Name:

Common Name:

Photo, Drawing, Seed Packet or Plant Marker:

Plant Type:
- ○ Annual
- ○ Biennial
- ○ Perennial

- ○ Fruit
- ○ Vegetable
- ○ Herb

- ○ Tree
- ○ Shrub
- ○ Vine
- ○ Bulb

Size at Maturity:

Height   Width   Root Depth

Attributes:

- ○ Disease Resistant
- ○ Pest Resistant
- ○ Deer Resistant

- ○ Invasive
- ○ Deciduous
- ○ Self-Propagating

Attracts
- ○ Butterflies
- ○ Hummingbirds
- ○ Birds:

☆ ☆ ☆ ☆ ☆

Sun Exposure:

Water Requirements:

Hardiness Zone:

Propagation:
- ○ Layering
- ○ Cutting:
  - ○ in Soil
  - ○ in Water
- ○ Seed
- ○ Dividing:
  - ○ Spring
  - ○ Fall
  - ○ Other

Uses:

Companion Plants:

Characteristics

Individual Plant Info

Soil Requirements:
- ○ Rich
- ○ Average
- ○ Poor

- ○ Moist
- ○ Dry
- ○ Sandy

- ○ Rocky
- ○ Sandy
- ○ Well-Drained

- ○ Alkaline
- ○ Acid
- ○ PH

Notes:

Sowing and Planting Dates:

Treatment and Dates:

- ○ Fertilize with: _____   Dates: _____
- ○ Spray with: _____   _____
- ○ Treat with:

Prune:
- ○ Spring
- ○ Fall
- ○ Summer
- ○ Anytime
- ○ After Bloom
- ○ Other

Tidy:
- ○ Deadhead
- ○ Pinch
- ○ Shear
- ○ Thin

Protect:
- ○ in Winter
- ○ from Wind
- ○ from Frost
- ○ Store indoors for Winter
- ○ Other

- ○ Stake
- ○ Mulch
- ○ Wrap trunk

Cultivation Notes:

Poisonous To:
- ○ People
- ○ Pets
- ○ Livestock

Part Poisonous:
- ○ Leaves
- ○ Flower
- ○ Stem
- ○ Roots

Problems:

Notes:

Botanical Name:

Common Name:

Photo, Drawing, Seed Packet or Plant Marker:

Plant Type:
- ○ Annual
- ○ Biennial
- ○ Perennial

- ○ Fruit
- ○ Vegetable
- ○ Herb

- ○ Tree
- ○ Shrub
- ○ Vine
- ○ Bulb

Size at Maturity:
Height   Width   Root Depth

Attributes:
- ○ Disease Resistant
- ○ Pest Resistant
- ○ Deer Resistant

- ○ Invasive
- ○ Deciduous
- ○ Self-Propagating

Attracts
- ○ Butterflies
- ○ Hummingbirds
- ○ Birds:

☆ ☆ ☆ ☆ ☆

Sun Exposure:

Water Requirements:

Hardiness Zone:

Propagation:
- ○ Layering
- ○ Cutting:
  - ○ in Soil
  - ○ in Water
- ○ Seed
- ○ Dividing:
  - ○ Spring
  - ○ Fall
  - ○ Other

Uses:

Companion Plants:

Characteristics

Individual Plant Info

Soil Requirements:
- ○ Rich
- ○ Average
- ○ Poor
- ○ Moist
- ○ Dry
- ○ Sandy
- ○ Rocky
- ○ Sandy
- ○ Well-Drained
- ○ Alkaline
- ○ Acid
- ○ PH

Notes:

Sowing and Planting Dates:

Treatment and Dates:
- ○ Fertilize with: _____ Dates: _____
- ○ Spray with: _____ _____
- ○ Treat with:

Prune:	Tidy:	Protect:	
○ Spring	○ Deadhead	○ in Winter	○ Stake
○ Fall	○ Pinch	○ from Wind	○ Mulch
○ Summer	○ Shear	○ from Frost	○ Wrap trunk
○ Anytime	○ Thin	○ Store indoors for Winter	
○ After Bloom		○ Other	
○ Other			

Cultivation Notes:

Poisonous To: ○ People ○ Pets ○ Livestock

Part Poisonous: ○ Leaves ○ Flower ○ Stem ○ Roots

Problems:

Notes:

Botanical Name:

Common Name:

Photo, Drawing, Seed Packet or Plant Marker:

Plant Type:
- ○ Annual
- ○ Biennial
- ○ Perennial
- ○ Fruit
- ○ Vegetable
- ○ Herb
- ○ Tree
- ○ Shrub
- ○ Vine
- ○ Bulb

Size at Maturity:

Height   Width   Root Depth

Attributes:
- ○ Disease Resistant
- ○ Pest Resistant
- ○ Deer Resistant
- ○ Invasive
- ○ Deciduous
- ○ Self-Propagating

Attracts
- ○ Butterflies
- ○ Hummingbirds
- ○ Birds:

☆ ☆ ☆ ☆ ☆

Sun Exposure:

Water Requirements:

Hardiness Zone:

Propagation:
- ○ Layering
- ○ Cutting:
  - ○ in Soil
  - ○ in Water
- ○ Seed
- ○ Dividing:
  - ○ Spring
  - ○ Fall
  - ○ Other

Uses:

Companion Plants:

Characteristics

Individual Plant Info

Soil Requirements:
- ○ Rich
- ○ Average
- ○ Poor

- ▪ Moist
- ▪ Dry
- ▪ Sandy

- ○ Rocky
- ○ Sandy
- ○ Well-Drained

- ○ Alkaline
- ○ Acid
- ○ PH

Notes:

Sowing and Planting Dates:

Treatment and Dates:

Dates:

- ○ Fertilize with: _____ _____
- ○ Spray with: _____ _____
- ○ Treat with:

Prune:
- ○ Spring
- ○ Fall
- ○ Summer
- ○ Anytime
- ○ After Bloom
- ○ Other

Tidy:
- ○ Deadhead
- ○ Pinch
- ○ Shear
- ○ Thin

Protect:
- ▪ in Winter
- ▪ from Wind
- ▪ from Frost
- ▪ Store indoors for Winter
- ▪ Other

- ▪ Stake
- ▪ Mulch
- ▪ Wrap trunk

Cultivation Notes:

Poisonous To: ○ People ○ Pets ○ Livestock

Part Poisonous: ▪ Leaves ▪ Flower ▪ Stem ○ Roots

Problems:

Notes:

Botanical Name:

Common Name:

Photo, Drawing, Seed Packet or Plant Marker:

Plant Type:

- ○ Annual
- ○ Biennial
- ○ Perennial

- ○ Fruit
- ○ Vegetable
- ○ Herb

- ▪ Tree
- ▪ Shrub
- ▪ Vine
- ▪ Bulb

Size at Maturity:

Height   Width   Root Depth

Attributes: **Attracts**
- ○ Disease Resistant   ○ Invasive   ○ Butterflies
- ○ Pest Resistant   ○ Deciduous   ○ Hummingbirds
- ○ Deer Resistant   ○ Self-Propagating ○ Birds:

☆ ☆ ☆ ☆ ☆

Sun Exposure:

Water Requirements:

Hardiness Zone:

Propagation:
- ○ Layering
- ○ Cutting:
  - ▪ in Soil
  - ▪ in Water
- ○ Seed
- ○ Dividing:
  - ▪ Spring
  - ▪ Fall
  - ○ Other

Uses:

Companion Plants:

Characteristics

Individual Plant Info

Soil Requirements:

- ○ Rich
- ○ Average
- ○ Poor
- ○ Moist
- ▢ Dry
- ▢ Sandy
- ▢ Rocky
- ▢ Sandy
- ▢ Well-Drained
- ▢ Alkaline
- ▢ Acid
- ▢ PH

Notes:

Sowing and Planting Dates:

Treatment and Dates:

Dates:

- ○ Fertilize with: _____ _____
- ○ Spray with: _____ _____
- ○ Treat with:

Prune:
- ○ Spring
- ○ Fall
- ○ Summer
- ○ Anytime
- ○ After Bloom
- ○ Other

Tidy:
- ▢ Deadhead
- ▢ Pinch
- ▢ Shear
- ▢ Thin

Protect:
- ▢ in Winter
- ▢ from Wind
- ▢ from Frost
- ▢ Store indoors for Winter
- ▢ Other

- ▢ Stake
- ▢ Mulch
- ▢ Wrap trunk

Cultivation Notes:

Poisonous To:
- ○ People
- ○ Pets
- ○ Livestock

Part Poisonous:
- ○ Leaves
- ○ Flower
- ○ Stem
- ○ Roots

Problems:

Notes:

Botanical Name:

Common Name:

Photo, Drawing, Seed Packet or Plant Marker:

Plant Type:

- ○ Annual
- ○ Biennial
- ○ Perennial
- ▢ Fruit
- ▢ Vegetable
- ▢ Herb
- ○ Tree
- ○ Shrub
- ○ Vine
- ○ Bulb

Size at Maturity:

Height   Width   Root Depth

Attributes:
- ○ Disease Resistant
- ○ Pest Resistant
- ○ Deer Resistant
- ○ Invasive
- ○ Deciduous
- ○ Self-Propagating

Attracts
- ○ Butterflies
- ○ Hummingbirds
- ○ Birds:

☆ ☆ ☆ ☆ ☆

Sun Exposure:

Water Requirements:

Hardiness Zone:

Propagation:
- ○ Layering
- ○ Cutting:
  - ▢ in Soil
  - ▢ in Water
- ○ Seed
- ○ Dividing:
  - ○ Spring
  - ○ Fall
  - ○ Other

Uses:

Companion Plants:

Characteristics

Individual Plant Info

Soil Requirements:
- ( ) Rich
- ( ) Average
- ( ) Poor
- ( ) Moist
- ( ) Dry
- ( ) Sandy
- ( ) Rocky
- ( ) Sandy
- ( ) Well-Drained
- ( ) Alkaline
- ( ) Acid
- ( ) PH

Notes:

Sowing and Planting Dates:

Treatment and Dates:

Dates:

- ( ) Fertilize with: _____   _____
- ( ) Spray with: _____   _____
- ( ) Treat with:

Prune:
- ( ) Spring
- ( ) Fall
- ( ) Summer
- ( ) Anytime
- ( ) After Bloom
- ( ) Other

Tidy:
- ( ) Deadhead
- ( ) Pinch
- ( ) Shear
- ( ) Thin

Protect:
- ( ) in Winter
- ( ) from Wind
- ( ) from Frost
- ( ) Store indoors for Winter
- ( ) Other
- ( ) Stake
- ( ) Mulch
- ( ) Wrap trunk

Cultivation Notes:

Poisonous To:
( ) People ( ) Pets ( ) Livestock

Part Poisonous:
( ) Leaves ( ) Flower ( ) Stem ( ) Roots

Problems:

Notes:

Botanical Name:

Common Name:

Photo, Drawing, Seed Packet or Plant Marker:

Plant Type:
- ( ) Annual
- ( ) Biennial
- ( ) Perennial
- ( ) Fruit
- ( ) Vegetable
- ( ) Herb
- ( ) Tree
- ( ) Shrub
- ( ) Vine
- ( ) Bulb

Size at Maturity:
Height   Width   Root Depth

Attributes:
- ( ) Disease Resistant
- ( ) Pest Resistant
- ( ) Deer Resistant
- ( ) Invasive
- ( ) Deciduous
- ( ) Self-Propagating

Attracts
- ( ) Butterflies
- ( ) Hummingbirds
- ( ) Birds:

☆ ☆ ☆ ☆ ☆

Sun Exposure:

Water Requirements:

Hardiness Zone:

Propagation:
- ( ) Layering
- ( ) Cutting:
  - ( ) in Soil
  - ( ) in Water
- ( ) Seed
- ( ) Dividing:
  - ( ) Spring
  - ( ) Fall
  - ( ) Other

Uses:

Companion Plants:

Characteristics

Individual Plant Info

Soil Requirements:
- ◉ Rich
- ◉ Average
- ◉ Poor
- ◉ Moist
- ◉ Dry
- ◉ Sandy
- ◉ Rocky
- ◉ Sandy
- ◉ Well-Drained
- ◉ Alkaline
- ◉ Acid
- ◉ PH

Notes:

Sowing and Planting Dates:

Treatment and Dates:

- ◯ Fertilize with: _____   Dates: _____
- ◯ Spray with: _____   _____
- ◯ Treat with:

Prune:	Tidy:	Protect:	
◯ Spring	◯ Deadhead	◯ in Winter	◯ Stake
◯ Fall	◯ Pinch	◯ from Wind	◯ Mulch
◯ Summer	◯ Shear	◯ from Frost	◯ Wrap trunk
◯ Anytime	◯ Thin	◯ Store indoors for Winter	
◯ After Bloom		◯ Other	
◯ Other			

Cultivation Notes:

Poisonous To:
- ◯ People
- ◯ Pets
- ◯ Livestock

Part Poisonous:
- ◯ Leaves
- ◯ Flower
- ◯ Stem
- ◯ Roots

Problems:

Notes:

Botanical Name:

Common Name:

Photo, Drawing, Seed Packet or Plant Marker:

Plant Type:

◯ Annual	◯ Fruit	◯ Tree
◯ Biennial	◯ Vegetable	◯ Shrub
◯ Perennial	◯ Herb	◯ Vine
		◯ Bulb

Size at Maturity:
Height   Width   Root Depth

Attributes: Attracts
- ◯ Disease Resistant
- ◯ Pest Resistant
- ◯ Deer Resistant
- ◯ Invasive
- ◯ Deciduous
- ◯ Self-Propagating
- ◯ Butterflies
- ◯ Hummingbirds
- ◯ Birds:

☆ ☆ ☆ ☆ ☆

Sun Exposure:

Water Requirements:

Hardiness Zone:

Propagation:
- ◯ Layering
- ◯ Cutling:
  - ☐ in Soil
  - ☐ in Water
- ◯ Seed
- ◯ Dividing:
  - ◯ Spring
  - ◯ Fall
  - ◯ Other

Uses:

Companion Plants:

Characteristics

Individual Plant Info

Soil Requirements:
- ○ Rich
- ○ Average
- ○ Poor
- ○ Moist
- ○ Dry
- ○ Sandy
- ● Rocky
- ○ Sandy
- ● Well-Drained
- ○ Alkaline
- ○ Acid
- ○ PH

Notes:

Sowing and Planting Dates:

Treatment and Dates:

Dates:

- ○ Fertilize with: _____ _____
- ○ Spray with: _____ _____
- ○ Treat with:

Prune:
- ● Spring
- ○ Fall
- ○ Summer
- ○ Anytime
- ○ After Bloom
- ○ Other

Tidy:
- ○ Deadhead
- ○ Pinch
- ○ Shear
- ○ Thin

Protect:
- ○ in Winter
- ○ from Wind
- ○ from Frost
- ○ Store indoors for Winter
- ○ Other

- ○ Stake
- ○ Mulch
- ○ Wrap trunk

Cultivation Notes:

Poisonous To:
- ○ People
- ○ Pets
- ○ Livestock

Part Poisonous:
- ○ Leaves
- ○ Flower
- ○ Stem
- ○ Roots

Problems:

Notes:

Botanical Name:

Common Name:

Photo, Drawing, Seed Packet or Plant Marker:

☆ ☆ ☆ ☆ ☆

Sun Exposure:

Water Requirements:

Hardiness Zone:

Propagation:
- ○ Layering
- ○ Cutting:
  - ○ in Soil
  - ○ in Water
- ○ Seed
- ○ Dividing:
  - ○ Spring
  - ○ Fall
  - ○ Other

Uses:

Companion Plants:

Characteristics

Plant Type:
- ○ Annual
- ○ Biennial
- ○ Perennial
- ○ Fruit
- ○ Vegetable
- ○ Herb
- ○ Tree
- ○ Shrub
- ○ Vine
- ○ Bulb

Size at Maturity:
Height   Width   Root Depth

Attributes:
- ○ Disease Resistant
- ○ Pest Resistant
- ○ Deer Resistant
- ○ Invasive
- ○ Deciduous
- ○ Self-Propagating

Attracts
- ○ Butterflies
- ○ Hummingbirds
- ○ Birds:

Individual Plant Info

Soil Requirements:
- ○ Rich
- ○ Average
- ○ Poor
- ○ Moist
- ○ Dry
- ○ Sandy
- ○ Rocky
- ○ Sandy
- ○ Well-Drained
- ○ Alkaline
- ○ Acid
- ○ PH

Notes:

Sowing and Planting Dates:

Treatment and Dates:

Dates:

- ○ Fertilize with: _____ _____
- ○ Spray with: _____ _____
- ○ Treat with:

Prune:
- ○ Spring
- ○ Fall
- ○ Summer
- ○ Anytime
- ○ After Bloom
- ○ Other

Tidy:
- ○ Deadhead
- ○ Pinch
- ○ Shear
- ○ Thin

Protect:
- ○ in Winter
- ○ from Wind
- ○ from Frost
- ○ Store indoors for Winter
- ○ Other
- ○ Stake
- ○ Mulch
- ○ Wrap trunk

Cultivation Notes:

Poisonous To:
- ○ People
- ○ Pets
- ○ Livestock

Part Poisonous:
- ○ Leaves
- ○ Flower
- ○ Stem
- ○ Roots

Problems:

Notes:

Botanical Name:

Common Name:

Photo, Drawing, Seed Packet or Plant Marker:

☆ ☆☆ ☆☆ ☆ ☆

Sun Exposure:

Water Requirements:

Hardiness Zone:

Propagation:
- ○ Layering
- ○ Cutting:
  - ○ in Soil
  - ○ in Water
- ○ Seed
- ○ Dividing:
  - ○ Spring
  - ○ Fall
  - ○ Other

Uses:

Companion Plants:

Characteristics

Plant Type:
- ○ Annual
- ○ Biennial
- ○ Perennial
- ○ Fruit
- ○ Vegetable
- ○ Herb
- ○ Tree
- ○ Shrub
- ○ Vine
- ○ Bulb

Size at Maturity:
Height   Width   Root Depth

Attributes:
- ○ Disease Resistant
- ○ Pest Resistant
- ○ Deer Resistant
- ○ Invasive
- ○ Deciduous
- ○ Self-Propagating

Attracts
- ○ Butterflies
- ○ Hummingbirds
- ○ Birds:

Individual Plant Info

Soil Requirements:
- ○ Rich
- ○ Average
- ○ Poor
- ○ Moist
- ○ Dry
- ○ Sandy
- ○ Rocky
- ○ Sandy
- ○ Well-Drained
- ○ Alkaline
- ○ Acid
- ○ PH

Notes:

Sowing and Planting Dates:

Treatment and Dates:

Dates:

- ○ Fertilize with: _____ _____
- ○ Spray with: _____ _____
- ○ Treat with:

Prune:
- ○ Spring
- ○ Fall
- ○ Summer
- ○ Anytime
- ○ After Bloom
- ○ Other

Tidy:
- ○ Deadhead
- ○ Pinch
- ○ Shear
- ○ Thin

Protect:
- ○ in Winter
- ○ from Wind
- ○ from Frost
- ○ Store indoors for Winter
- ○ Other
- ○ Stake
- ○ Mulch
- ○ Wrap trunk

Cultivation Notes:

| Poisonous To: | ○ People | ○ Pets | ○ Livestock |
| Part Poisonous: | ○ Leaves | ○ Flower | ○ Stem | ○ Roots |

Problems:

Notes:

Botanical Name:

Common Name:

Photo, Drawing, Seed Packet or Plant Marker:

Plant Type:
- ○ Annual
- ○ Biennial
- ○ Perennial
- ○ Fruit
- ○ Vegetable
- ○ Herb
- ○ Tree
- ○ Shrub
- ○ Vine
- ○ Bulb

Size at Maturity:
Height   Width   Root Depth

Attributes:
- ○ Disease Resistant
- ○ Pest Resistant
- ○ Deer Resistant
- ○ Invasive
- ○ Deciduous
- ○ Self-Propagating

Attracts
- ○ Butterflies
- ○ Hummingbirds
- ○ Birds:

☆ ☆ ☆ ☆ ☆

Sun Exposure:

Water Requirements:

Hardiness Zone:

Propagation:
- ○ Layering
- ○ Cutting:
  - ○ in Soil
  - ○ in Water
- ○ Seed
- ○ Dividing:
  - ○ Spring
  - ○ Fall
  - ○ Other

Uses:

Companion Plants:

Characteristics

Individual Plant Info

Soil Requirements:

- ○ Rich
- ○ Average
- ○ Poor

- ○ Moist
- ○ Dry
- ○ Sandy

- ○ Rocky
- ○ Sandy
- ○ Well-Drained

- ○ Alkaline
- ○ Acid
- ○ PH

Notes:

Sowing and Planting Dates:

Treatment and Dates:

Dates:

- ○ Fertilize with: _____ _____
- ○ Spray with: _____ _____
- ○ Treat with:

Prune:	Tidy:	Protect:	
○ Spring	○ Deadhead	○ in Winter	○ Stake
○ Fall	○ Pinch	○ from Wind	○ Mulch
○ Summer	○ Shear	○ from Frost	○ Wrap trunk
○ Anytime	○ Thin	○ Store indoors for Winter	
○ After Bloom		○ Other	
○ Other			

Cultivation Notes:

Poisonous To: ○ People   ○ Pets   ○ Livestock

Part Poisonous: ○ Leaves   ○ Flower   ○ Stem   ○ Roots

Problems:

Notes:

Botanical Name:

Common Name:

Photo, Drawing, Seed Packet or Plant Marker:

Plant Type:

- ○ Annual
- ○ Biennial
- ○ Perennial

- ○ Fruit
- ○ Vegetable
- ○ Herb

- ○ Tree
- ○ Shrub
- ○ Vine
- ○ Bulb

Size at Maturity:

Height   Width   Root Depth

Attributes:		Attracts	
○ Disease Resistant	○ Invasive		○ Butterflies
○ Pest Resistant	○ Deciduous		○ Hummingbirds
○ Deer Resistant	○ Self-Propagating		○ Birds:

☆ ☆ ☆ ☆ ☆

Sun Exposure:

Water Requirements:

Hardiness Zone:

Propagation:

- ○ Layering
- ○ Cutting:
  - ○ in Soil
  - ○ in Water
- ○ Seed
- ○ Dividing:
  - ○ Spring
  - ○ Fall
  - ○ Other

Uses:

Companion Plants:

Characteristics

Individual Plant Info

Soil Requirements:
- ○ Rich
- ○ Average
- ○ Poor
- ○ Moist
- ○ Dry
- ○ Sandy
- ○ Rocky
- ○ Sandy
- ○ Well-Drained
- ○ Alkaline
- ○ Acid
- ○ PH

Notes:

Sowing and Planting Dates:

Treatment and Dates:

Dates:
- ○ Fertilize with: _____ _____
- ○ Spray with: _____ _____
- ○ Treat with:

Prune:
- ○ Spring
- ○ Fall
- ○ Summer
- ○ Anytime
- ○ After Bloom
- ○ Other

Tidy:
- ○ Deadhead
- ○ Pinch
- ○ Shear
- ○ Thin

Protect:
- ○ in Winter
- ○ from Wind
- ○ from Frost
- ○ Store indoors for Winter
- ○ Other
- ○ Stake
- ○ Mulch
- ○ Wrap trunk

Cultivation Notes:

Poisonous To:
- ○ People
- ○ Pets
- ○ Livestock

Part Poisonous:
- ○ Leaves
- ○ Flower
- ○ Stem
- ○ Roots

Problems:

Notes:

Botanical Name:

Common Name:

Photo, Drawing, Seed Packet or Plant Marker:

Plant Type:
- ○ Annual
- ○ Biennial
- ○ Perennial
- ○ Fruit
- ○ Vegetable
- ○ Herb
- ○ Tree
- ○ Shrub
- ○ Vine
- ○ Bulb

Size at Maturity:
Height   Width   Root Depth

Attributes:
- ○ Disease Resistant
- ○ Pest Resistant
- ○ Deer Resistant
- ○ Invasive
- ○ Deciduous
- ○ Self-Propagating

Attracts
- ○ Butterflies
- ○ Hummingbirds
- ○ Birds:

☆ ☆ ☆ ☆ ☆

Sun Exposure:

Water Requirements:

Hardiness Zone:

Propagation:
- ○ Layering
- ○ Cutting:
  - ○ in Soil
  - ○ in Water
- ○ Seed
- ○ Dividing:
  - ○ Spring
  - ○ Fall
  - ○ Other

Uses:

Companion Plants:

Characteristics

Individual Plant Info

Soil Requirements:
- ○ Rich
- ○ Average
- ○ Poor
- ○ Moist
- ○ Dry
- ○ Sandy
- ○ Rocky
- ○ Sandy
- ○ Well-Drained
- ○ Alkaline
- ○ Acid
- ○ PH

Notes:

Sowing and Planting Dates:

Treatment and Dates:

Dates:

- ○ Fertilize with: _____ _____
- ○ Spray with: _____ _____
- ○ Treat with:

Prune:
- ○ Spring
- ○ Fall
- ○ Summer
- ○ Anytime
- ○ After Bloom
- ○ Other

Tidy:
- ○ Deadhead
- ○ Pinch
- ○ Shear
- ○ Thin

Protect:
- ○ in Winter
- ○ from Wind
- ○ from Frost
- ○ Store indoors for Winter
- ○ Other
- ○ Stake
- ○ Mulch
- ○ Wrap trunk

Cultivation Notes:

Poisonous To: ○ People ○ Pets ○ Livestock

Part Poisonous: ○ Leaves ○ Flower ○ Stem ○ Roots

Problems:

Notes:

Botanical Name:

Common Name:

Photo, Drawing, Seed Packet or Plant Marker:

Plant Type:
- ○ Annual
- ○ Biennial
- ○ Perennial
- ○ Fruit
- ○ Vegetable
- ○ Herb
- ○ Tree
- ○ Shrub
- ○ Vine
- ○ Bulb

Size at Maturity:

Height   Width   Root Depth

Attributes:
- ○ Disease Resistant
- ○ Pest Resistant
- ○ Deer Resistant
- ○ Invasive
- ○ Deciduous
- ○ Self-Propagating

Attracts
- ○ Butterflies
- ○ Hummingbirds
- ○ Birds:

☆ ☆ ☆ ☆ ☆

Sun Exposure:

Water Requirements:

Hardiness Zone:

Propagation:
- ○ Layering
- ○ Cutting:
  - ○ in Soil
  - ○ in Water
- ○ Seed
- ○ Dividing:
  - ○ Spring
  - ○ Fall
  - ○ Other

Uses:

Companion Plants:

Characteristics

Individual Plant Info

Soil Requirements:

- ○ Rich
- ○ Average
- ○ Poor
- ○ Moist
- ○ Dry
- ○ Sandy
- ○ Rocky
- ○ Sandy
- ○ Well-Drained
- ○ Alkaline
- ○ Acid
- ○ PH

Notes:

Sowing and Planting Dates:

Treatment and Dates:

Dates:

- ○ Fertilize with: _____   _____
- ○ Spray with: _____   _____
- ○ Treat with:

Prune:
- ○ Spring
- ○ Fall
- ○ Summer
- ○ Anytime
- ○ After Bloom
- ○ Other

Tidy:
- ○ Deadhead
- ○ Pinch
- ○ Shear
- ○ Thin

Protect:
- ○ in Winter
- ○ from Wind
- ○ from Frost
- ○ Store indoors for Winter
- ○ Other
- ○ Stake
- ○ Mulch
- ○ Wrap trunk

Cultivation Notes:

Poisonous To:
- ○ People
- ○ Pets
- ○ Livestock

Part Poisonous:
- ○ Leaves
- ○ Flower
- ○ Stem
- ○ Roots

Problems:

Notes:

Botanical Name:

Common Name:

Photo, Drawing, Seed Packet or Plant Marker:

Plant Type:
- ○ Annual
- ○ Biennial
- ○ Perennial
- ○ Fruit
- ○ Vegetable
- ○ Herb
- ○ Tree
- ○ Shrub
- ○ Vine
- ○ Bulb

Size at Maturity:

Height   Width   Root Depth

Attributes:
- ○ Disease Resistant
- ○ Pest Resistant
- ○ Deer Resistant
- ○ Invasive
- ○ Deciduous
- ○ Self-Propagating

Attracts
- ○ Butterflies
- ○ Hummingbirds
- ○ Birds:

☆ ☆ ☆ ☆ ☆

Sun Exposure:

Water Requirements:

Hardiness Zone:

Propagation:
- ○ Layering
- ○ Cutting:
  - ○ in Soil
  - ○ in Water
- ○ Seed
- ○ Dividing:
  - ○ Spring
  - ○ Fall
  - ○ Other

Uses:

Companion Plants:

Characteristics

Individual Plant Info

Soil Requirements:
- ○ Rich
- ○ Average
- ○ Poor
- ○ Moist
- ○ Dry
- ○ Sandy
- ○ Rocky
- ○ Sandy
- ○ Well-Drained
- ○ Alkaline
- ○ Acid
- ○ PH

Notes:

Sowing and Planting Dates :

Treatment and Dates :

- ○ Fertilize with: _____ Dates: _____
- ○ Spray with: _____ _____
- ○ Treat with:

Prune:
- ○ Spring
- ○ Fall
- ○ Summer
- ○ Anytime
- ○ After Bloom
- ○ Other

Tidy:
- ○ Deadhead
- ○ Pinch
- ○ Shear
- ○ Thin

Protect:
- ○ in Winter
- ○ from Wind
- ○ from Frost
- ○ Store indoors for Winter
- ○ Other
- ○ Stake
- ○ Mulch
- ○ Wrap trunk

Cultivation Notes :

Poisonous To:
- ○ People
- ○ Pets
- ○ Livestock

Part Poisonous:
- ○ Leaves
- ○ Flower
- ○ Stem
- ○ Roots

Problems:

Notes:

Botanical Name :

Common Name :

Photo, Drawing, Seed Packet or Plant Marker :

Plant Type:
- ○ Annual
- ○ Biennial
- ○ Perennial
- ○ Fruit
- ○ Vegetable
- ○ Herb
- ○ Tree
- ○ Shrub
- ○ Vine
- ○ Bulb

Size at Maturity :

Height	Width	Root Depth

Attributes:
- ○ Disease Resistant
- ○ Pest Resistant
- ○ Deer Resistant
- ○ Invasive
- ○ Deciduous
- ○ Self-Propagating

Attracts
- ○ Butterflies
- ○ Hummingbirds
- ○ Birds:

☆ ☆ ☆ ☆ ☆

Sun Exposure :

Water Requirements :

Hardiness Zone:

Propagation:
- ○ Layering
- ○ Cutting:
  - ○ in Soil
  - ○ in Water
- ○ Seed
- ○ Dividing:
  - ○ Spring
  - ○ Fall
  - ○ Other

Uses :

Companion Plants:

Characteristics

Individual Plant Info

Soil Requirements:
- ○ Rich
- ○ Average
- ○ Poor
- ○ Moist
- ○ Dry
- ○ Sandy
- ○ Rocky
- ○ Sandy
- ○ Well-Drained
- ○ Alkaline
- ○ Acid
- ○ PH

Notes:

Sowing and Planting Dates:

Treatment and Dates:

Dates:

- ○ Fertilize with: _____   _____
- ○ Spray with: _____   _____
- ○ Treat with:

Prune:
- ○ Spring
- ○ Fall
- ○ Summer
- ○ Anytime
- ○ After Bloom
- ○ Other

Tidy:
- ○ Deadhead
- ○ Pinch
- ○ Shear
- ○ Thin

Protect:
- ○ in Winter
- ○ from Wind
- ○ from Frost
- ○ Store indoors for Winter
- ○ Other
- ○ Stake
- ○ Mulch
- ○ Wrap trunk

Cultivation Notes:

Poisonous To:
- ○ People
- ○ Pets
- ○ Livestock

Part Poisonous:
- ○ Leaves
- ○ Flower
- ○ Stem
- ○ Roots

Problems:

Notes:

Botanical Name:

Common Name:

Photo, Drawing, Seed Packet or Plant Marker:

Plant Type:
- ○ Annual
- ○ Biennial
- ○ Perennial
- ○ Fruit
- ○ Vegetable
- ○ Herb
- ○ Tree
- ○ Shrub
- ○ Vine
- ○ Bulb

Size at Maturity:
Height   Width   Root Depth

Attributes:
- ○ Disease Resistant
- ○ Pest Resistant
- ○ Deer Resistant
- ○ Invasive
- ○ Deciduous
- ○ Self-Propagating

Attracts
- ○ Butterflies
- ○ Hummingbirds
- ○ Birds:

☆ ☆ ☆ ☆ ☆

Sun Exposure:

Water Requirements:

Hardiness Zone:

Propagation:
- ○ Layering
- ○ Cutting:
  - ○ in Soil
  - ○ in Water
- ○ Seed
- ○ Dividing:
  - ○ Spring
  - ○ Fall
  - ○ Other

Uses:

Companion Plants:

Characteristics

Individual Plant Info

Soil Requirements:
- ○ Rich
- ○ Average
- ○ Poor
- ○ Moist
- ☐ Dry
- ○ Sandy
- ☐ Rocky
- ○ Sandy
- ☐ Well-Drained
- ☐ Alkaline
- ☐ Acid
- ☐ PH

Notes:

Sowing and Planting Dates:

Treatment and Dates:

Dates:
- ○ Fertilize with: _____   _____
- ○ Spray with: _____   _____
- ○ Treat with:

Prune:
- ○ Spring
- ○ Fall
- ○ Summer
- ○ Anytime
- ○ After Bloom
- ○ Other

Tidy:
- ○ Deadhead
- ○ Pinch
- ○ Shear
- ○ Thin

Protect:
- ○ in Winter
- ○ from Wind
- ○ from Frost
- ○ Store indoors for Winter
- ○ Other
- ○ Stake
- ○ Mulch
- ○ Wrap trunk

Cultivation Notes:

Poisonous To:
- ○ People
- ○ Pets
- ○ Livestock

Part Poisonous:
- ○ Leaves
- ○ Flower
- ○ Stem
- ○ Roots

Problems:

Notes:

Botanical Name:

Common Name:

Photo, Drawing, Seed Packet or Plant Marker:

Plant Type:
- ○ Annual
- ○ Biennial
- ○ Perennial
- ☐ Fruit
- ☐ Vegetable
- ○ Herb
- ☐ Tree
- ○ Shrub
- ○ Vine
- ○ Bulb

Size at Maturity:
Height   Width   Root Depth

Attributes:
- ○ Disease Resistant
- ■ Pest Resistant
- ○ Deer Resistant
- ○ Invasive
- ○ Deciduous
- ○ Self-Propagating

Attracts
- ○ Butterflies
- ○ Hummingbirds
- ○ Birds:

☆ ☆ ☆ ☆ ☆

Sun Exposure:

Water Requirements:

Hardiness Zone:

Propagation:
- ○ Layering
- ○ Cutting:
  - ○ in Soil
  - ○ in Water
- ○ Seed
- ○ Dividing:
  - ○ Spring
  - ○ Fall
  - ○ Other

Uses:

Companion Plants:

Characteristics

Individual Plant Info

Soil Requirements:

- ○ Rich
- ○ Average
- ○ Poor
- ● Moist
- ● Dry
- ● Sandy
- ■ Rocky
- ■ Sandy
- ■ Well-Drained
- ○ Alkaline
- ○ Acid
- ○ PH

Notes:

Sowing and Planting Dates:

Treatment and Dates:

Dates:

- ○ Fertilize with: _____ _____
- ○ Spray with: _____ _____
- ○ Treat with:

Prune:	Tidy:	Protect:	
○ Spring	○ Deadhead	○ in Winter	● Stake
○ Fall	○ Pinch	○ from Wind	● Mulch
○ Summer	○ Shear	○ from Frost	○ Wrap trunk
○ Anytime	○ Thin	○ Store indoors for Winter	
○ After Bloom		○ Other	
○ Other			

Cultivation Notes:

Poisonous To: ○ People ○ Pets ○ Livestock

Part Poisonous: ○ Leaves ○ Flower ○ Stem ○ Roots

Problems:

Notes:

Botanical Name:

Common Name:

Photo, Drawing, Seed Packet or Plant Marker:

Plant Type:

- ○ Annual
- ○ Biennial
- ○ Perennial
- ○ Fruit
- ○ Vegetable
- ○ Herb
- ● Tree
- ● Shrub
- ● Vine
- ● Bulb

Size at Maturity:

Height   Width   Root Depth

Attributes:		Attracts	
● Disease Resistant	○ Invasive	○ Butterflies	
○ Pest Resistant	○ Deciduous	○ Hummingbirds	
○ Deer Resistant	○ Self-Propagating	○ Birds:	

☆ ☆ ☆ ☆ ☆

Sun Exposure:

Water Requirements:

Hardiness Zone:

Propagation:

- ○ Layering
- ○ Cutting:
  - ■ in Soil
  - ■ in Water
- ● Seed
- ● Dividing:
  - ○ Spring
  - ○ Fall
  - ○ Other

Uses:

Companion Plants:

Characteristics

Individual Plant Info

Soil Requirements:
- Rich
- Average
- Poor
- Moist
- Dry
- Sandy
- Rocky
- Sandy
- Well-Drained
- Alkaline
- Acid
- PH

Notes:

Sowing and Planting Dates:

Treatment and Dates:

Dates:

- Fertilize with: _____   _____
- Spray with: _____   _____
- Treat with:

Prune:
- Spring
- Fall
- Summer
- Anytime
- After Bloom
- Other

Tidy:
- Deadhead
- Pinch
- Shear
- Thin

Protect:
- in Winter
- from Wind
- from Frost
- Store indoors for Winter
- Other
- Stake
- Mulch
- Wrap trunk

Cultivation Notes:

Poisonous To:
- People
- Pets
- Livestock

Part Poisonous:
- Leaves
- Flower
- Stem
- Roots

Problems:

Notes:

Botanical Name:

Common Name:

Photo, Drawing, Seed Packet or Plant Marker:

Plant Type:
- Annual
- Biennial
- Perennial
- Fruit
- Vegetable
- Herb
- Tree
- Shrub
- Vine
- Bulb

Size at Maturity:
Height   Width   Root Depth

Attributes:
- Disease Resistant
- Pest Resistant
- Deer Resistant
- Invasive
- Deciduous
- Self-Propagating

Attracts
- Butterflies
- Hummingbirds
- Birds:

☆ ☆ ☆ ☆ ☆

Sun Exposure:

Water Requirements:

Hardiness Zone:

Propagation:
- Layering
- Cutting:
  - in Soil
  - in Water
- Seed
- Dividing:
  - Spring
  - Fall
  - Other

Uses:

Companion Plants:

Characteristics

Individual Plant Info

Soil Requirements:
- ◯ Rich
- ◯ Average
- ◯ Poor
- ◼ Moist
- ◼ Dry
- ◼ Sandy
- ◼ Rocky
- ◼ Sandy
- ◼ Well-Drained
- ◼ Alkaline
- ◼ Acid
- ◼ PH

Notes:

Sowing and Planting Dates:

Treatment and Dates:

Dates:

- ◯ Fertilize with: _____ _____
- ◯ Spray with: _____ _____
- ◯ Treat with:

Prune:
- ◯ Spring
- ◯ Fall
- ◯ Summer
- ◯ Anytime
- ◯ After Bloom
- ◯ Other

Tidy:
- ◼ Deadhead
- ◼ Pinch
- ◼ Shear
- ◼ Thin

Protect:
- ◼ in Winter
- ◼ from Wind
- ◼ from Frost
- ◼ Store indoors for Winter
- ◼ Other
- ◼ Stake
- ◼ Mulch
- ◼ Wrap trunk

Cultivation Notes:

Poisonous To:
- ◼ People
- ◼ Pets
- ◼ Livestock

Part Poisonous:
- ◼ Leaves
- ◼ Flower
- ◼ Stem
- ◯ Roots

Problems:

Notes:

Botanical Name:

Common Name:

Photo, Drawing, Seed Packet or Plant Marker:

Plant Type:
- ◯ Annual
- ◯ Biennial
- ◯ Perennial
- ◼ Fruit
- ◼ Vegetable
- ◼ Herb
- ◼ Tree
- ◼ Shrub
- ◼ Vine
- ◼ Bulb

Size at Maturity:
Height   Width   Root Depth

Attributes:
- ◯ Disease Resistant
- ◯ Pest Resistant
- ◯ Deer Resistant
- ◯ Invasive
- ◯ Deciduous
- ◯ Self-Propagating

Attracts
- ◯ Butterflies
- ◯ Hummingbirds
- ◯ Birds:

☆ ☆ ☆ ☆ ☆

Sun Exposure:

Water Requirements:

Hardiness Zone:

Propagation:
- ◯ Layering
- ◯ Cutting:
  - ◼ in Soil
  - ◼ in Water
- ◯ Seed
- ◯ Dividing:
  - ◼ Spring
  - ◼ Fall
  - ◼ Other

Uses:

Companion Plants:

Characteristics

Individual Plant Info

Soil Requirements:
- ◯ Rich
- ◯ Average
- ◯ Poor
- ◼ Moist
- ◼ Dry
- ◼ Sandy
- ◼ Rocky
- ◼ Sandy
- ◼ Well-Drained
- ◼ Alkaline
- ◼ Acid
- ◼ PH

Notes:

Sowing and Planting Dates:

Treatment and Dates:

Dates:

- ◯ Fertilize with: _____ _____
- ◯ Spray with: _____ _____
- ◯ Treat with:

Prune:
- ◯ Spring
- ◯ Fall
- ◯ Summer
- ◯ Anytime
- ◯ After Bloom
- ◯ Other

Tidy:
- ◼ Deadhead
- ◼ Pinch
- ◼ Shear
- ◼ Thin

Protect:
- ◼ in Winter
- ◼ from Wind
- ◼ from Frost
- ◯ Store indoors for Winter
- ◼ Other

- ◼ Stake
- ◼ Mulch
- ◼ Wrap trunk

Cultivation Notes:

Poisonous To:
- ◯ People
- ◯ Pets
- ◼ Livestock

Part Poisonous:
- ◼ Leaves
- ◼ Flower
- ◼ Stem
- ◯ Roots

Problems:

Notes:

Botanical Name:

Common Name:

Photo, Drawing, Seed Packet or Plant Marker:

Plant Type:
- ◯ Annual
- ◯ Biennial
- ◯ Perennial
- ◼ Fruit
- ◼ Vegetable
- ◼ Herb
- ◼ Tree
- ◼ Shrub
- ◼ Vine
- ◼ Bulb

Size at Maturity:
Height   Width   Root Depth

Attributes:
- ◯ Disease Resistant
- ◯ Pest Resistant
- ◯ Deer Resistant
- ◼ Invasive
- ◼ Deciduous
- ◼ Self-Propagating

Attracts
- ◯ Butterflies
- ◯ Hummingbirds
- ◯ Birds:

☆ ☆☆ ☆☆ ☆ ☆

Sun Exposure:

Water Requirements:

Hardiness Zone:

Propagation:
- ◯ Layering
- ◯ Cutting:
  - ◼ in Soil
  - ◼ in Water
- ◯ Seed
- ◯ Dividing:
  - ◼ Spring
  - ◼ Fall
  - ◼ Other

Uses:

Companion Plants:

Characteristics

Individual Plant Info

Soil Requirements:
- ○ Rich
- ○ Average
- ○ Poor
- ■ Moist
- ■ Dry
- ■ Sandy
- ■ Rocky
- ■ Sandy
- ■ Well-Drained
- ■ Alkaline
- ○ Acid
- ○ PH

Notes:

Sowing and Planting Dates:

Treatment and Dates:

Dates:

- ○ Fertilize with: _____ _____
- ○ Spray with: _____ _____
- ○ Treat with:

Prune:	Tidy:	Protect:	
○ Spring	■ Deadhead	■ in Winter	■ Stake
○ Fall	○ Pinch	■ from Wind	■ Mulch
○ Summer	○ Shear	■ from Frost	○ Wrap trunk
○ Anytime	○ Thin	■ Store indoors for Winter	
○ After Bloom		○ Other	
○ Other			

Cultivation Notes:

Poisonous To:	○ People	○ Pets	○ Livestock	
Part Poisonous:	○ Leaves	○ Flower	○ Stem	○ Roots

Problems:

Notes:

Botanical Name:

Common Name:

Photo, Drawing, Seed Packet or Plant Marker:

Plant Type:
○ Annual	■ Fruit	○ Tree
○ Biennial	■ Vegetable	○ Shrub
○ Perennial	■ Herb	○ Vine
		○ Bulb

Size at Maturity:

Height	Width	Root Depth

Attributes:
		Attracts
○ Disease Resistant	○ Invasive	○ Butterflies
○ Pest Resistant	○ Deciduous	○ Hummingbirds
○ Deer Resistant	○ Self-Propagating	○ Birds:

☆ ☆ ☆ ☆ ☆

Sun Exposure:

Water Requirements:

Hardiness Zone:

Propagation:
- ○ Layering
- ○ Cutting:
  - ■ in Soil
  - ■ in Water
- ○ Seed
- ○ Dividing:
  - ■ Spring
  - ■ Fall
  - ■ Other

Uses:

Companion Plants:

Characteristics

Individual Plant Info

Soil Requirements:
- ◯ Rich
- ◯ Average
- ◯ Poor
- ◯ Moist
- ◯ Dry
- ◯ Sandy
- ◯ Rocky
- ◯ Sandy
- ◯ Well-Drained
- ◯ Alkaline
- ◯ Acid
- ◯ PH

Notes:

Sowing and Planting Dates:

Treatment and Dates:

- ◯ Fertilize with: _____   Dates: _____
- ◯ Spray with: _____   _____
- ◯ Treat with:

Prune:
- ◯ Spring
- ◯ Fall
- ◯ Summer
- ◯ Anytime
- ◯ After Bloom
- ◯ Other

Tidy:
- ◯ Deadhead
- ◯ Pinch
- ◯ Shear
- ◯ Thin

Protect:
- ◯ in Winter
- ◯ from Wind
- ◯ from Frost
- ◯ Store indoors for Winter
- ◯ Other
- ◯ Stake
- ◯ Mulch
- ◯ Wrap trunk

Cultivation Notes:

Poisonous To:
- ◯ People
- ◯ Pets
- ◯ Livestock

Part Poisonous:
- ◯ Leaves
- ◯ Flower
- ◯ Stem
- ◯ Roots

Problems:

Notes:

Botanical Name:

Common Name:

Photo, Drawing, Seed Packet or Plant Marker:

Plant Type:
- ◯ Annual
- ◯ Biennial
- ◯ Perennial
- ◯ Fruit
- ◯ Vegetable
- ◯ Herb
- ◯ Tree
- ◯ Shrub
- ◯ Vine
- ◯ Bulb

Size at Maturity:
Height   Width   Root Depth

Attributes:
- ◯ Disease Resistant
- ◯ Pest Resistant
- ◯ Deer Resistant
- ◯ Invasive
- ◯ Deciduous
- ◯ Self-Propagating

Attracts
- ◯ Butterflies
- ◯ Hummingbirds
- ◯ Birds:

☆ ☆ ☆ ☆ ☆

Sun Exposure:

Water Requirements:

Hardiness Zone:

Propagation:
- ◯ Layering
- ◯ Cutting:
  - ◯ in Soil
  - ◯ in Water
- ◯ Seed
- ◯ Dividing:
  - ◯ Spring
  - ◯ Fall
  - ◯ Other

Uses:

Companion Plants:

Characteristics

Individual Plant Info

Soil Requirements:
- ○ Rich
- ○ Average
- ○ Poor
- ○ Moist
- ○ Dry
- ○ Sandy
- ● Rocky
- ● Sandy
- ● Well-Drained
- ● Alkaline
- ● Acid
- ● PH

Notes:

Sowing and Planting Dates:

Treatment and Dates:

Dates:

- ○ Fertilize with: _____   _____
- ○ Spray with: _____   _____
- ○ Treat with:

Prune:
- ○ Spring
- ○ Fall
- ○ Summer
- ○ Anytime
- ○ After Bloom
- ○ Other

Tidy:
- ● Deadhead
- ● Pinch
- ● Shear
- ● Thin

Protect:
- ● in Winter
- ● from Wind
- ● from Frost
- ● Store indoors for Winter
- ○ Other
- ● Stake
- ● Mulch
- ● Wrap trunk

Cultivation Notes:

Poisonous To:
- ○ People
- ○ Pets
- ○ Livestock

Part Poisonous:
- ● Leaves
- ○ Flower
- ○ Stem
- ○ Roots

Problems:

Notes:

Botanical Name:

Common Name:

Photo, Drawing, Seed Packet or Plant Marker:

Plant Type:
- ○ Annual
- ○ Biennial
- ○ Perennial
- ○ Fruit
- ● Vegetable
- ○ Herb
- ○ Tree
- ○ Shrub
- ○ Vine
- ○ Bulb

Size at Maturity:
Height   Width   Root Depth

Attributes:
- ○ Disease Resistant
- ○ Pest Resistant
- ○ Deer Resistant
- ○ Invasive
- ○ Deciduous
- ○ Self-Propagating

Attracts
- ○ Butterflies
- ○ Hummingbirds
- ○ Birds:

☆ ☆ ☆ ☆ ☆

Sun Exposure:

Water Requirements:

Hardiness Zone:

Propagation:
- ○ Layering
- ○ Cutting:
  - ● in Soil
  - ● in Water
- ○ Seed
- ○ Dividing:
  - ● Spring
  - ● Fall
  - ● Other

Uses:

Companion Plants:

Characteristics

Annual Log

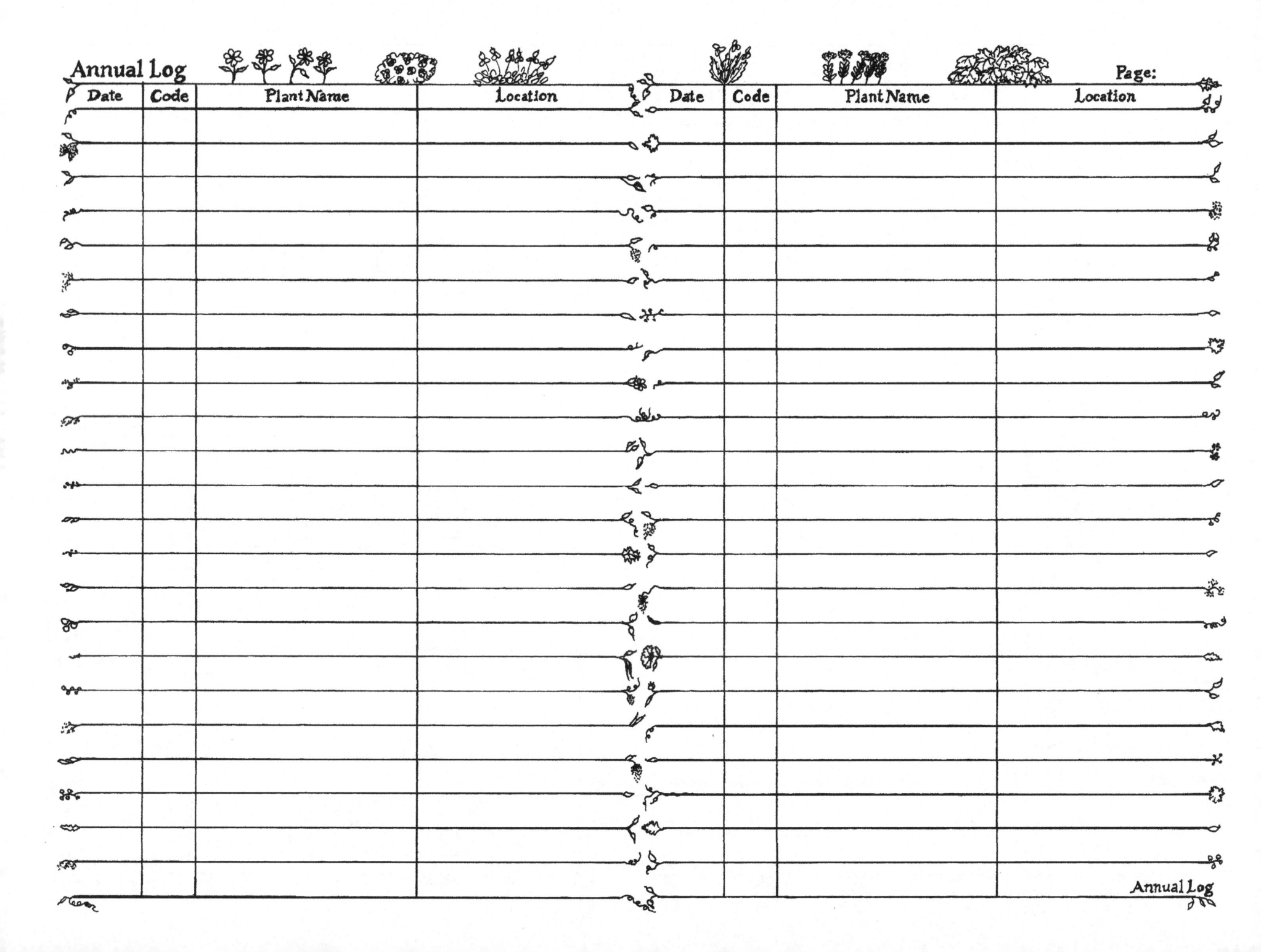

Date	Code	Plant Name	Location	Date	Code	Plant Name	Location

Page:

Annual Log

Annual Log

Date	Code	Plant Name	Location	Date	Code	Plant Name	Location

Annual Log

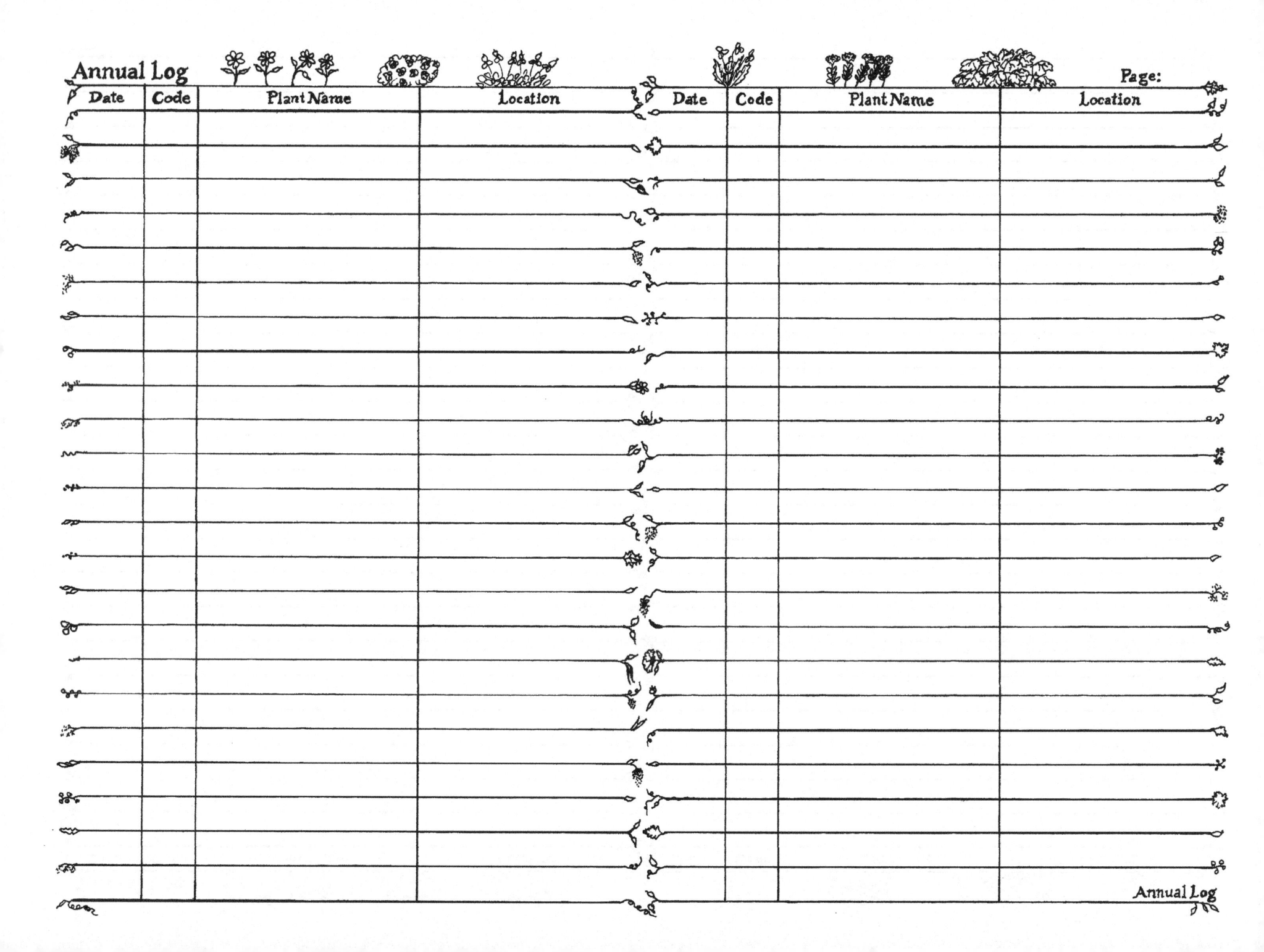

Annual Log

Date	Code	Plant Name	Location	Date	Code	Plant Name	Location

Annual Log

Date	Code	Plant Name	Location	Date	Code	Plant Name	Location

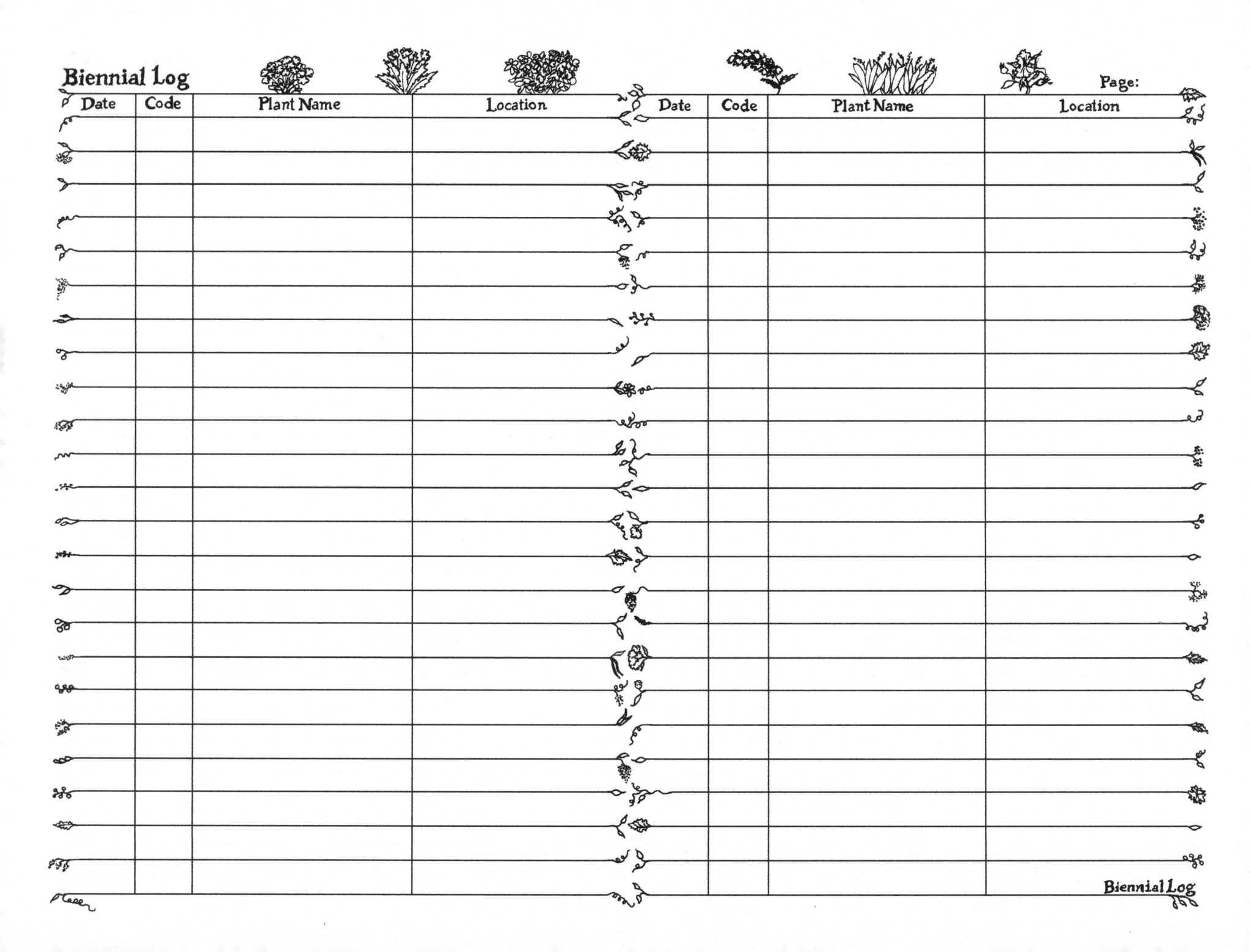

Biennial Log

Page:

Date	Code	Plant Name	Location	Date	Code	Plant Name	Location

Biennial Log

Biennial Log

Date	Code	Plant Name	Location	Date	Code	Plant Name	Location

Biennial Log

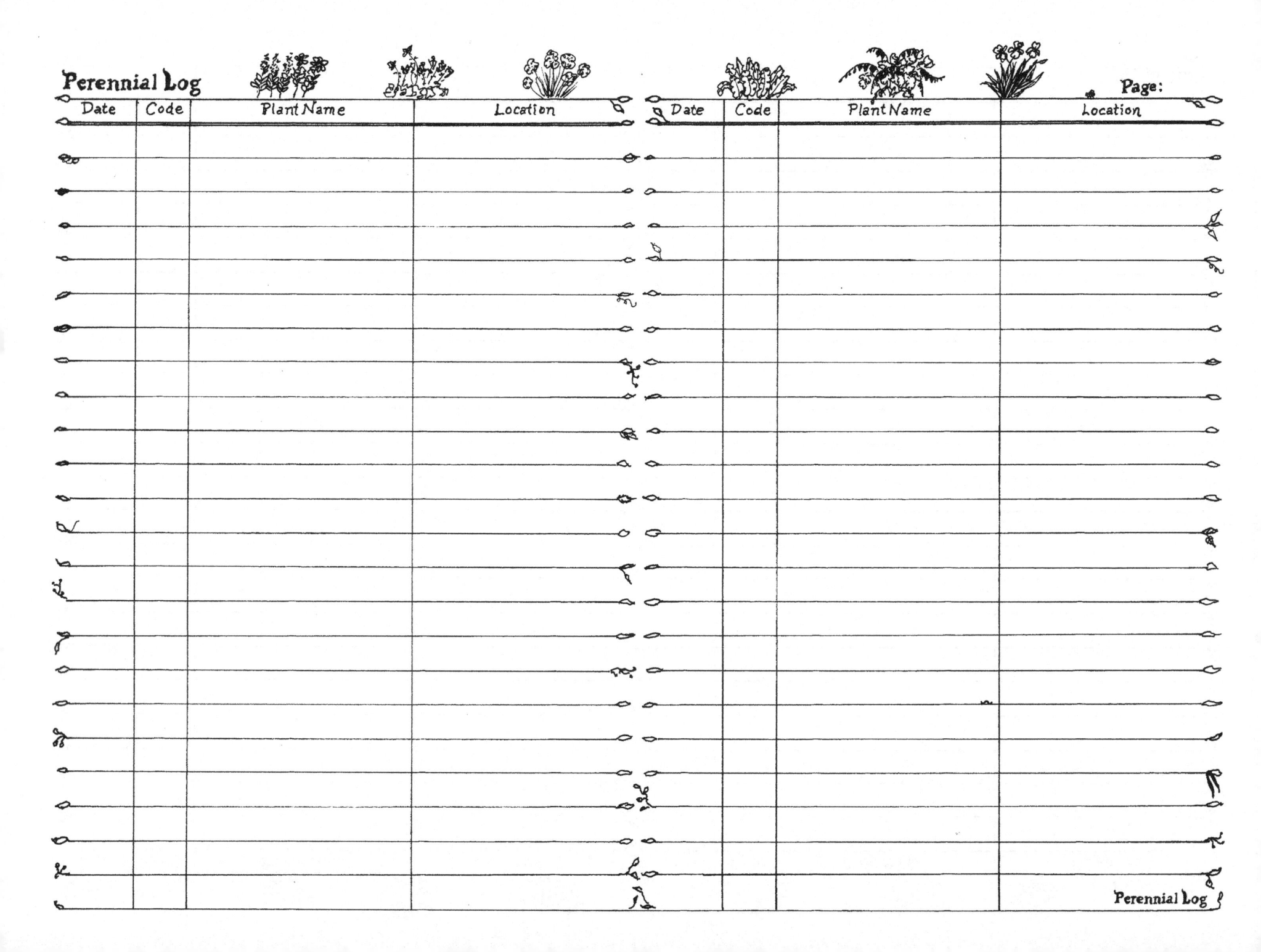

Perennial Log

Page:

Date	Code	Plant Name	Location	Date	Code	Plant Name	Location

Perennial Log

Perennial Log

Page:

Date	Code	Plant Name	Location	Date	Code	Plant Name	Location

Perennial Log

Perennial Log

Date	Code	Plant Name	Location	Date	Code	Plant Name	Location

Page:

Perennial Log

Perennial Log

Date	Code	Plant Name	Location	Date	Code	Plant Name	Location

Perennial Log

Flower Log

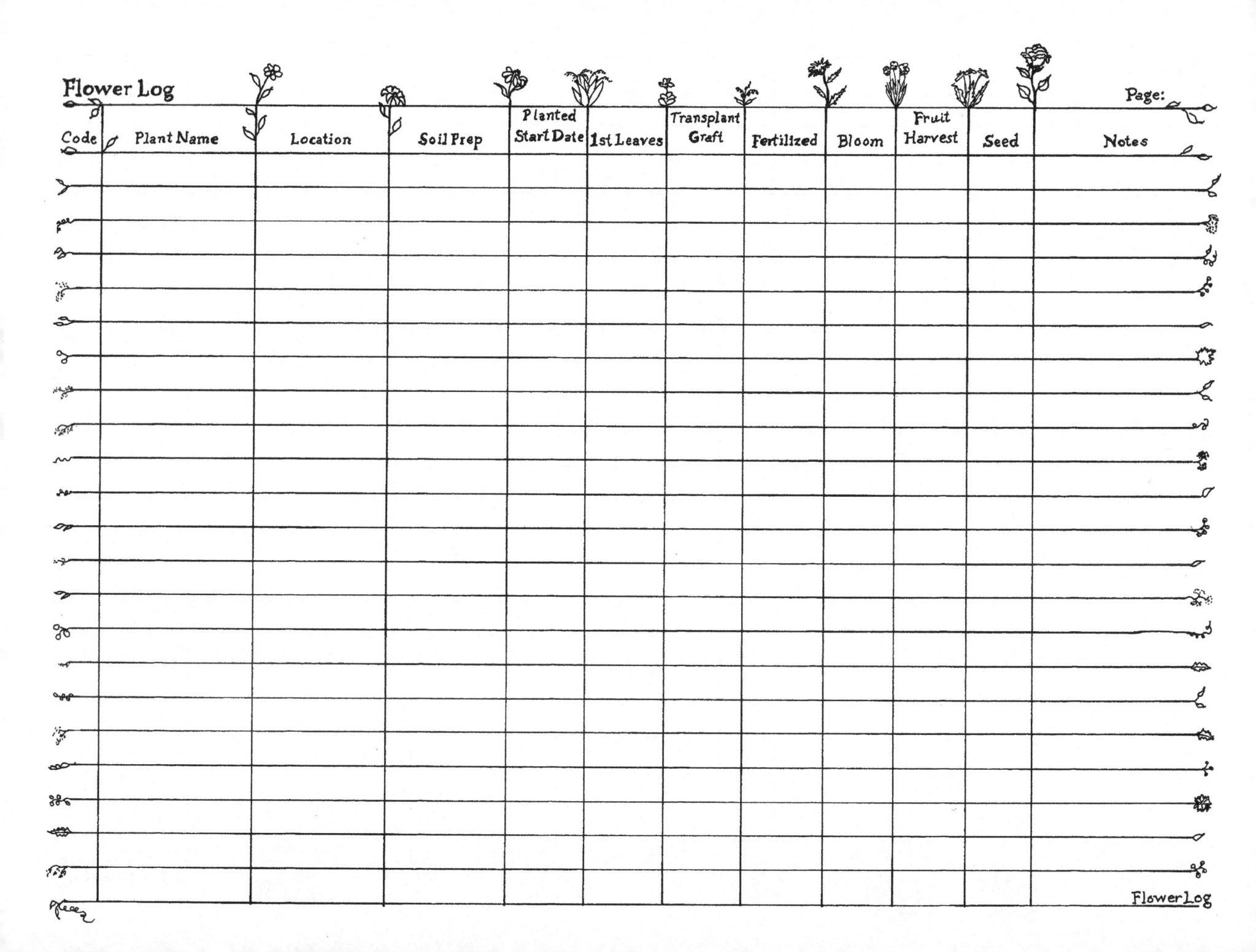

Code	Plant Name	Location	Soil Prep	Planted Start Date	1st Leaves	Transplant Graft	Fertilized	Bloom	Fruit Harvest	Seed	Notes

Flower Log

Code	Plant Name	Location	Soil Prep	Planted Start Date	1st Leaves	Transplant Graft	Fertilized	Bloom	Fruit Harvest	Seed	Notes

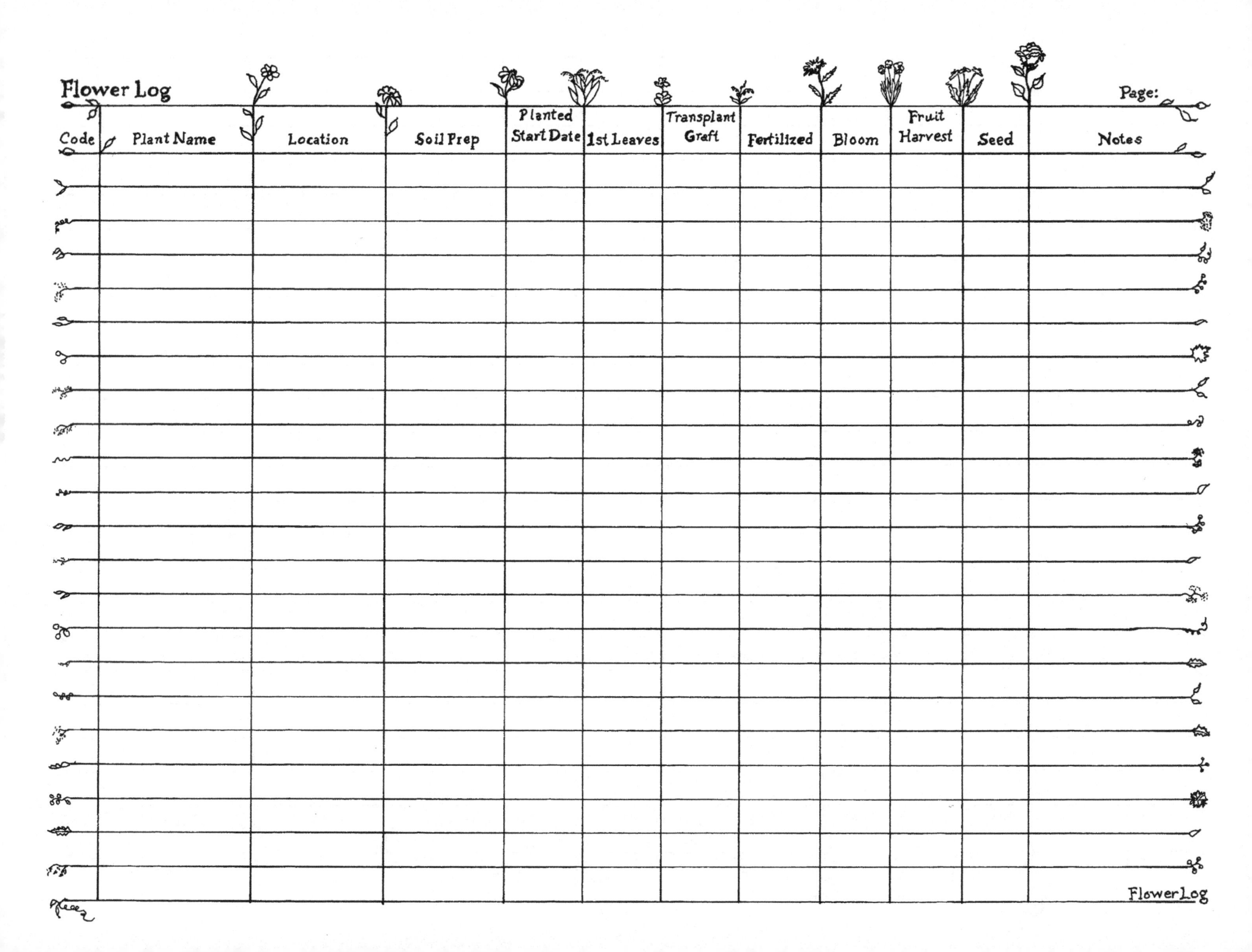

Flower Log

Page:

Code	Plant Name	Location	Soil Prep	Planted Start Date	1st Leaves	Transplant Graft	Fertilized	Bloom	Fruit Harvest	Seed	Notes

FlowerLog

Flower Log

Code	Plant Name	Location	Soil Prep	Planted Start Date	1st Leaves	Transplant Graft	Fertilized	Bloom	Fruit Harvest	Seed	Notes

Flower Log

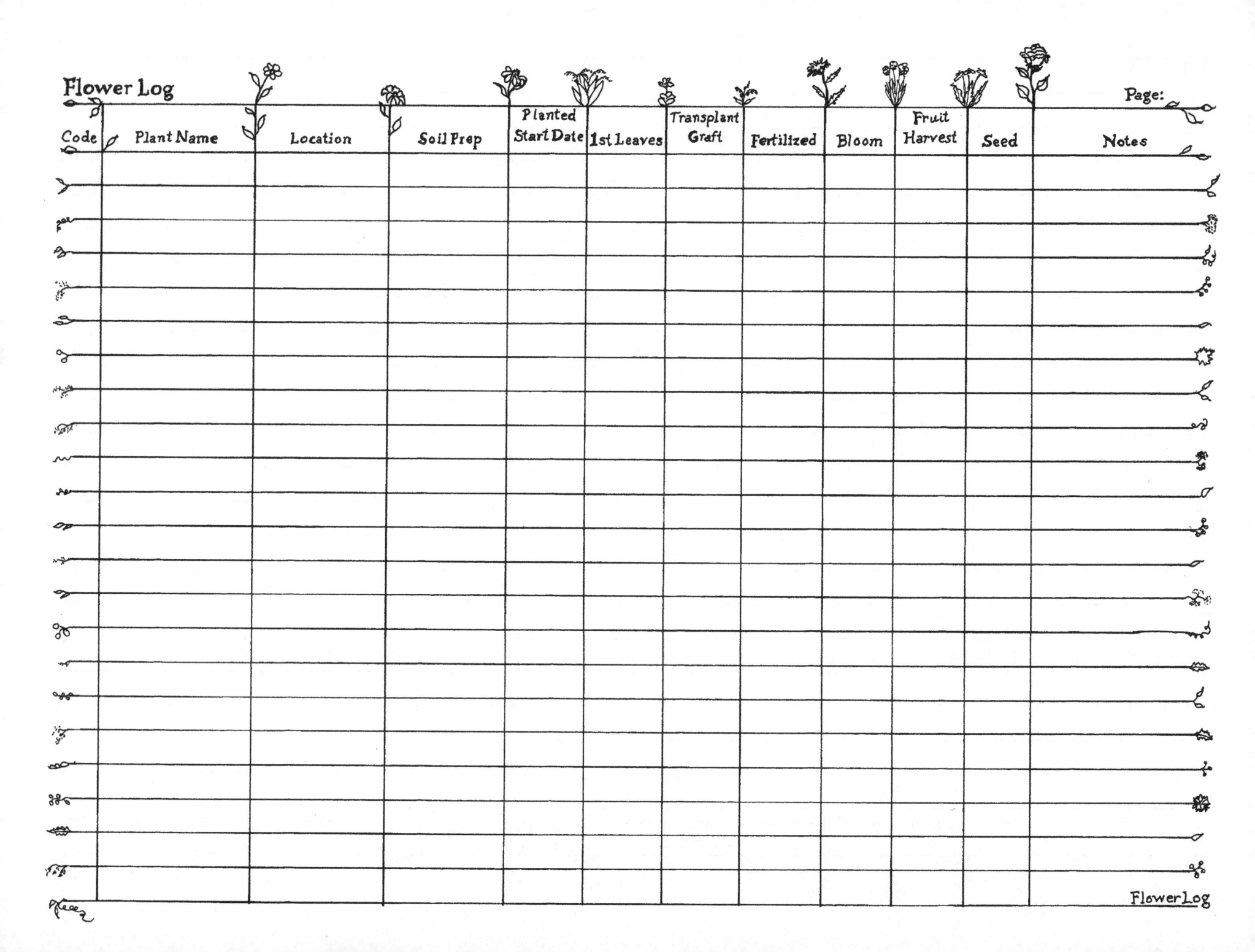

Flower Log

Page:

Code	Plant Name	Location	Soil Prep	Planted Start Date	1st Leaves	Transplant Graft	Fertilized	Bloom	Fruit Harvest	Seed	Notes

Flower Log

Bulb, Tuber and Rhizome Log

Page:

Code	Plant Name	Location	Soil Prep	Planted Start Date	1st Leaves	Transplant Graft	Fertilized	Bloom	Fruit-Harvest	Seed	Notes

Bulb, Tuber & Rhizome Log

Fruit Log

Page:

Code	Plant Name	Location	Soil Prep	Planted Start Date	1st Leaves	Transplant Graft	Fertilized	Bloom	Fruit Harvest	Sprayed	Notes

Fruit Log

Fruit Log

Page:

Code	Plant Name	Location	Soil Prep	Planted Start Date	1st Leaves	Transplant Graft	Fertilized	Bloom	Fruit Harvest	Sprayed	Notes

Fruit Log

Fruit Log

Page:

Code	Plant Name	Location	Soil Prep	Planted Start Date	1st Leaves	Transplant Graft	Fertilized	Bloom	Fruit Harvest	Sprayed	Notes

Vegetable Log

Page:

Code	Plant Name	Location	Soil Prep	Planted Start Date	1st Leaves	Transplant ~ Graft	Fertilized	Bloom	Fruit Harvest	Seed	Notes

Vegetable Log

Vegetable Log

Page:

Code	Plant Name	Location	Soil Prep	Planted Start Date	1st Leaves	Transplant ~ Graft	Fertilized	Bloom	Fruit Harvest	Seed	Notes

Vegetable Log

Vegetable Log

Code	Plant Name	Location	Soil Prep	Planted Start Date	1st Leaves	Transplant ~ Graft	Fertilized	Bloom	Fruit Harvest	Seed	Notes

Page:

Vegetable Log

Vegetable Log

Page:

Code	Plant Name	Location	Soil Prep	Planted Start Date	1st Leaves	Transplant ~ Graft	Fertilized	Bloom	Fruit Harvest	Seed	Notes

Vegetable Log

Vegetable Log

Page:

Code	Plant Name	Location	Soil Prep	Planted Start Date	1st Leaves	Transplant ~ Graft	Fertilized	Bloom	Fruit Harvest	Seed	Notes

Herb Log

Page:

Code	Plant Name	Location	Soil Prep	Planted Start Date	1st Leaves	Transplant ~ Graft	Fertilized	Bloom	Fruit- Harvest	Seed	Notes

Herb Log

Vine Log

Code	Plant Name	Location	Soil Prep	Planted Start Date	1st Leaves	Transplant ~ Graft	Fertilized	Bloom	Fruit Harvest	Seed	Notes

Shrub Log

Code	Plant Name	Location	Soil Prep	Planted Start Date	1st Leaves	Transplant Graft	Fertilized	Bloom	Fruit Harvest	Seed	Notes

Shrub Log

Shrub Log

Page:

Code	Plant Name	Location	Soil Prep	Planted Start Date	1st Leaves	Transplant Graft	Fertilized	Bloom	Fruit Harvest	Seed	Notes

Shrub Log

Tree Log

Code	Plant Name	Location	Soil Prep	Planted Start Date	1st Leaves	Transplant Graft	Fertilized	Pruned	Bloom	Fruit/ Harvest	Seed	Fall Color Leaf Fall

Page:

Tree Log

Hardscaping Log

Page:

Code	Name	Location	Feature(s)	Installation Time	Difficulty	Rating	Notes

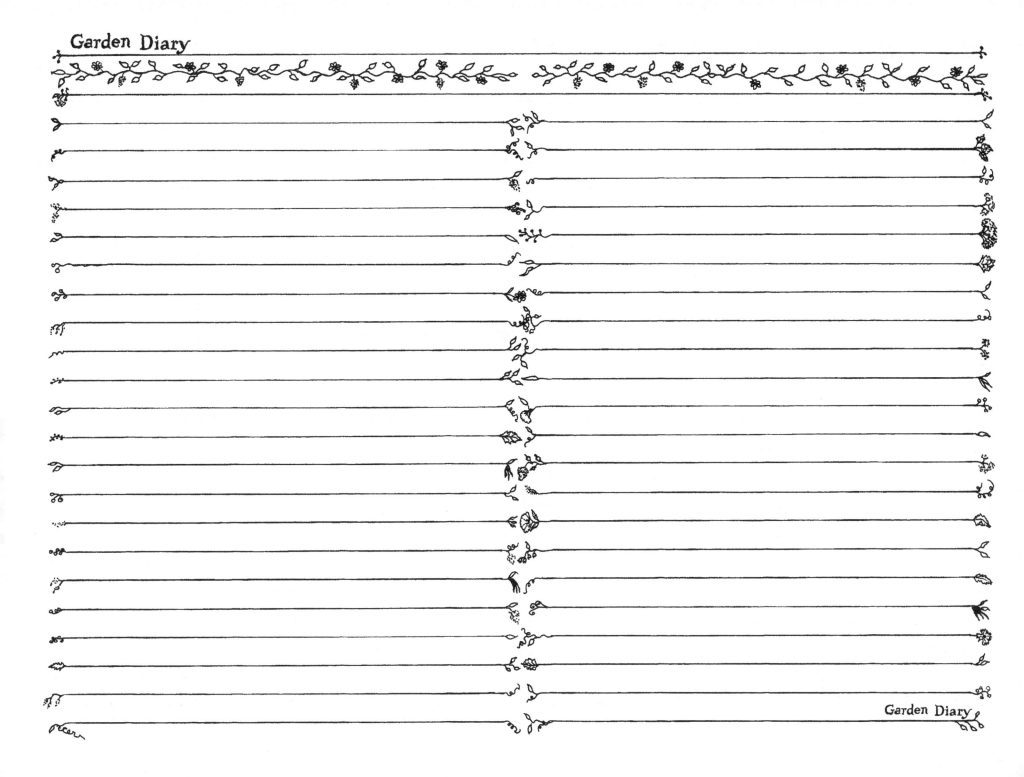

Garden Diary

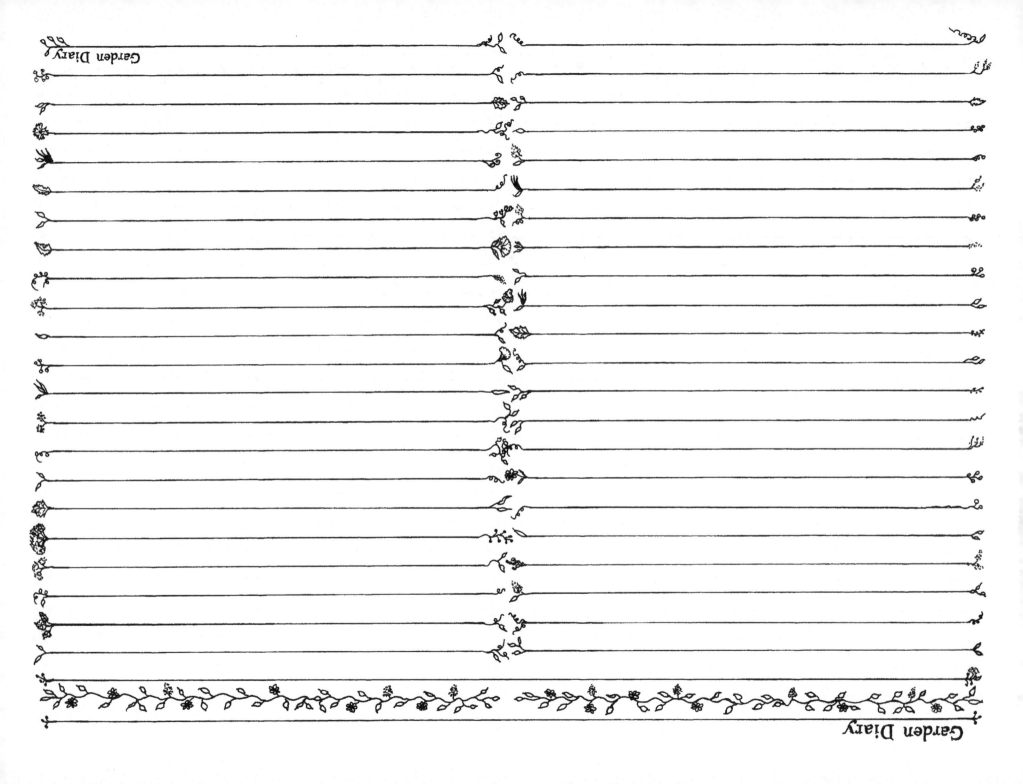

Garden Diary

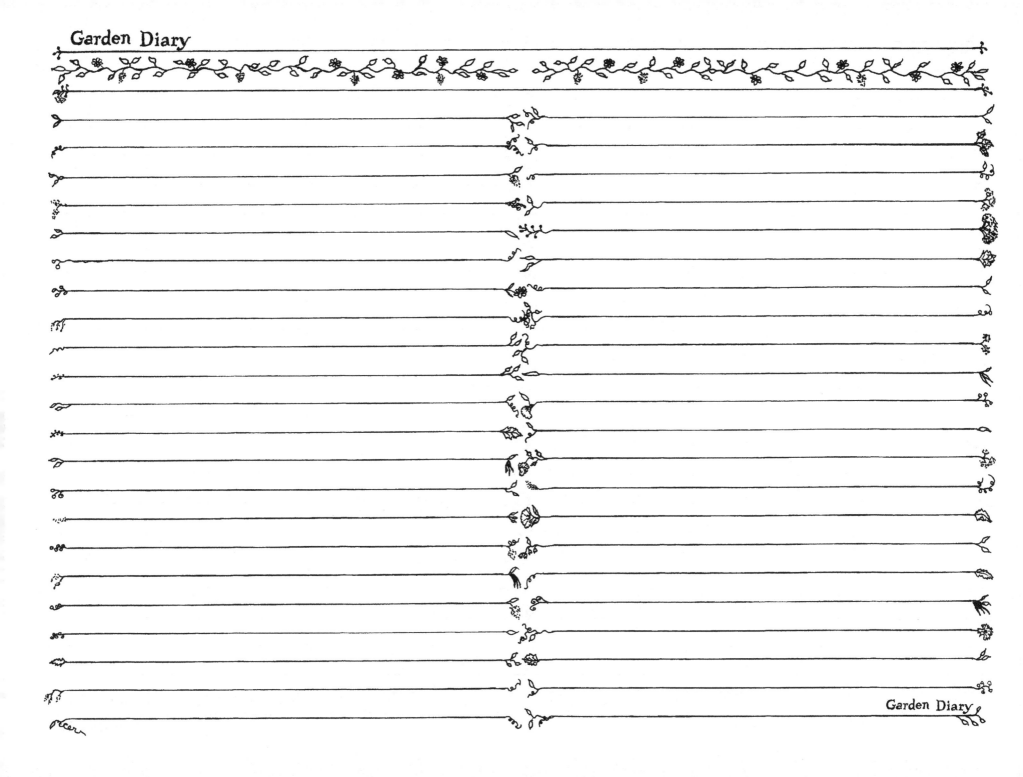

Garden Diary

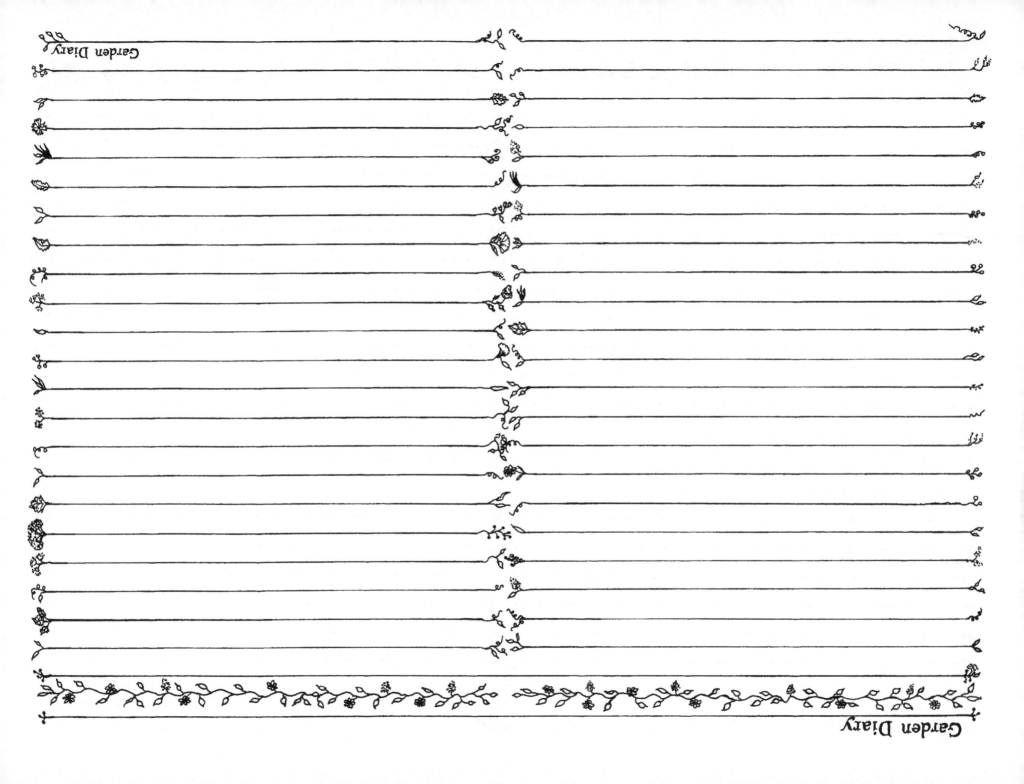

Garden Diary

Garden Diary

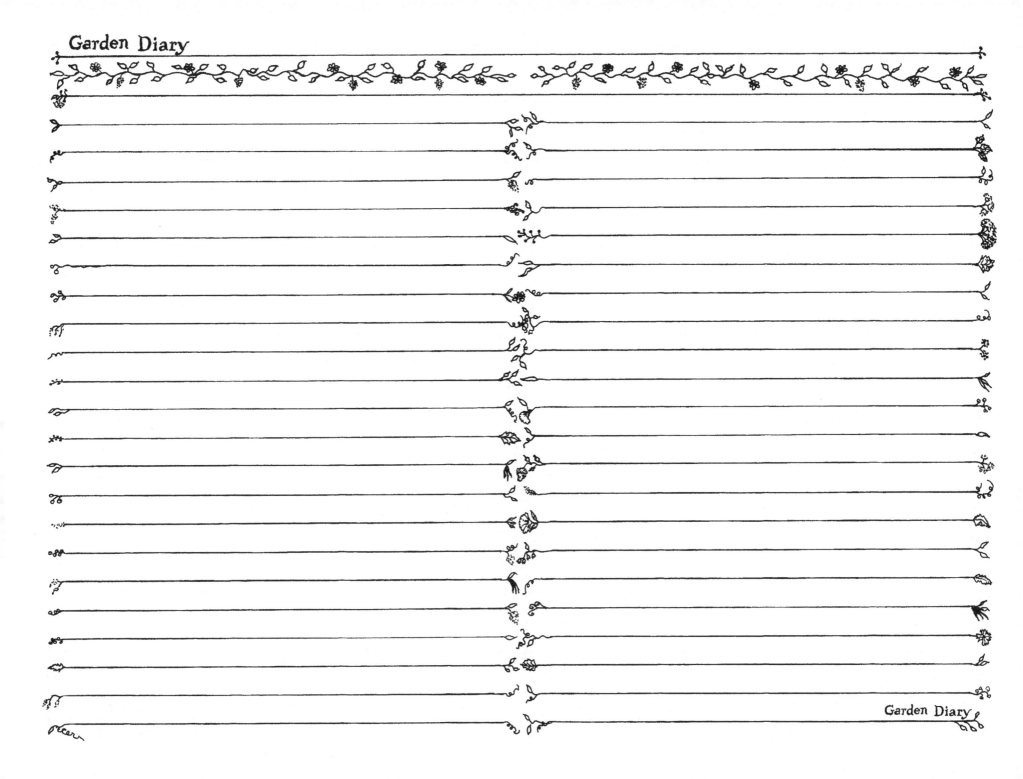

Garden Diary

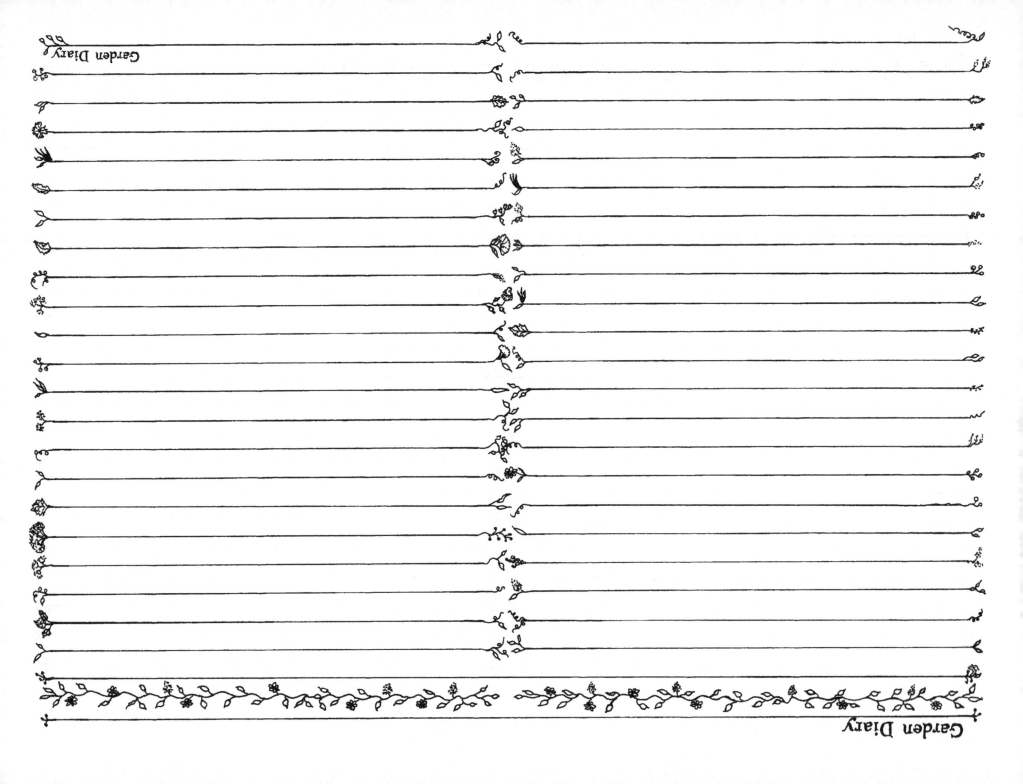

Garden Diary

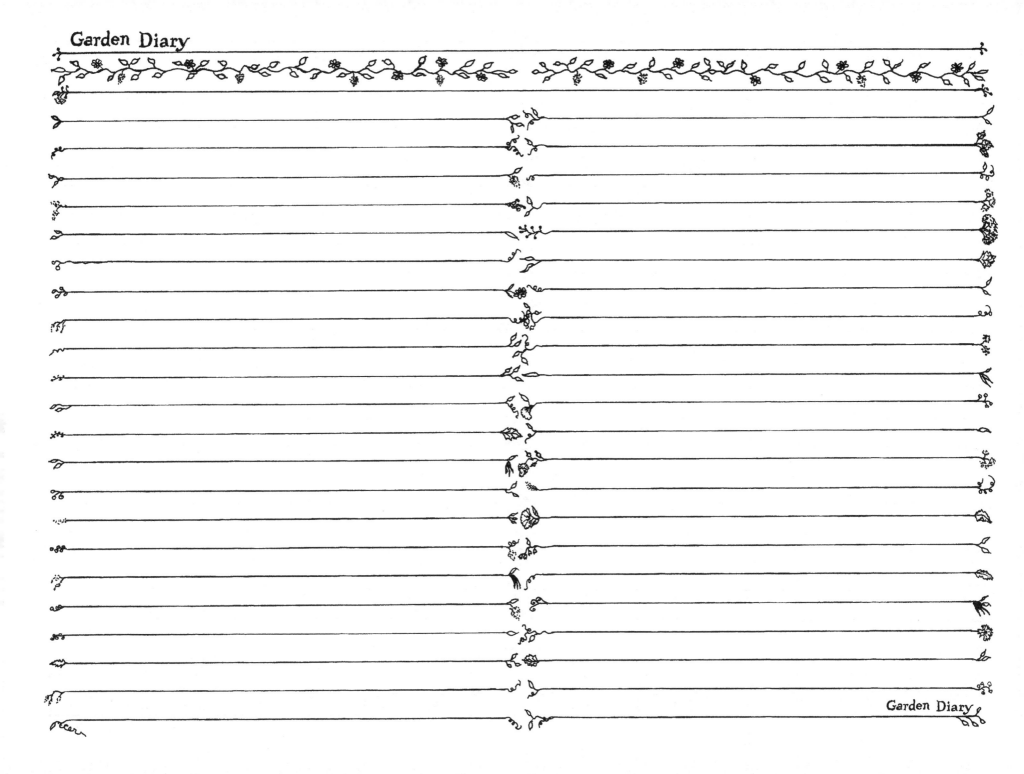

Garden Diary

Garden Diary

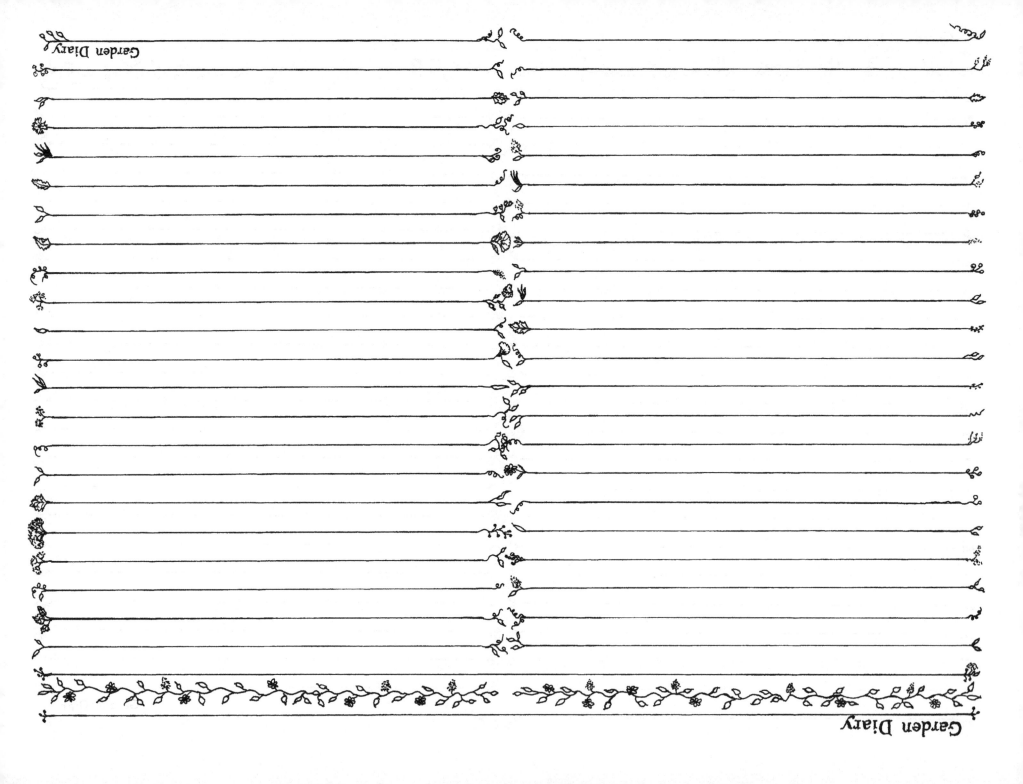

Garden Diary

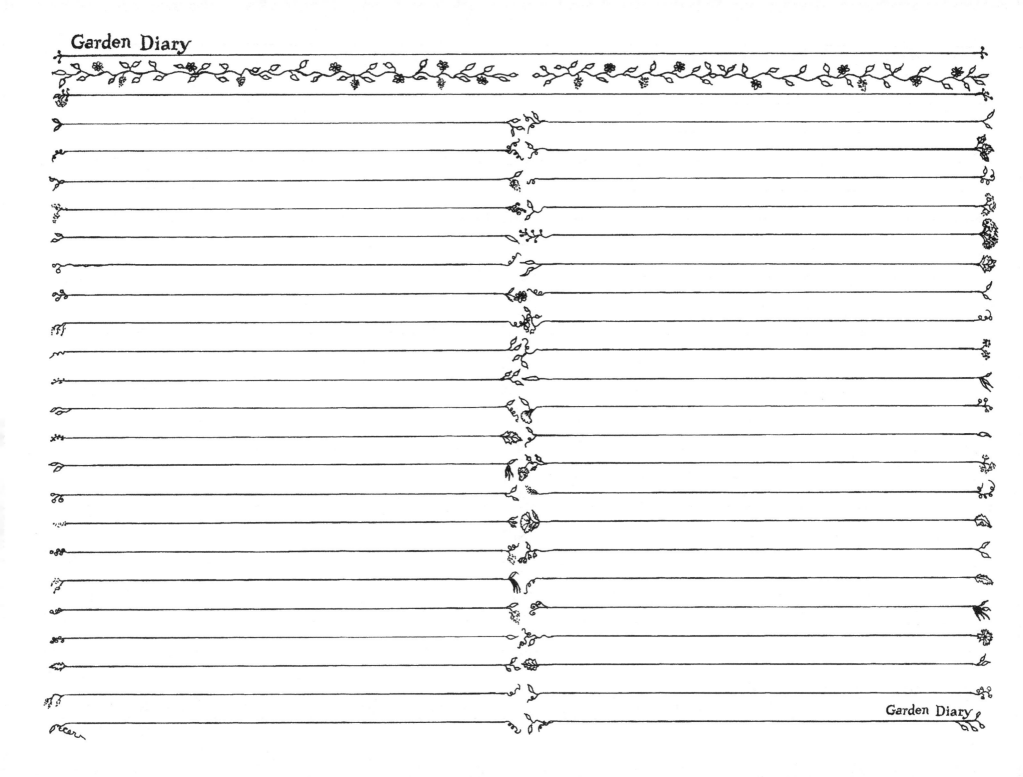

Garden Diary

Garden Diary

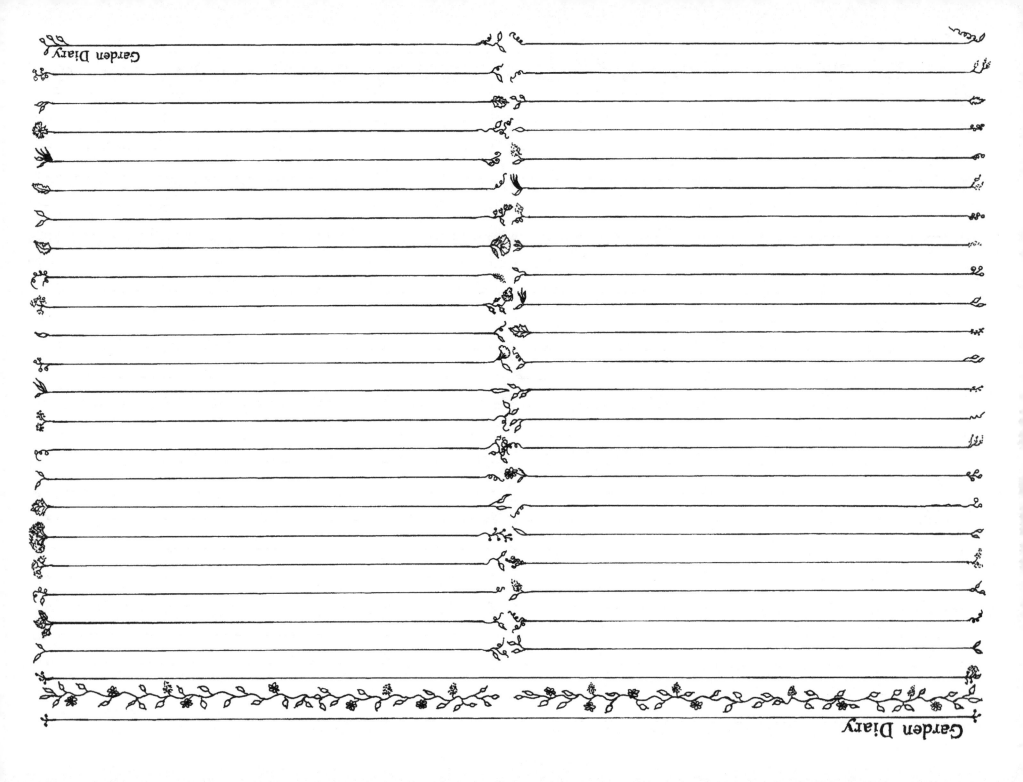

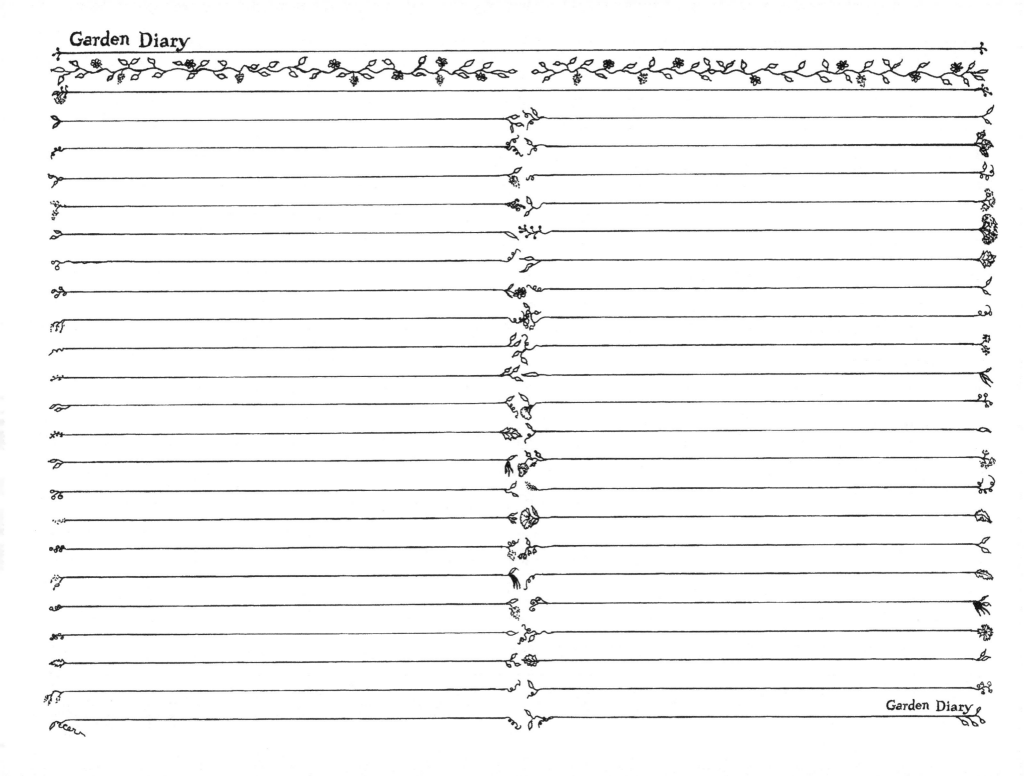

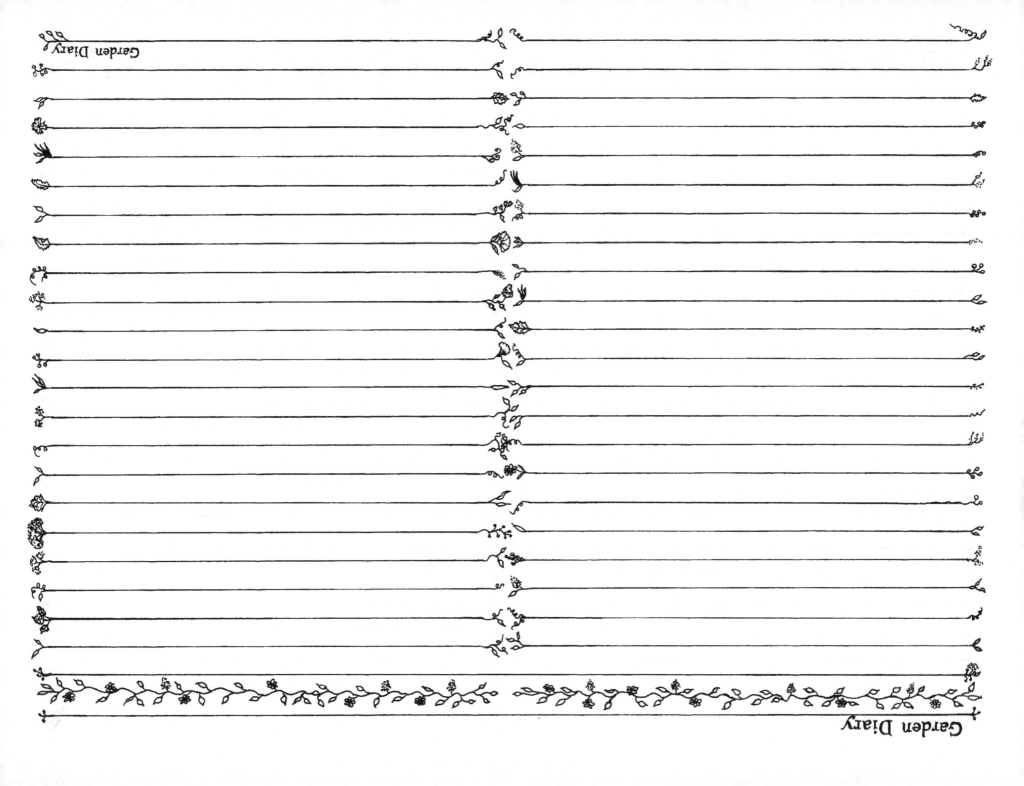

Garden Diary

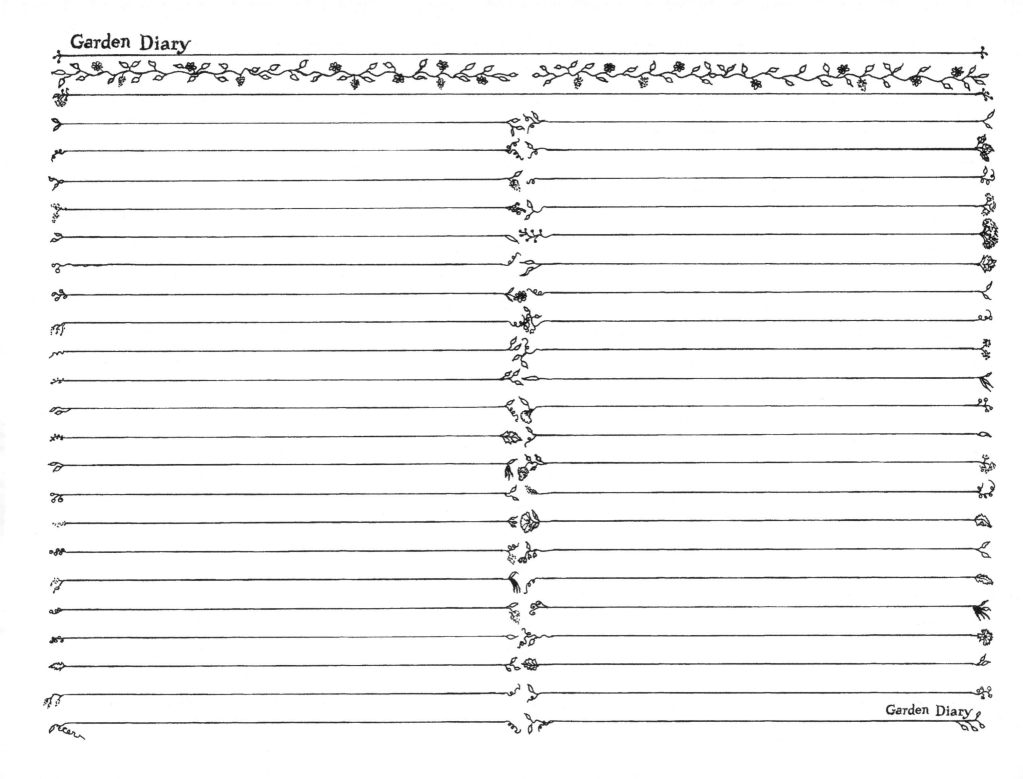

Garden Diary

Garden Diary

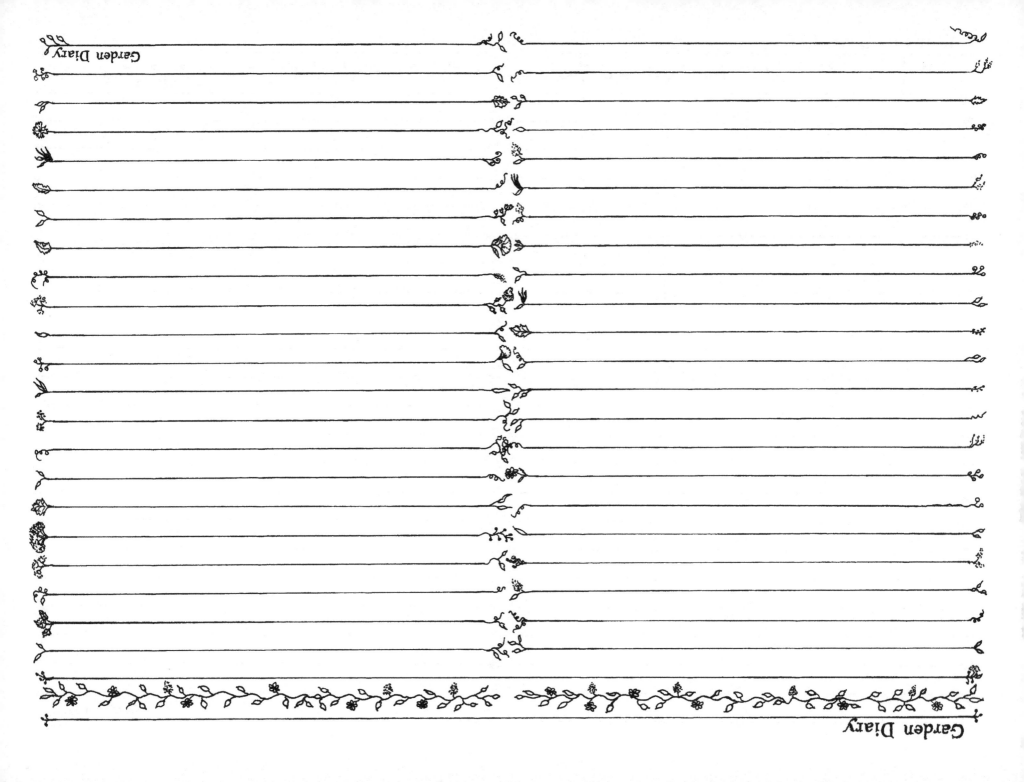

Garden Diary

Garden Diary

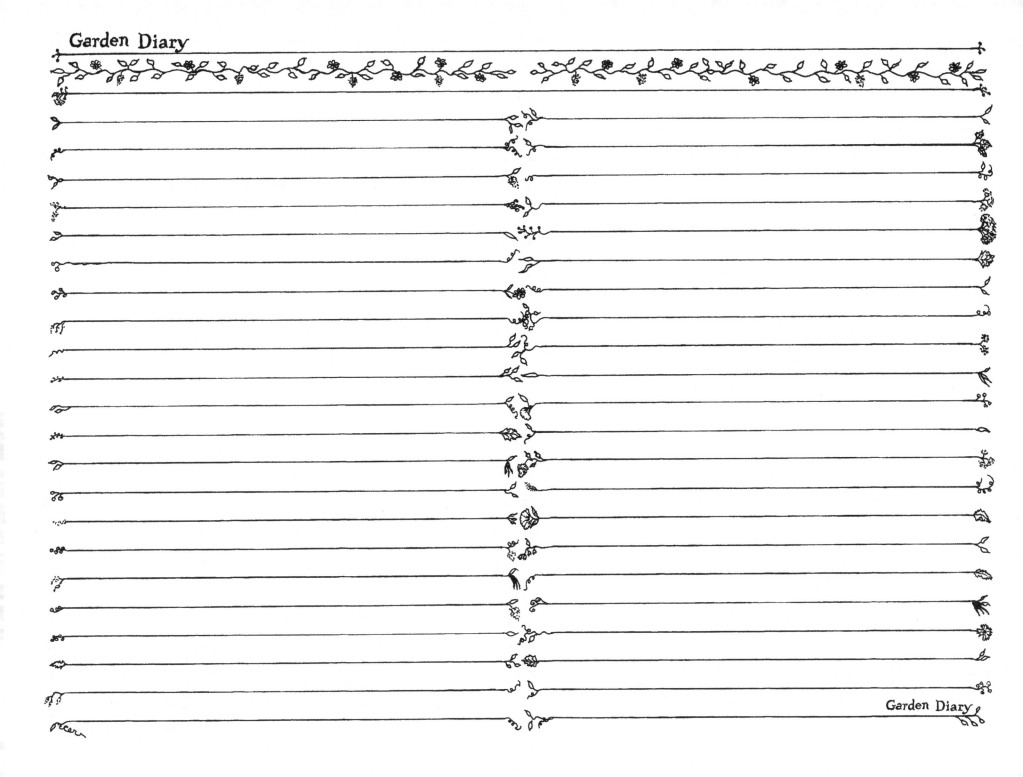

Garden Diary

Garden Diary

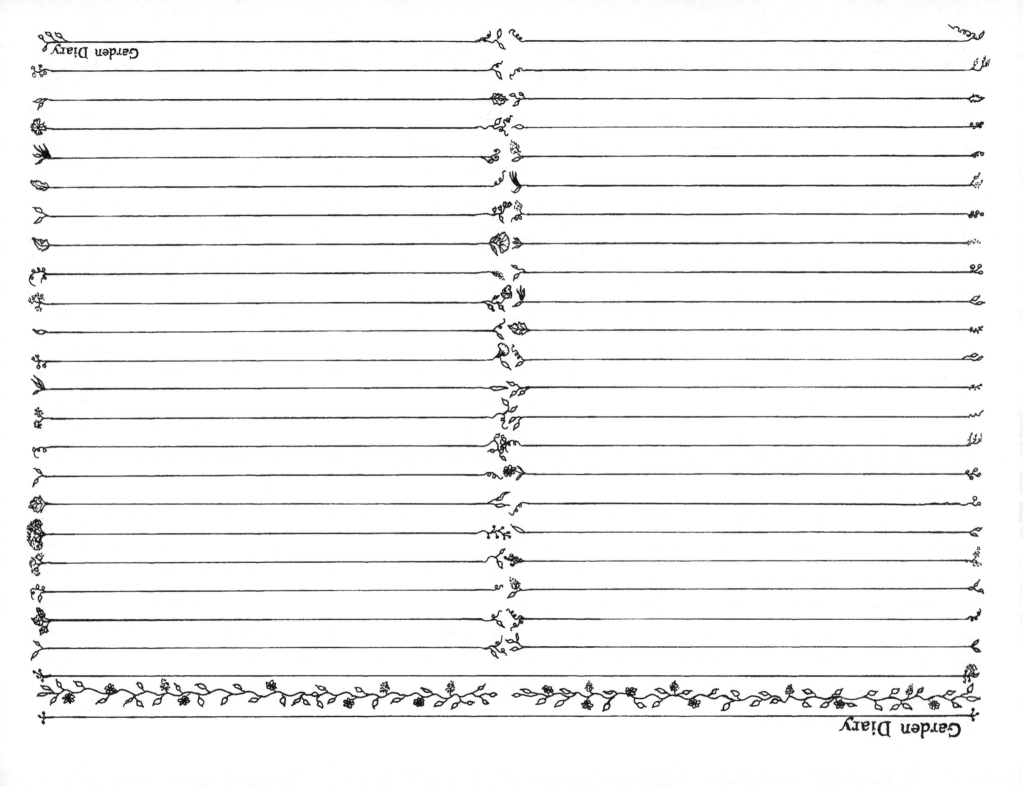

Garden Diary

Garden Diary

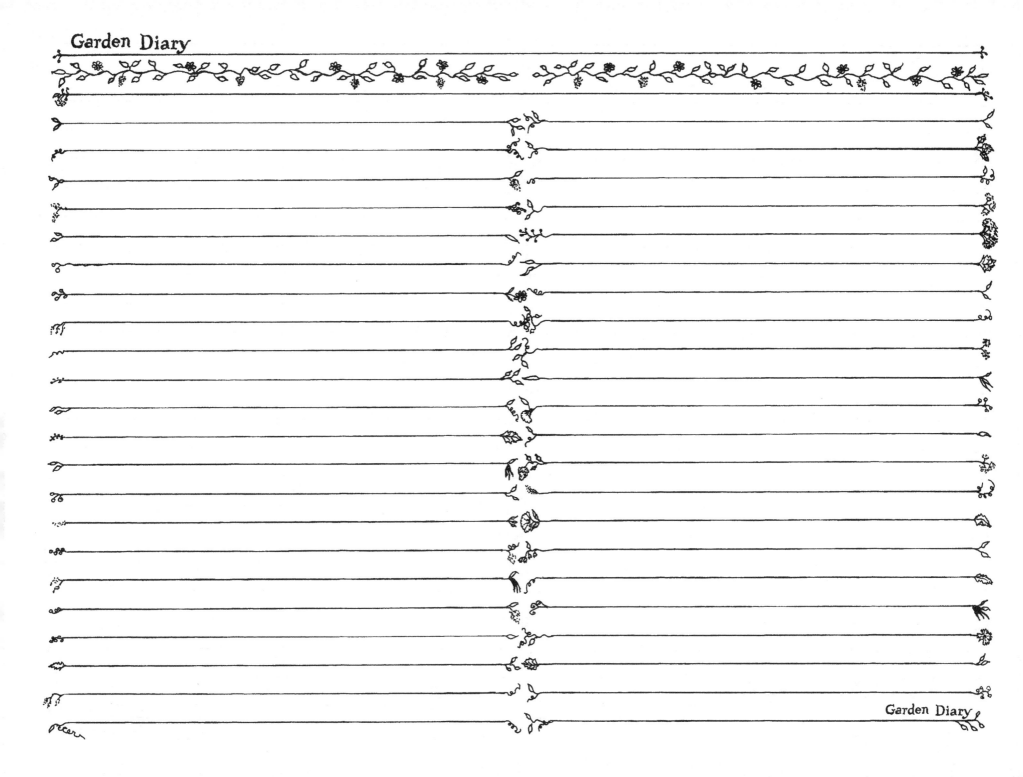

Garden Diary

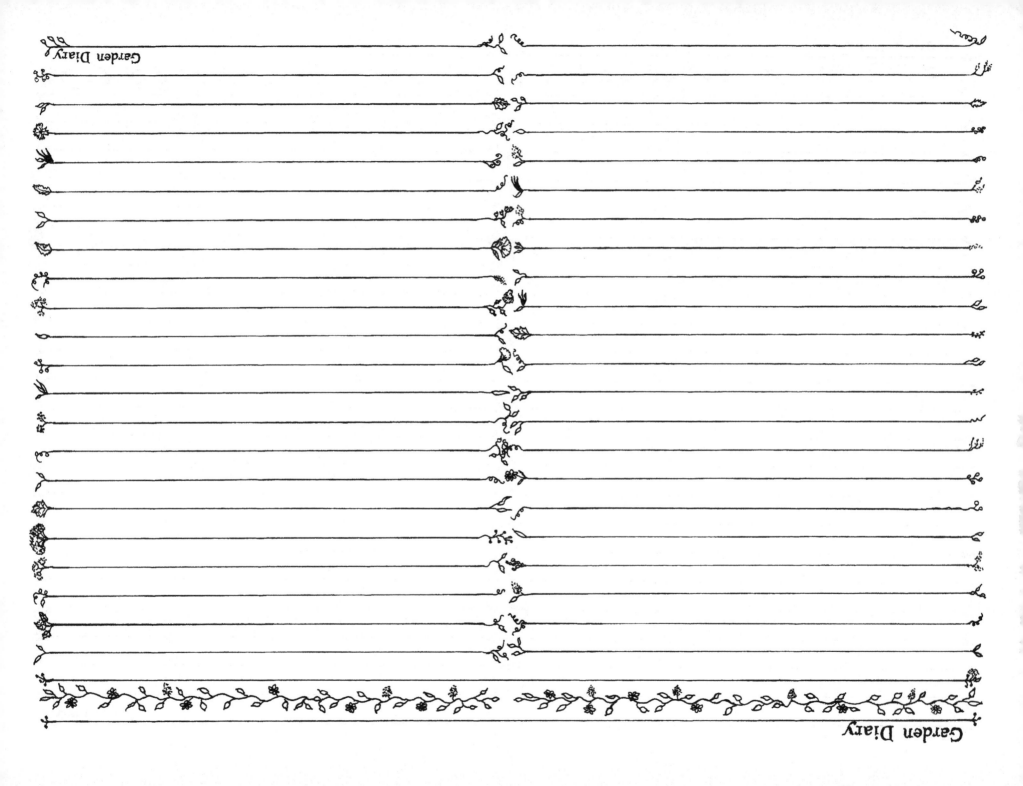

Garden Diary

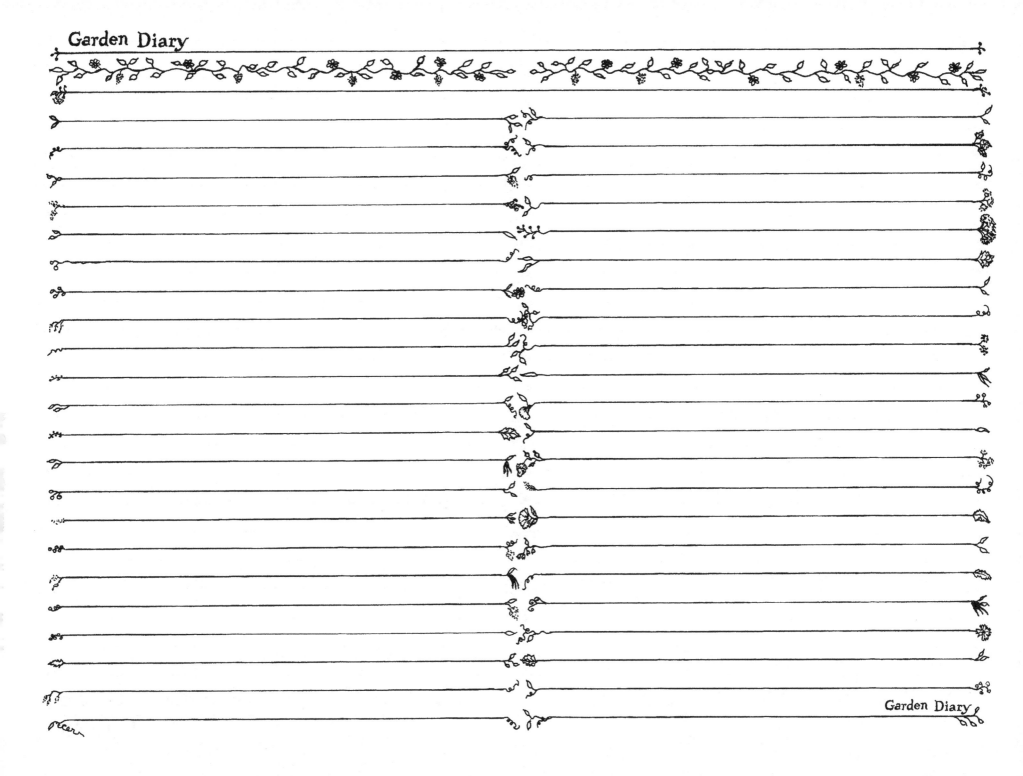

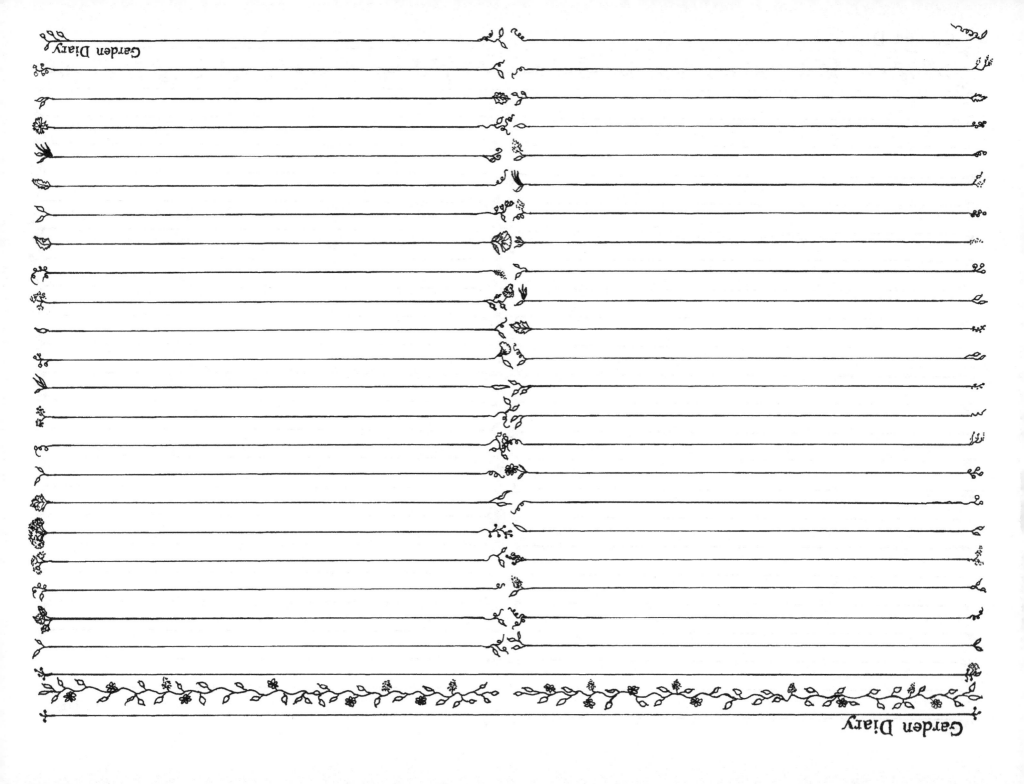

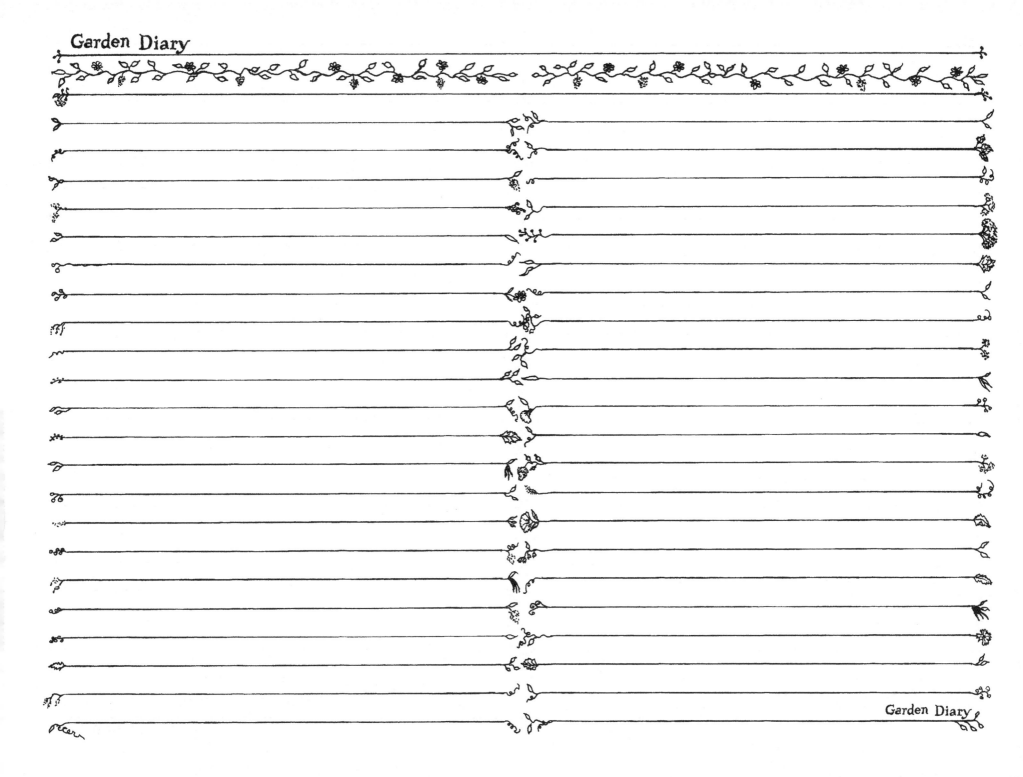

Garden Diary

Garden Diary

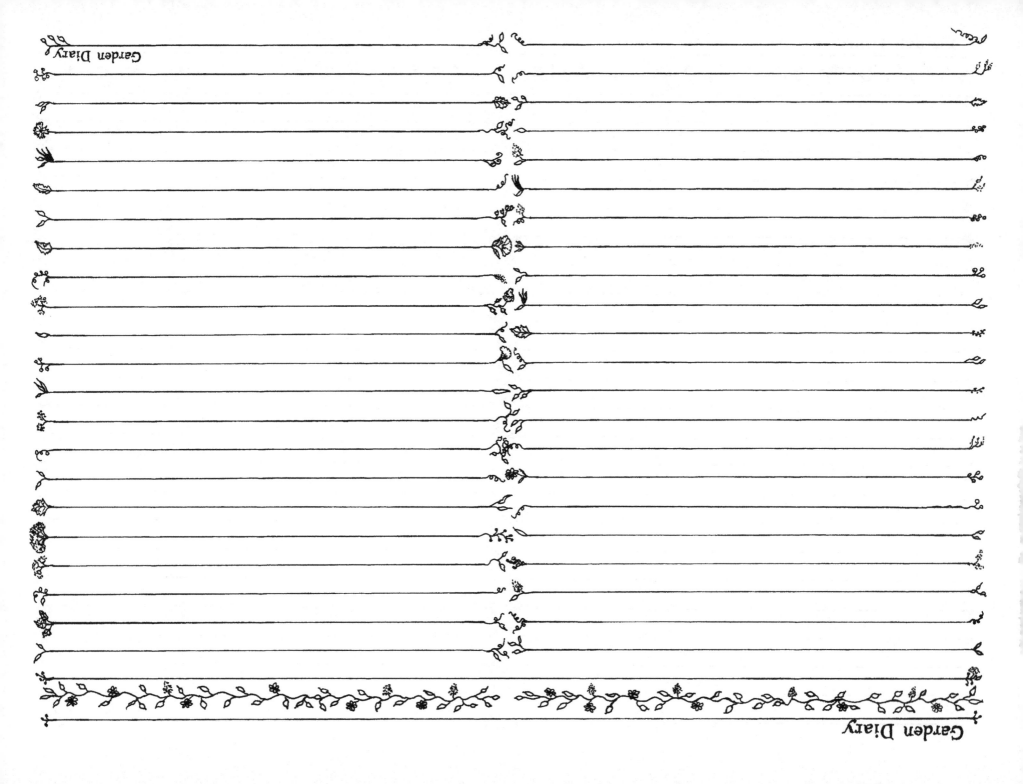

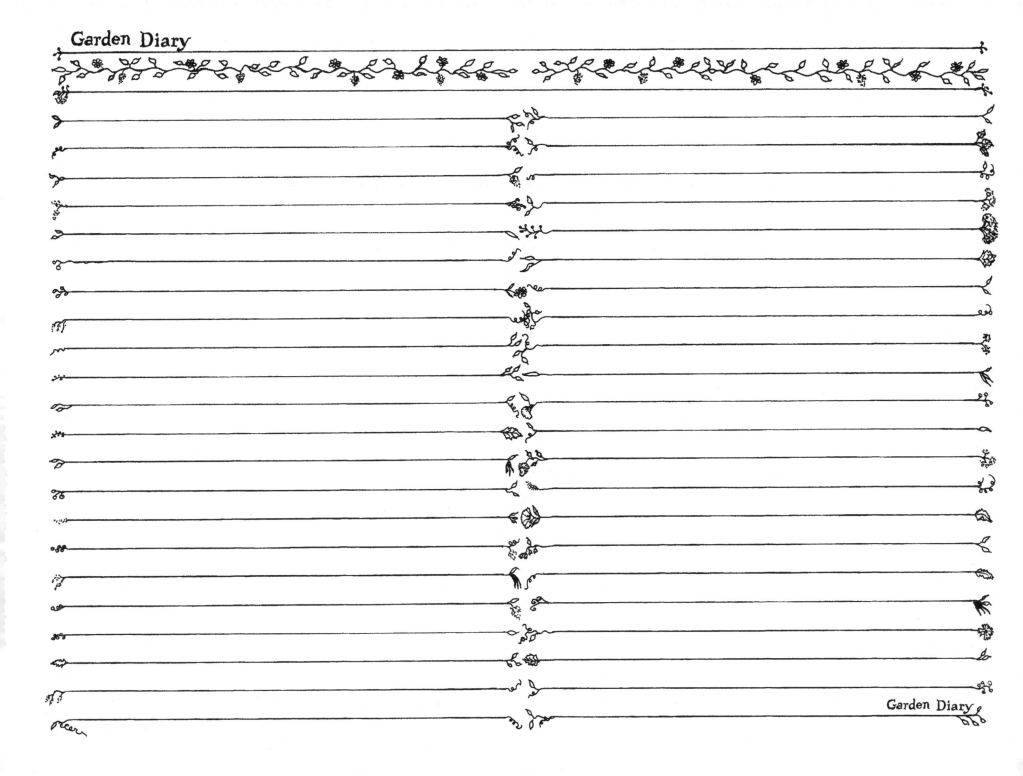

Garden Diary

Garden Diary

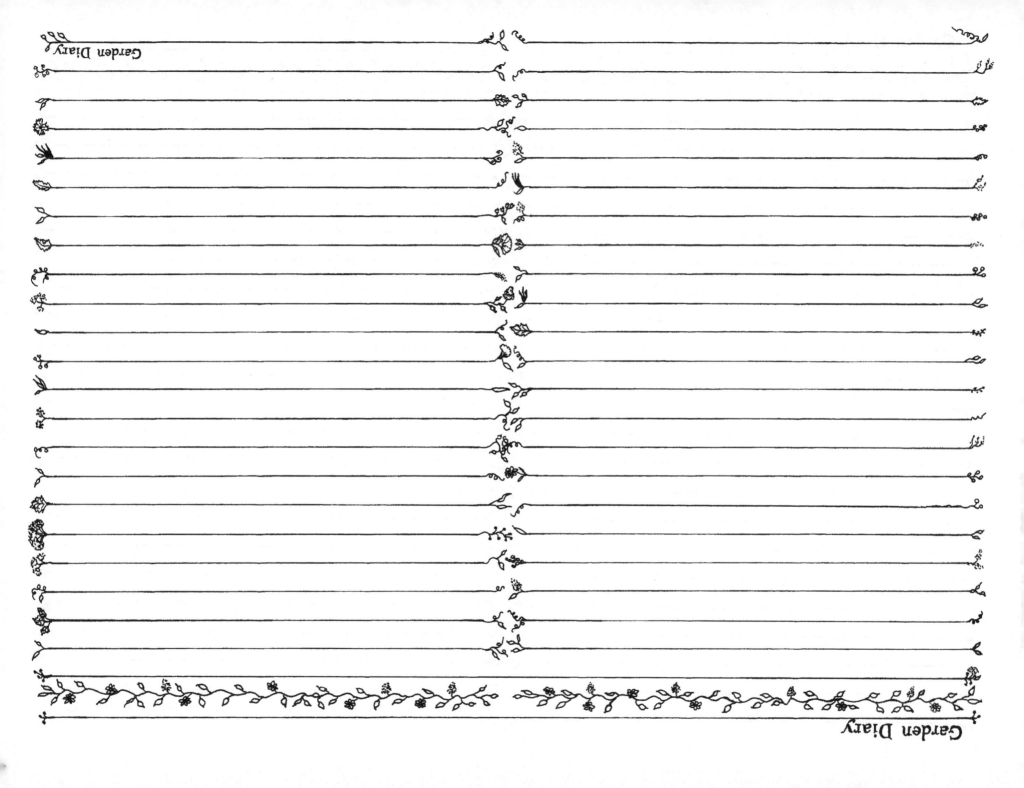

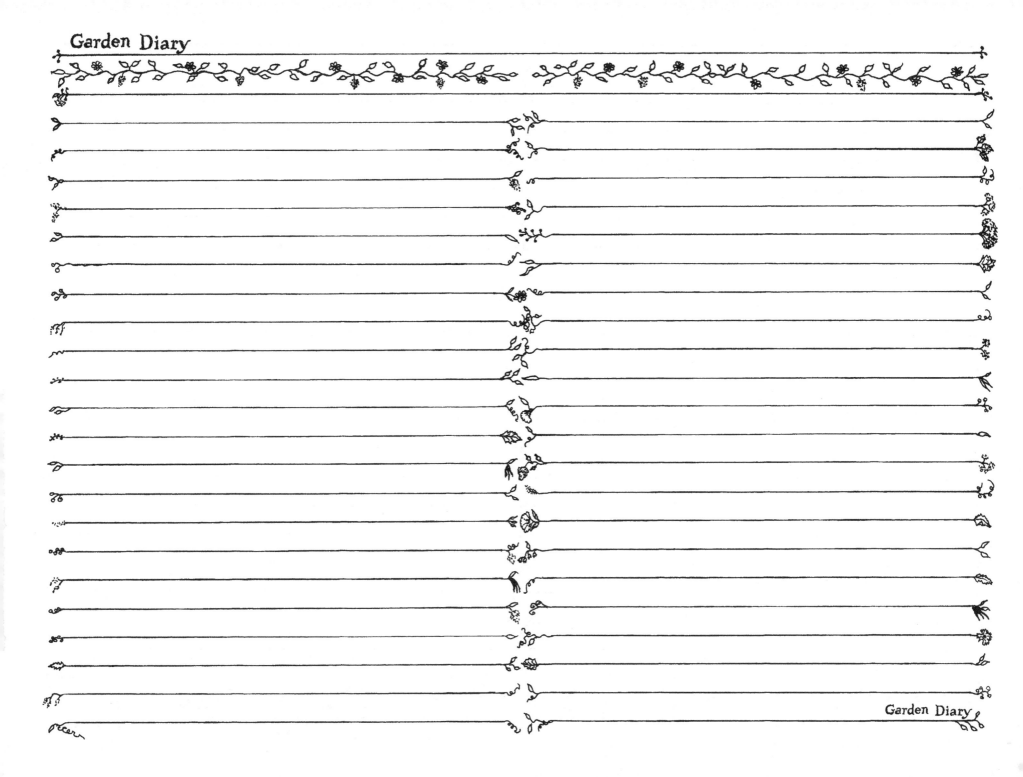

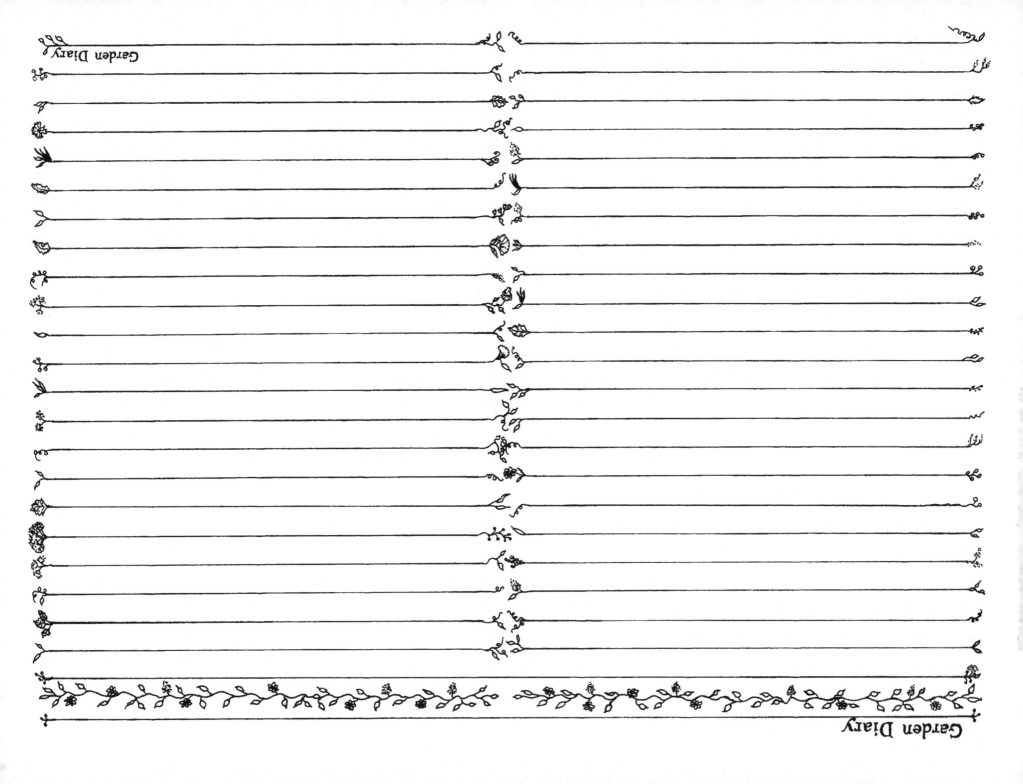

Garden Diary

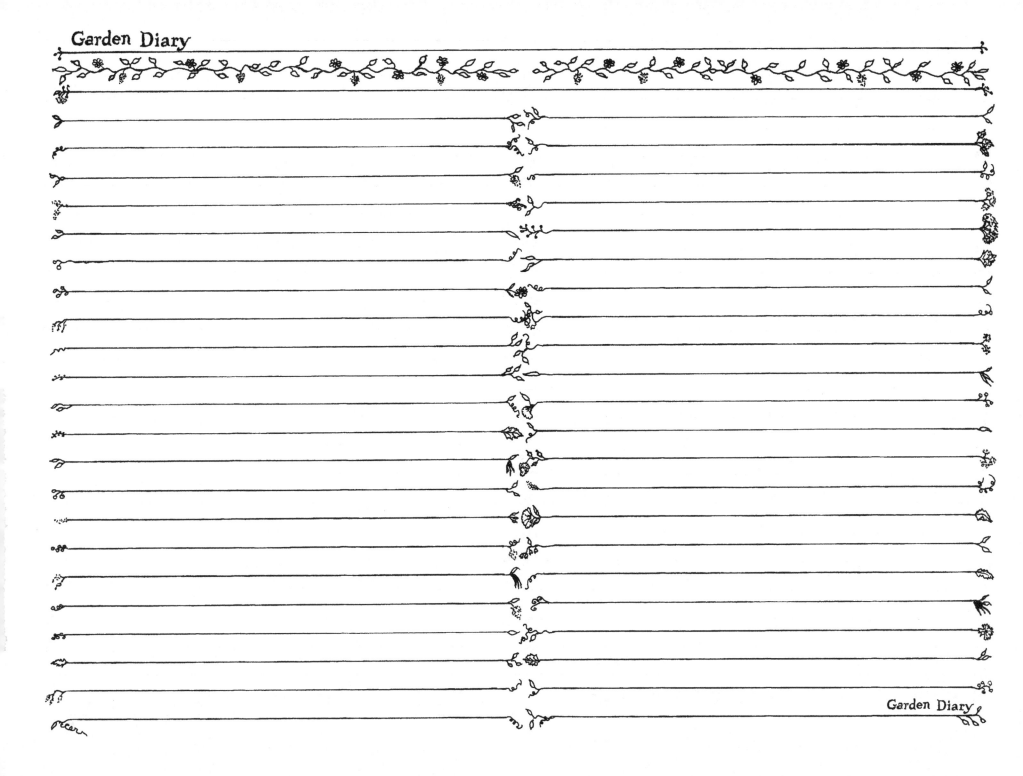

Garden Diary

Garden Diary

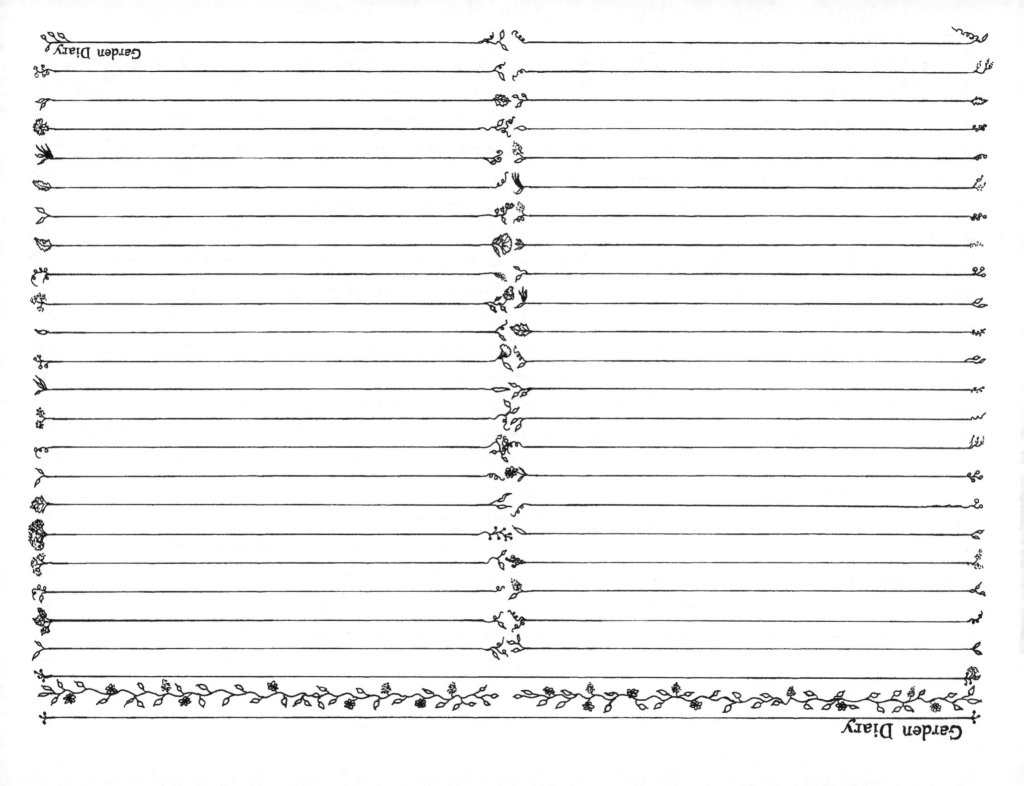

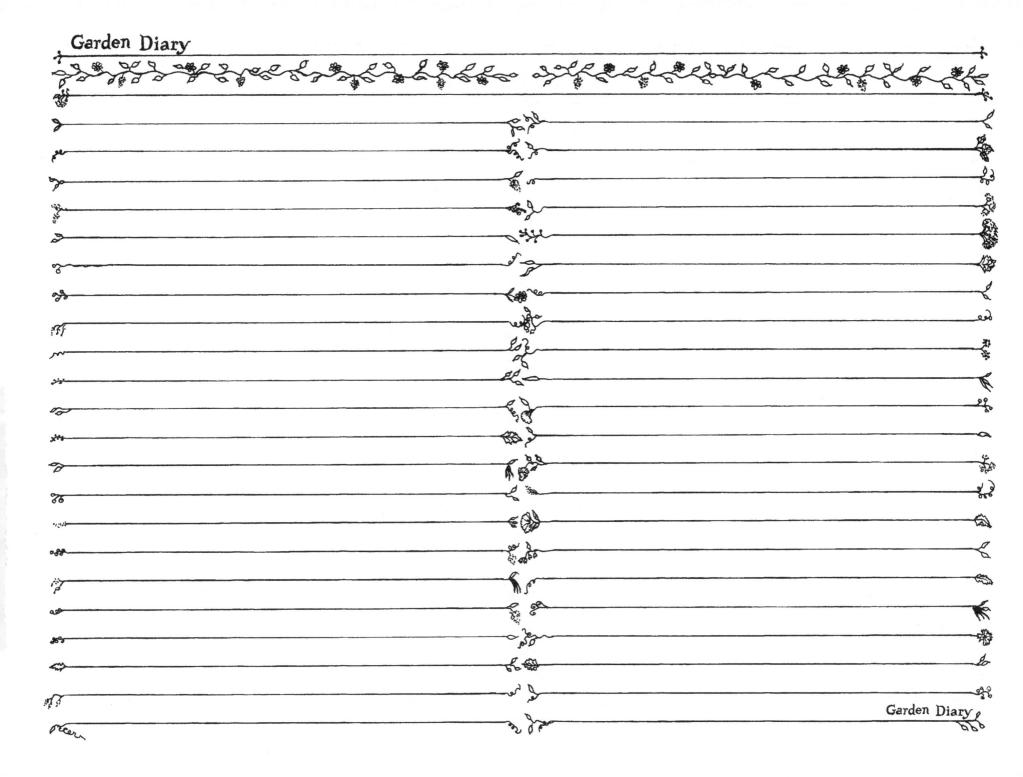

Garden Diary

Garden Diary

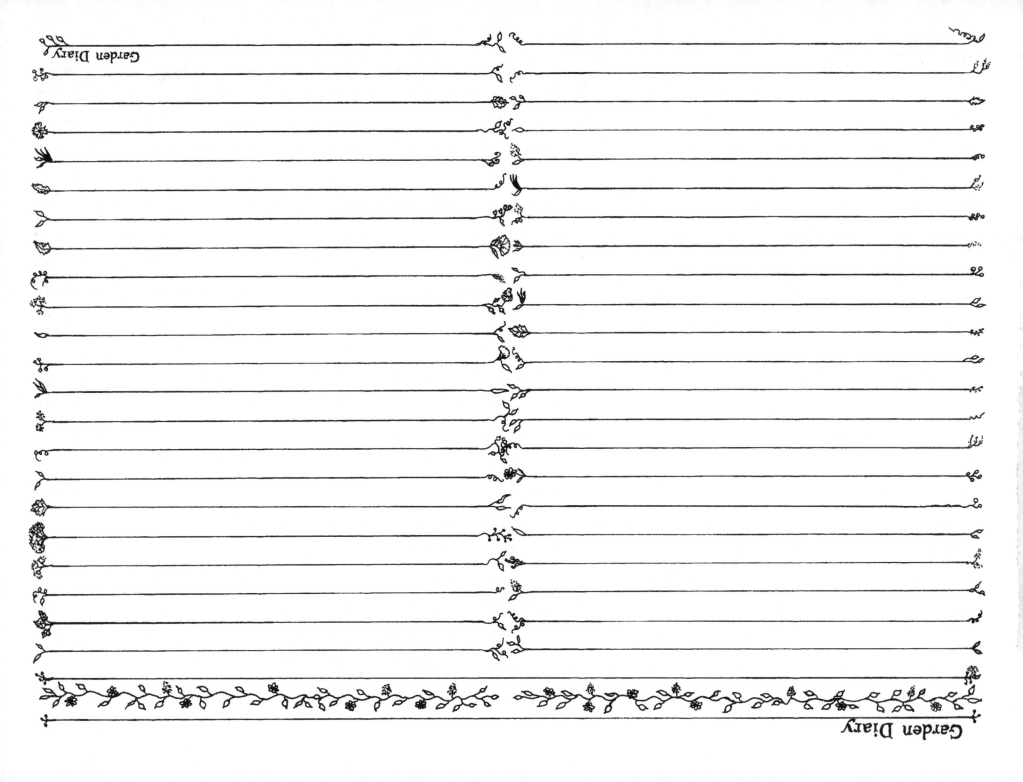

Garden Diary

Garden Diary

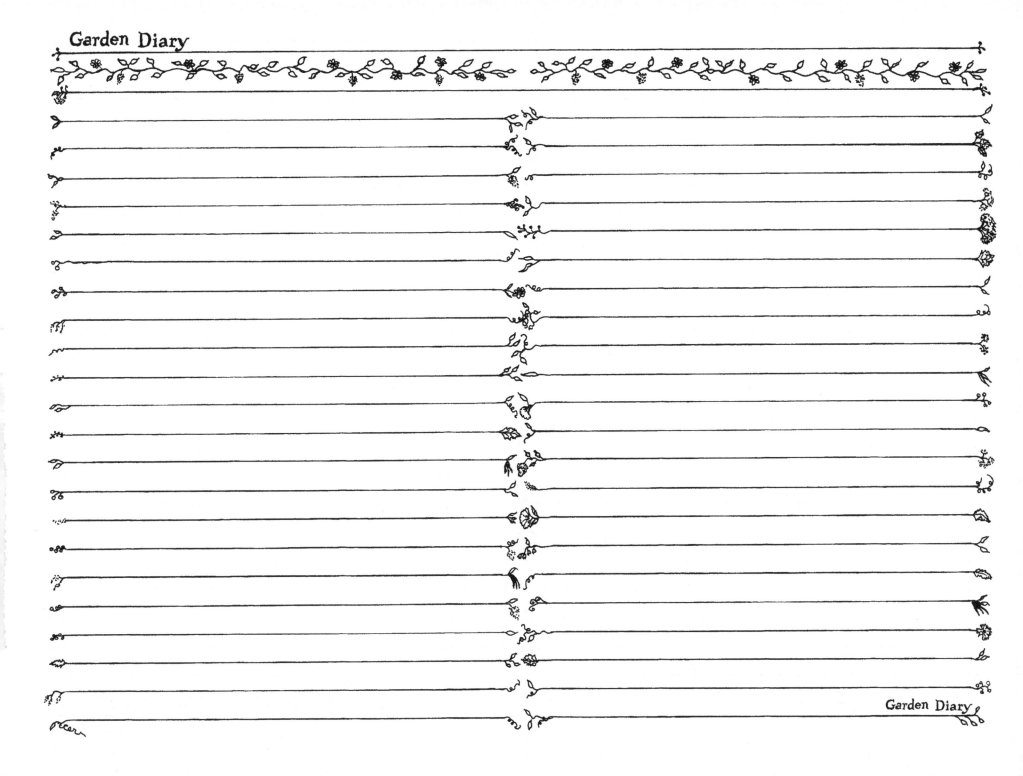

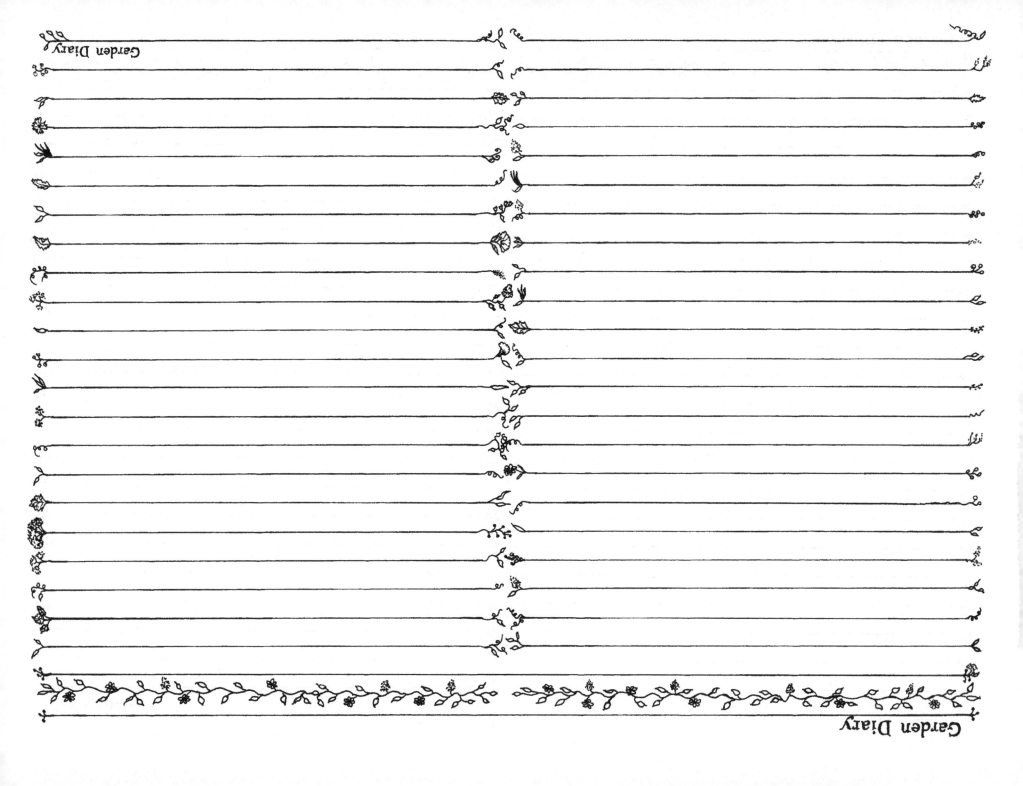

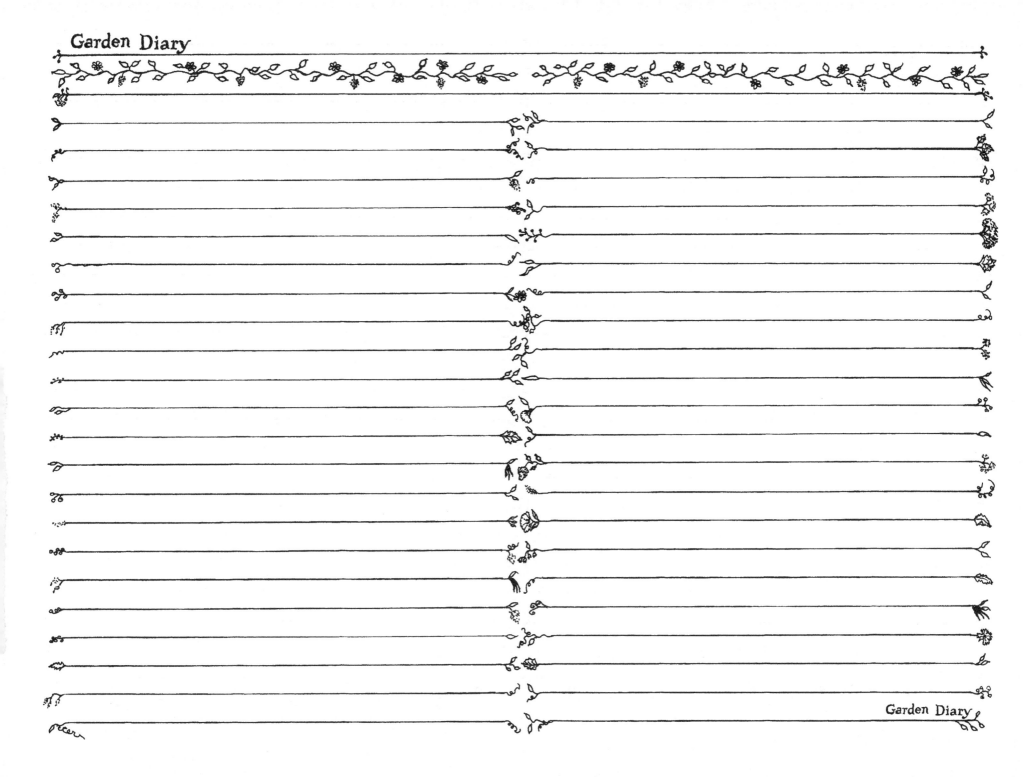

Garden Diary

Garden Diary

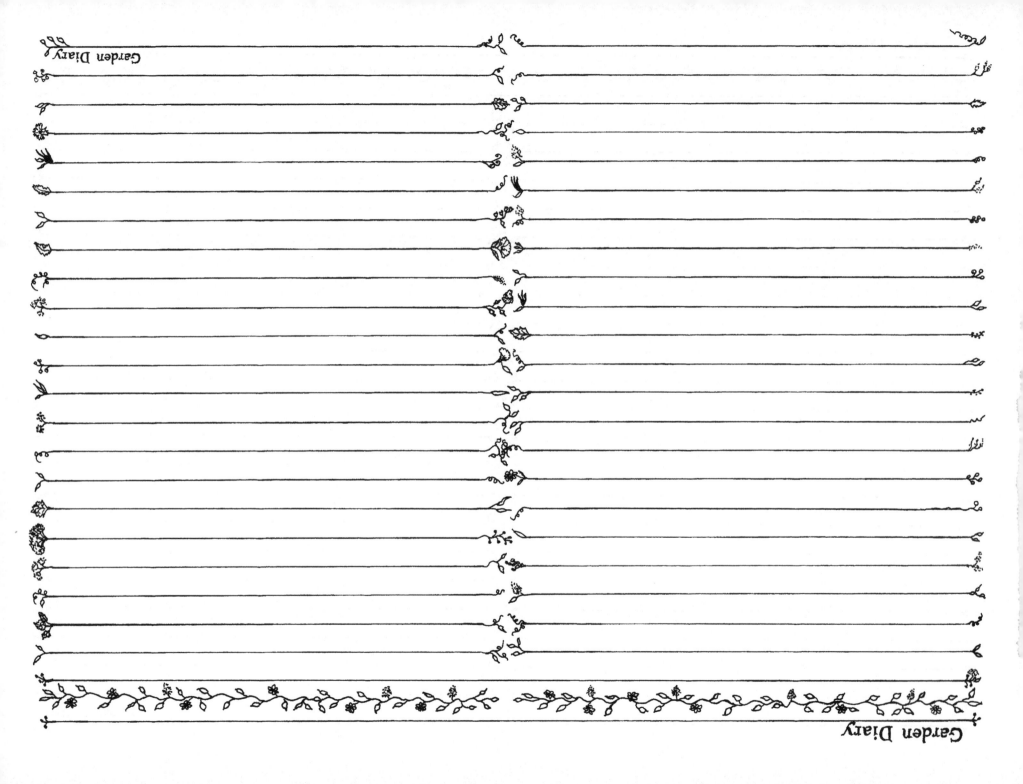

Garden Diary

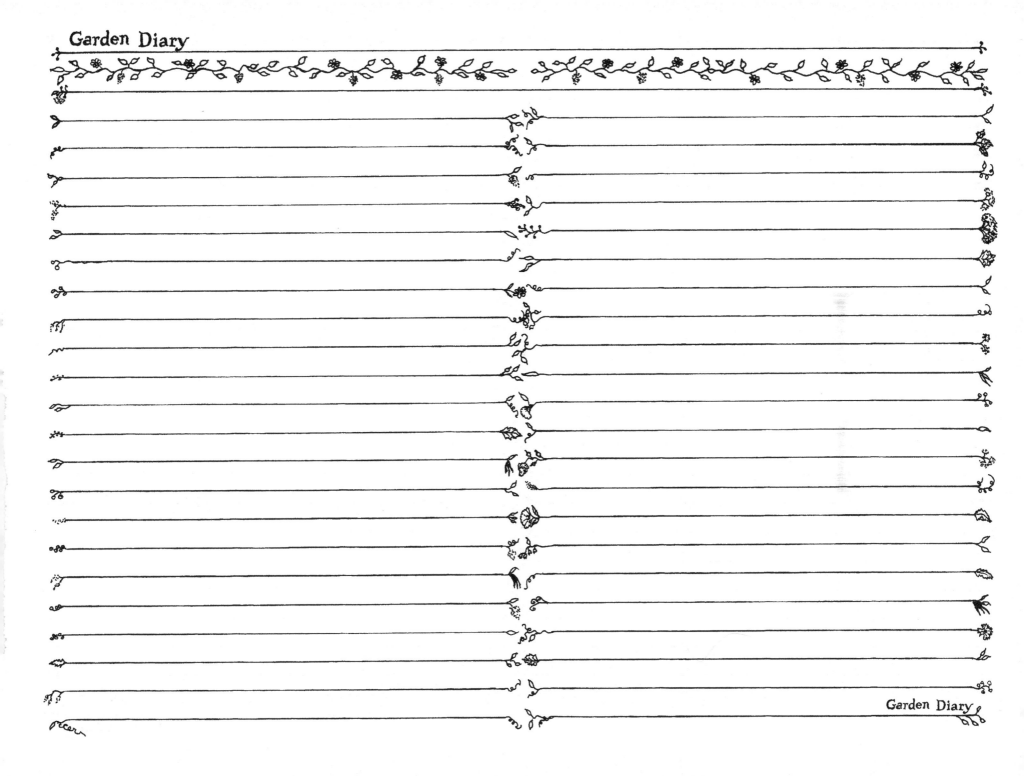

Garden Diary

Garden Diary

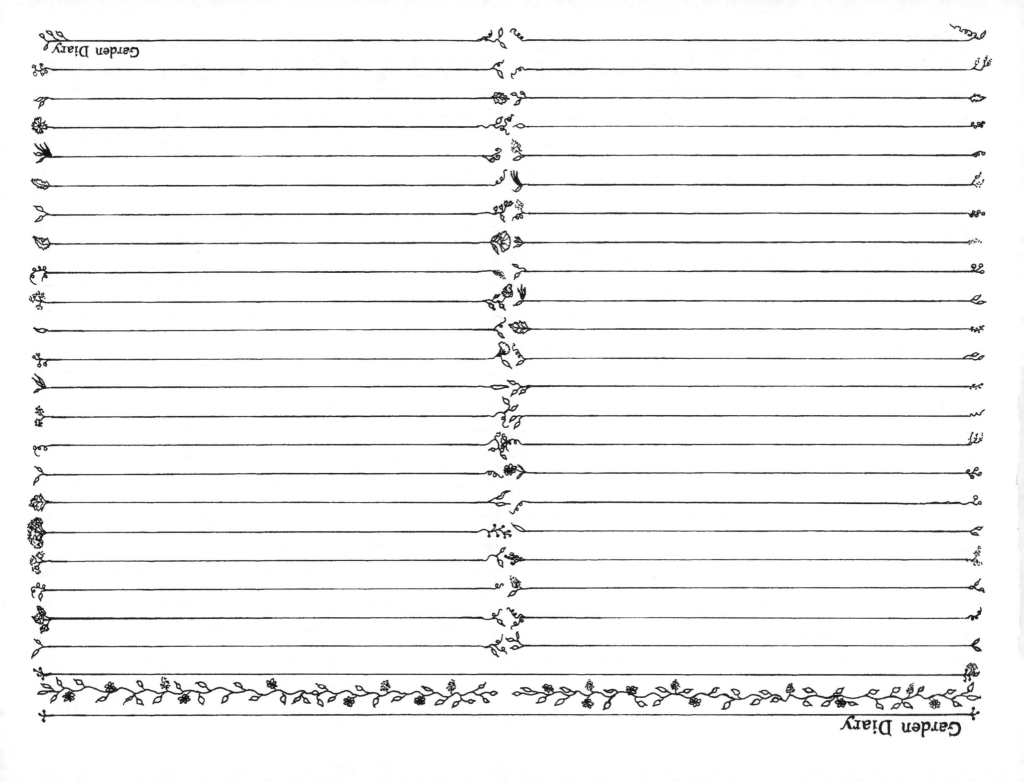

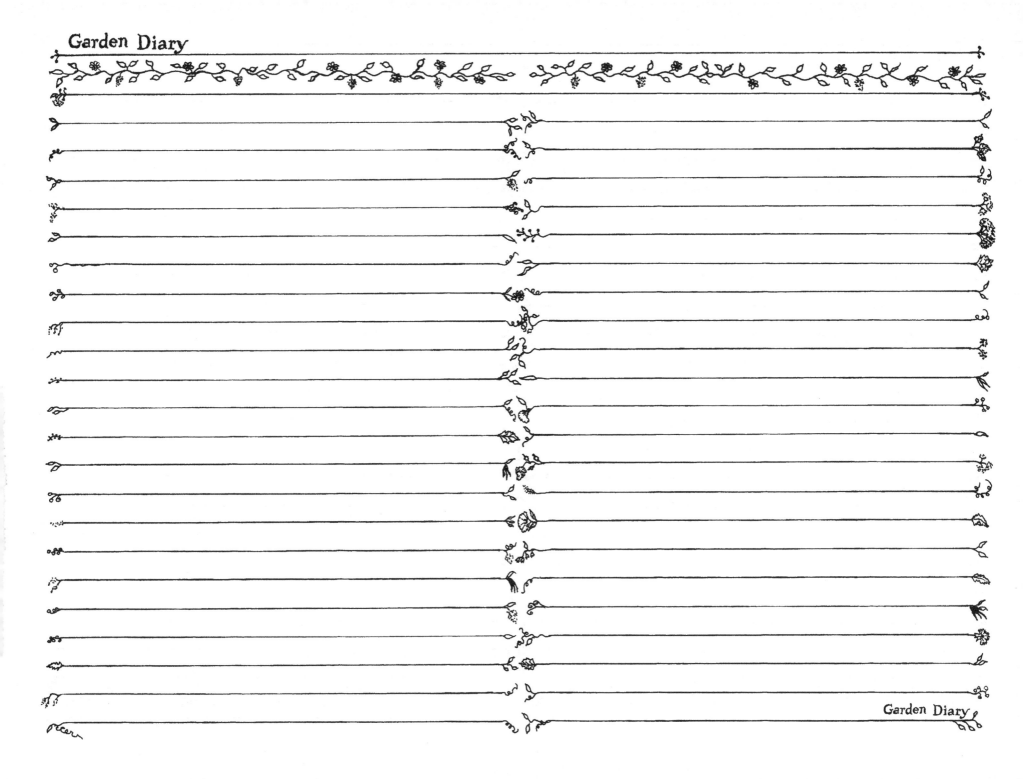

Garden Diary

Garden Diary

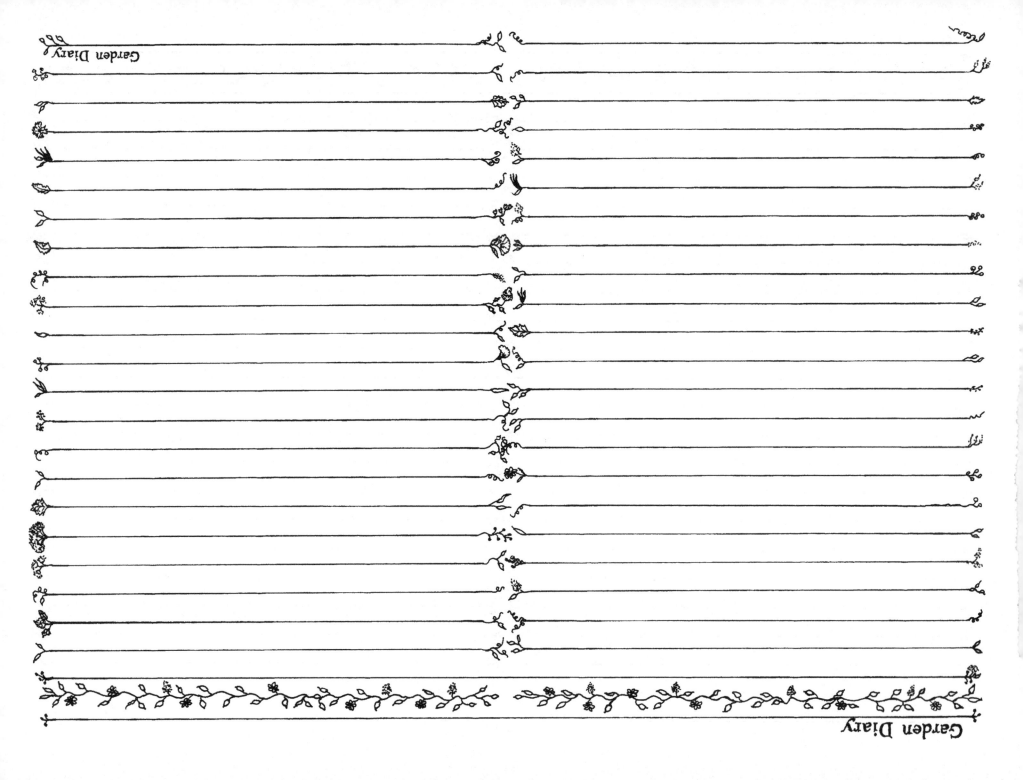

Garden Diary

Garden Diary

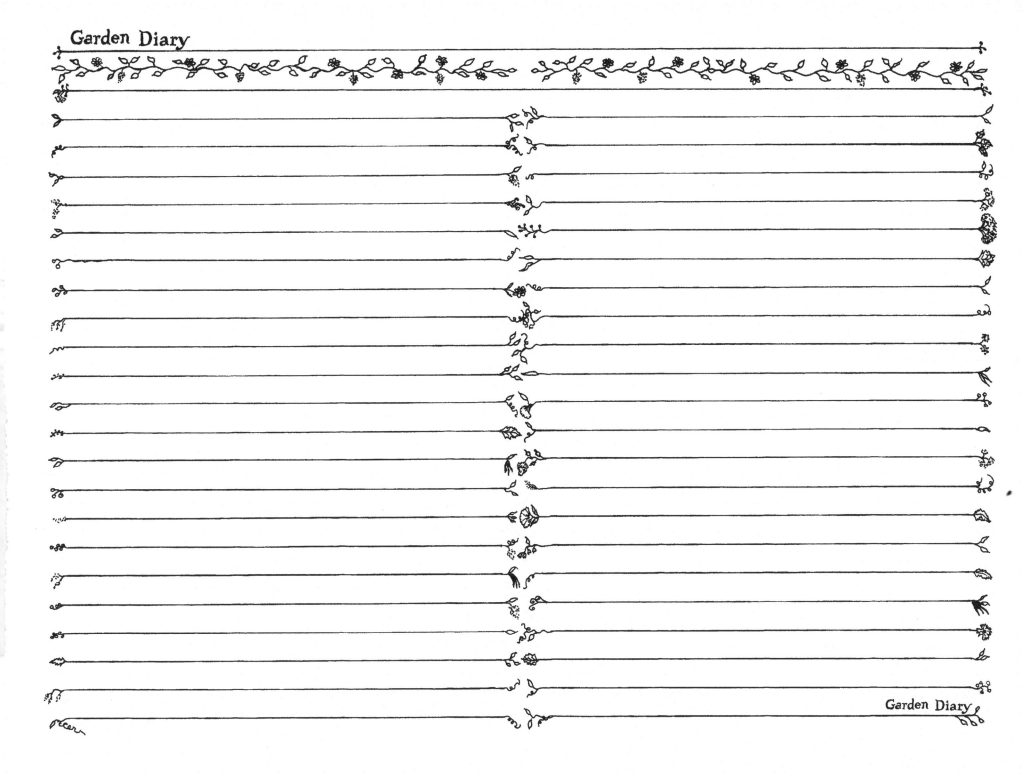

Garden Diary

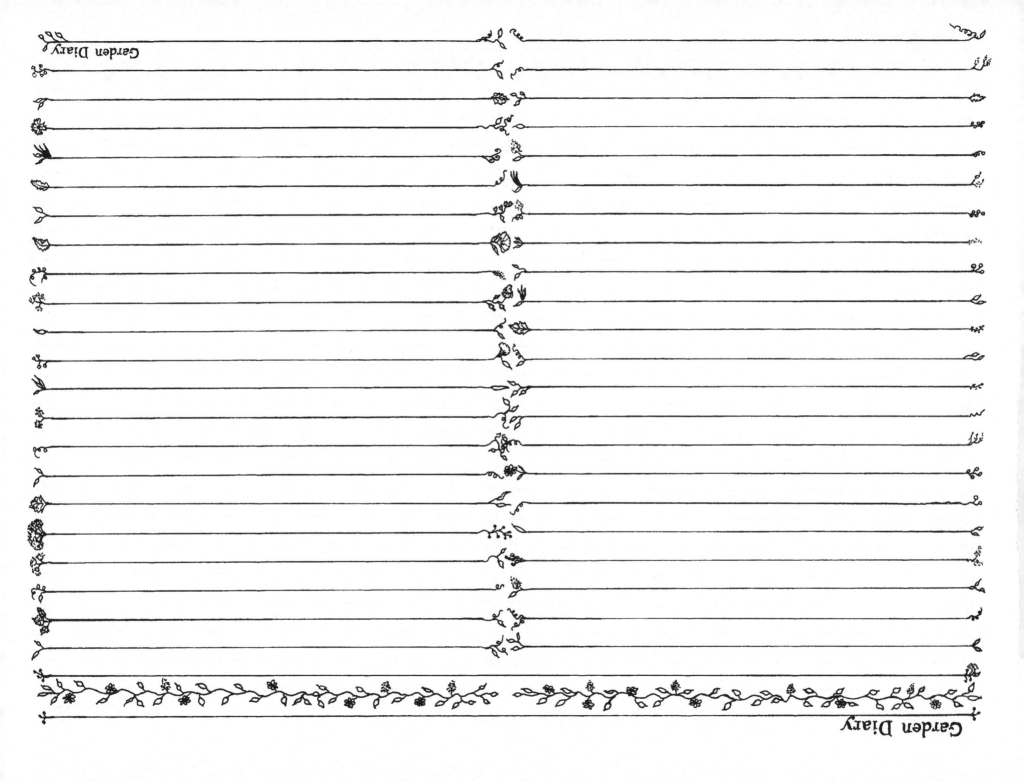

Garden Diary

Garden Diary

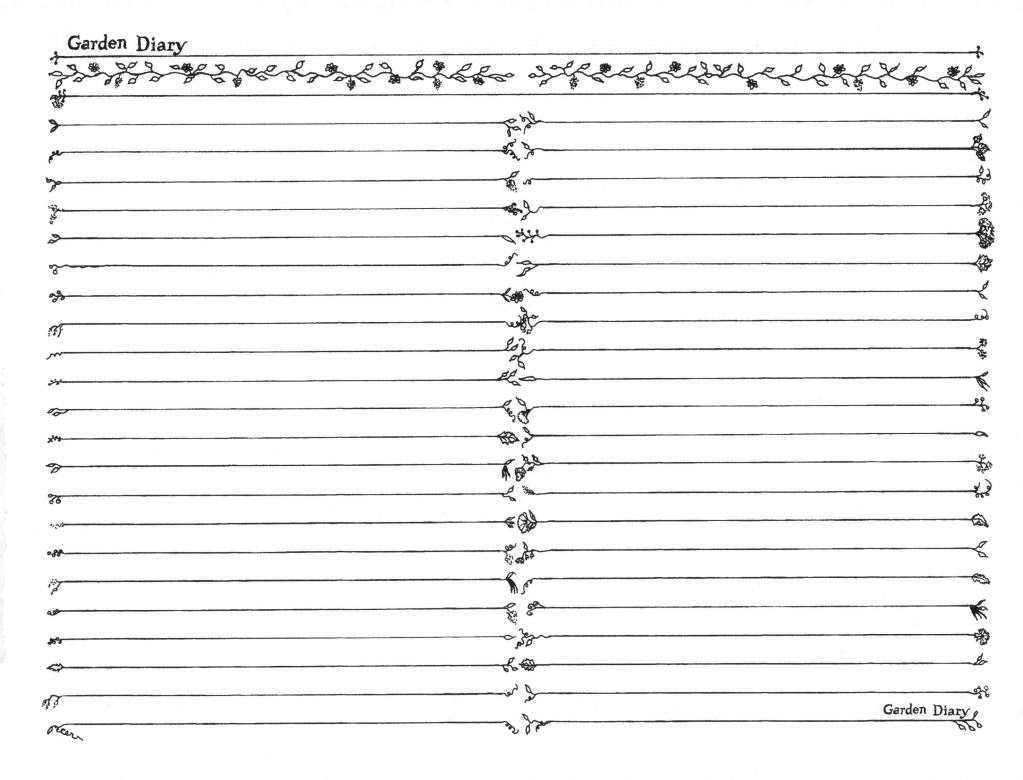

Garden Diary

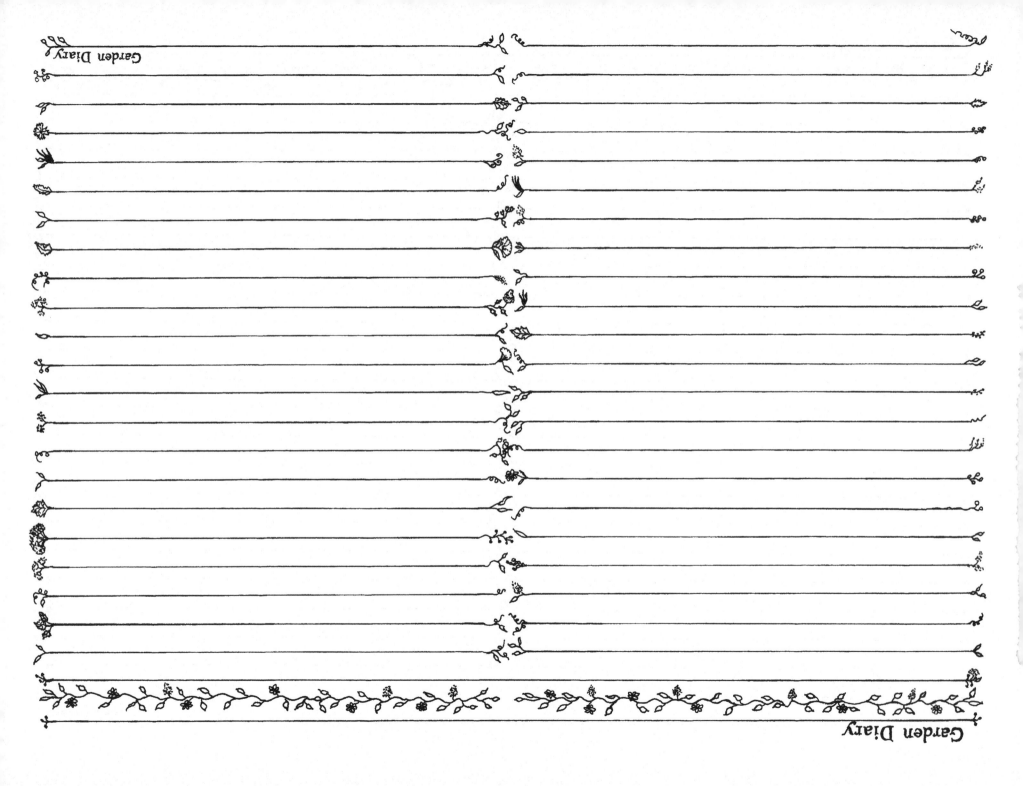

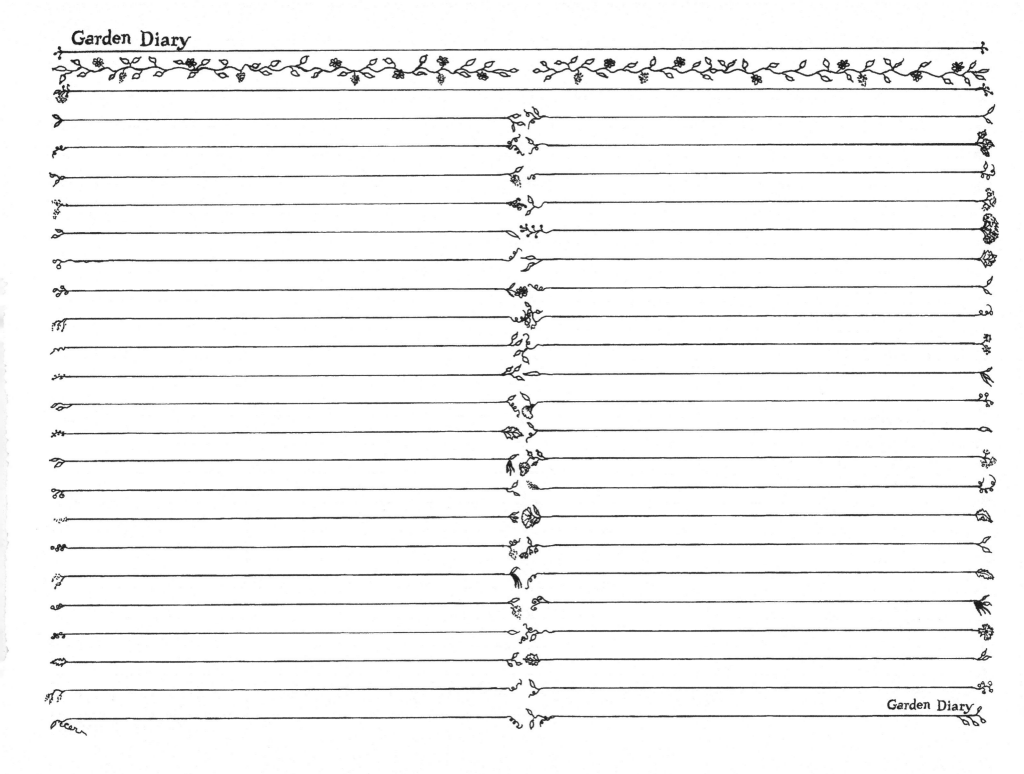

Garden Diary

Garden Diary

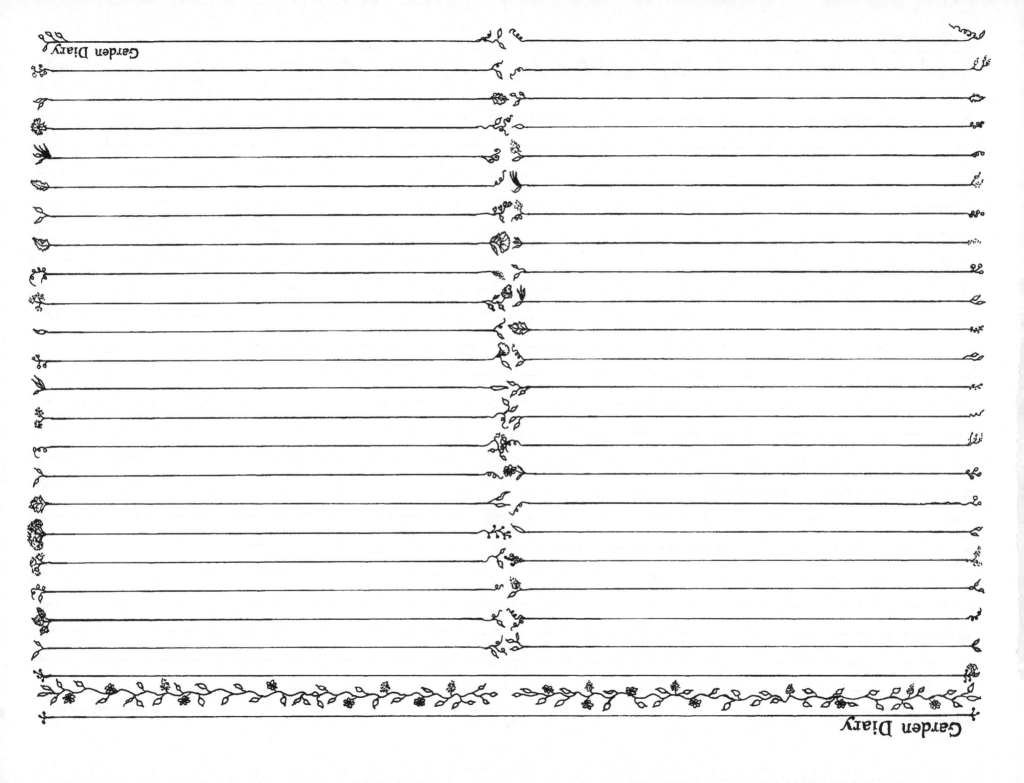

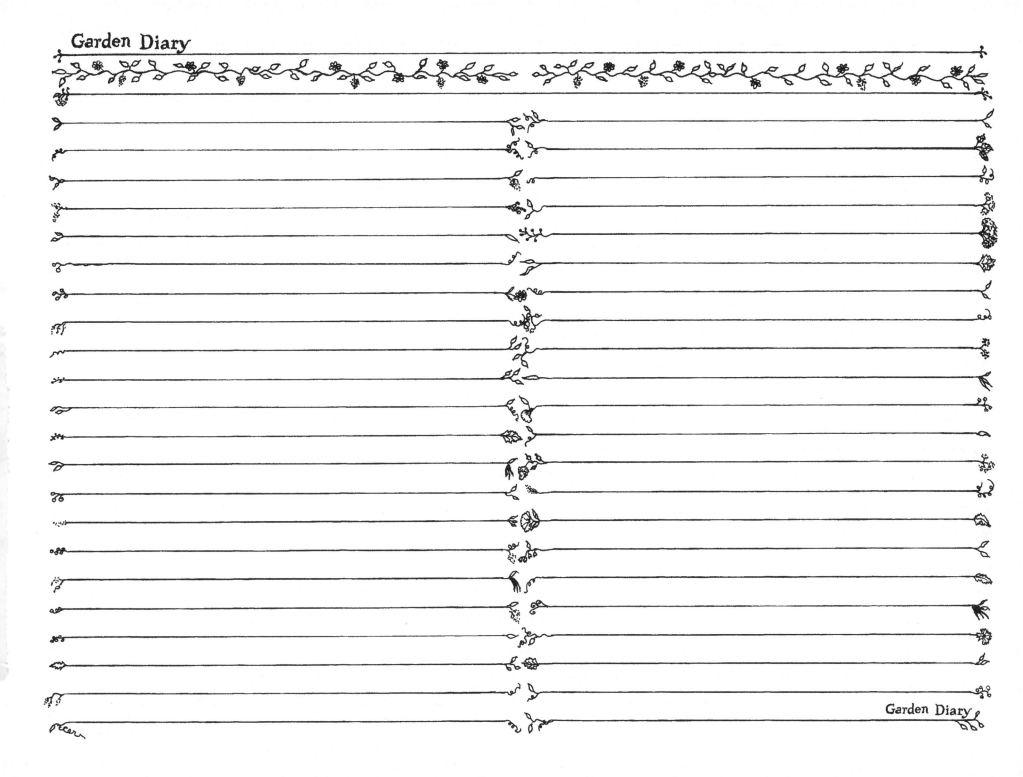

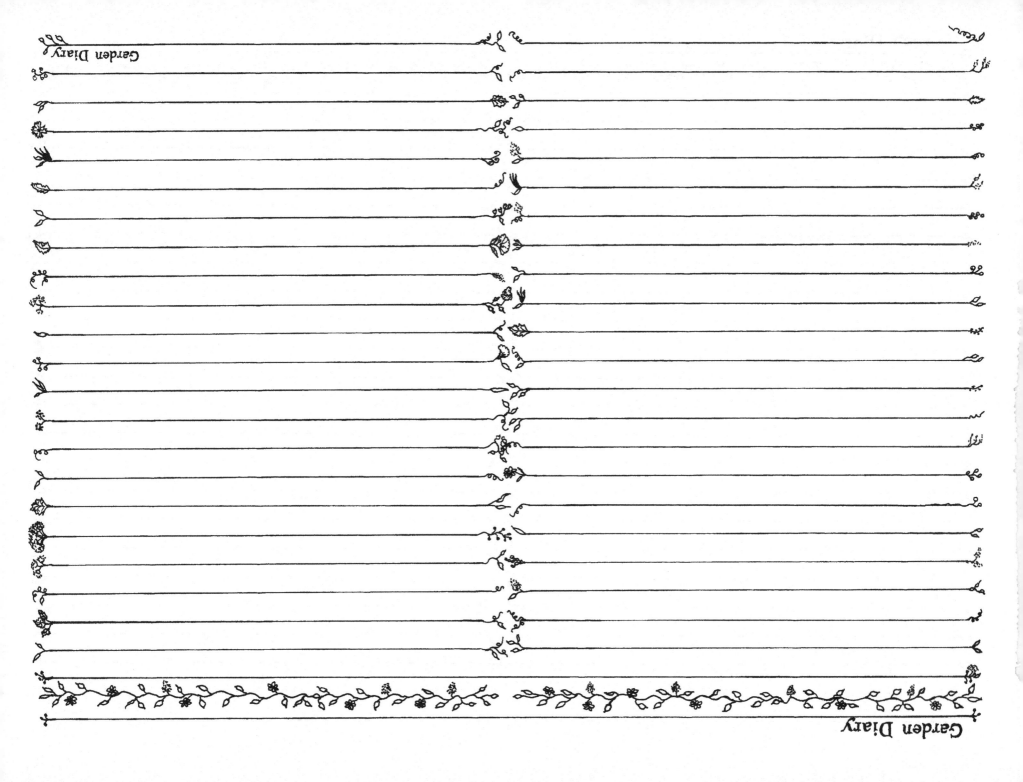

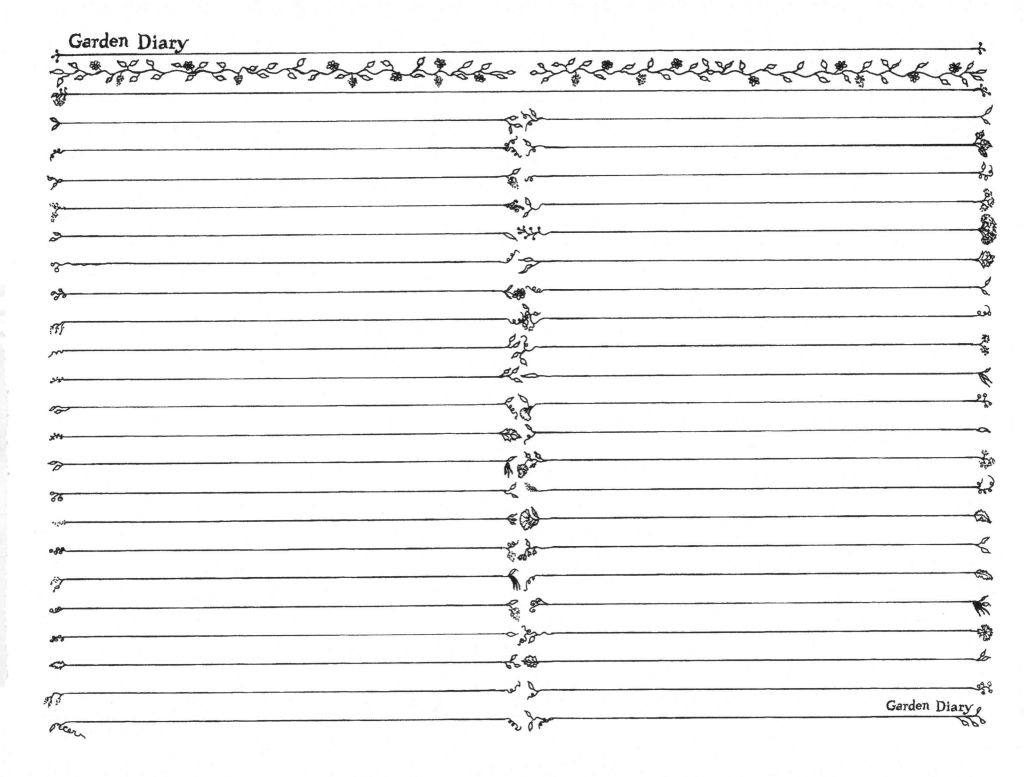

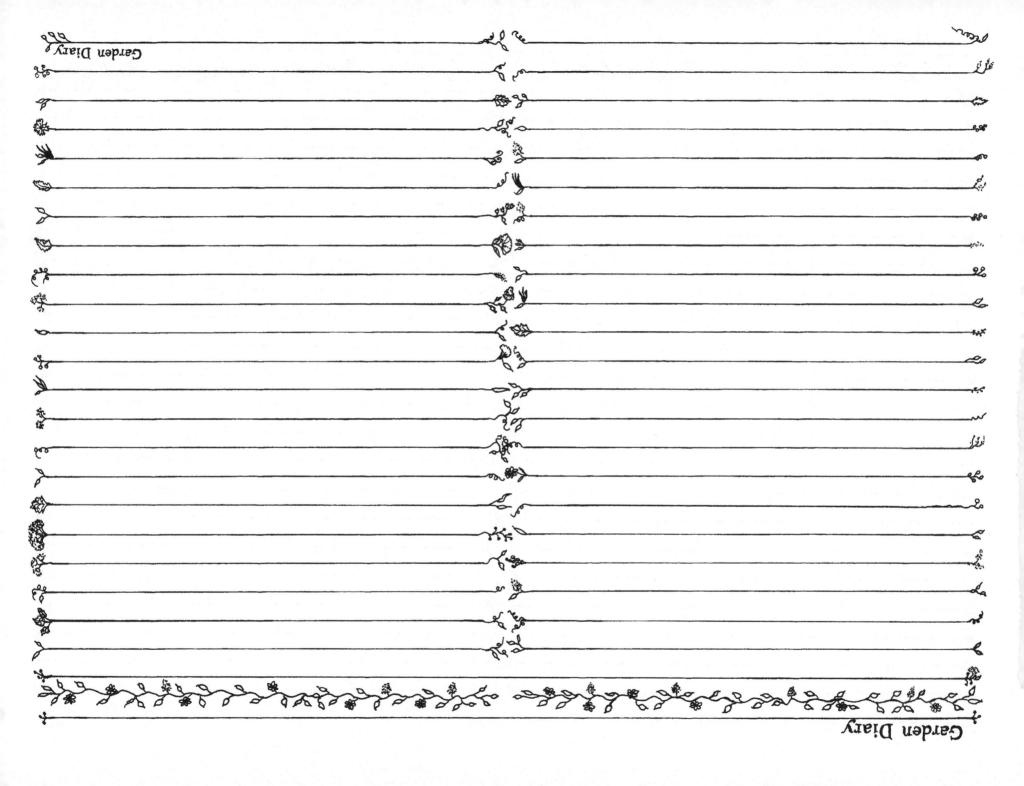

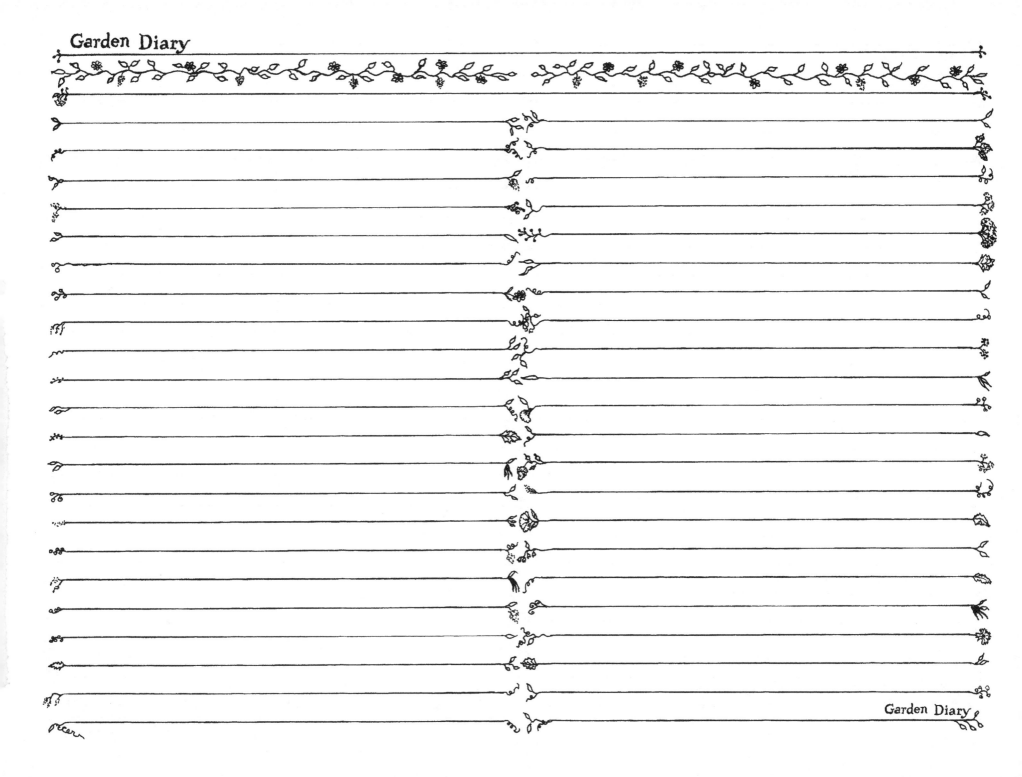

Garden Diary

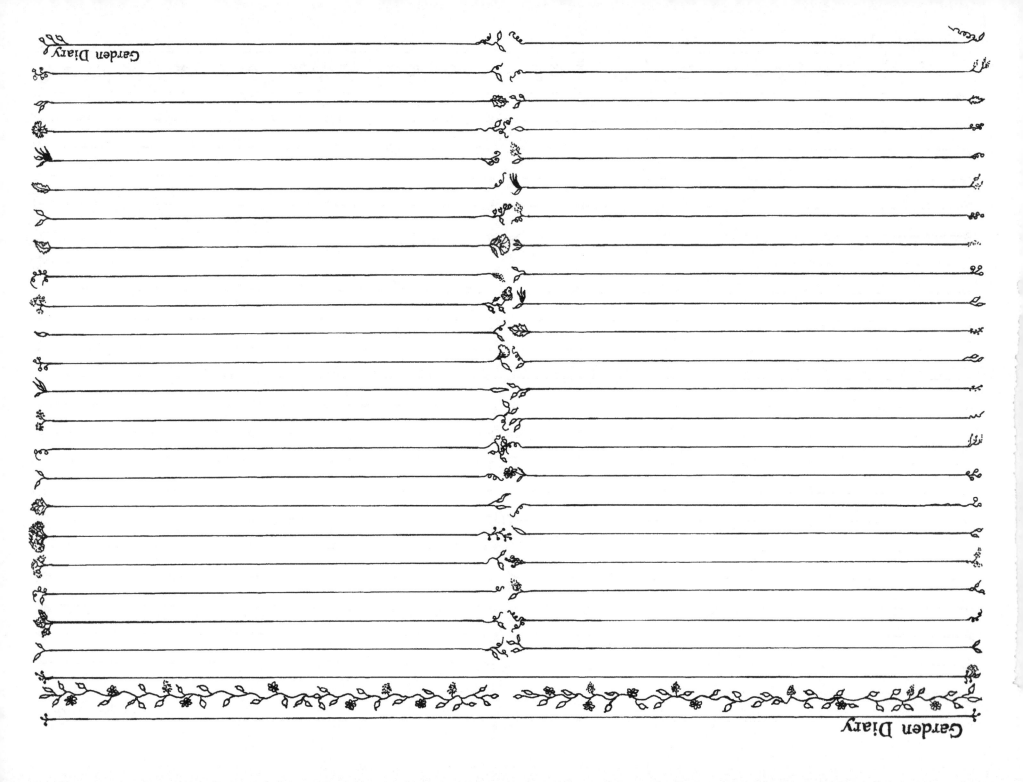

Garden Diary

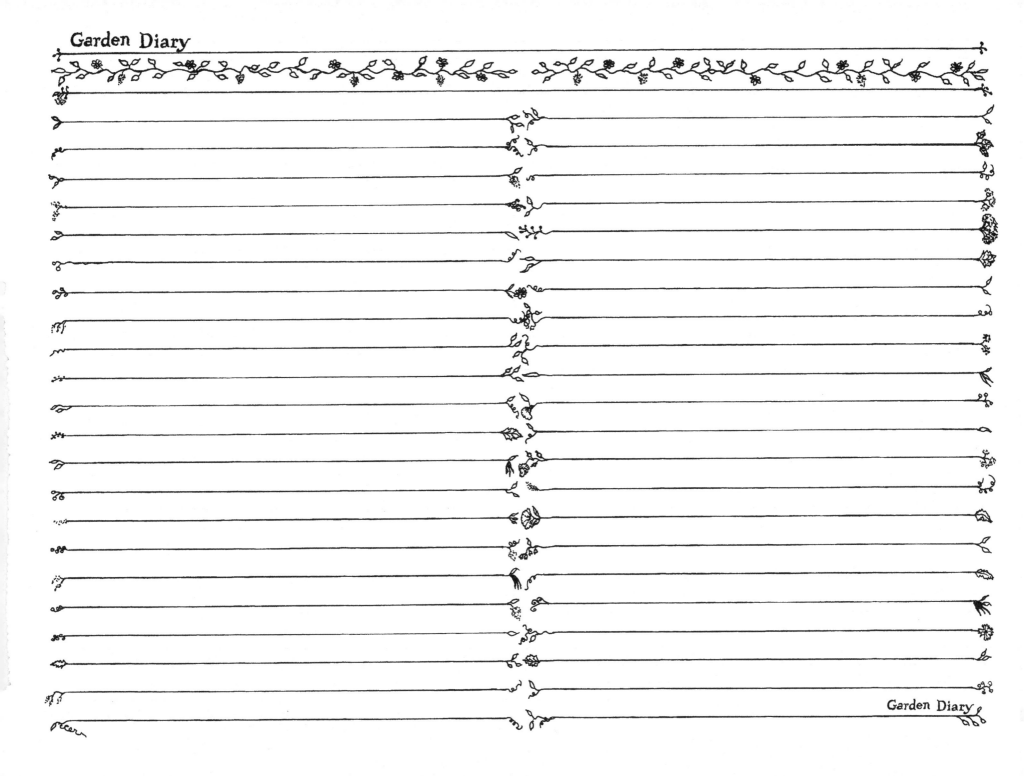

Garden Diary

One-Year Plan   Month:

One Year Plan

One-Year Plan

Month:

One-Year Plan

Month:

One Year Plan

Month:

One-Year Plan

One-Year Plan   Month:

Month:

One-Year Plan

Month: _____

One-Year Plan

Month:

One Year Plan

One-Year Plan

Month: _____

_____

_____

One Year Plan

One-Year Plan

Month:

~ Pruning Guidelines ~

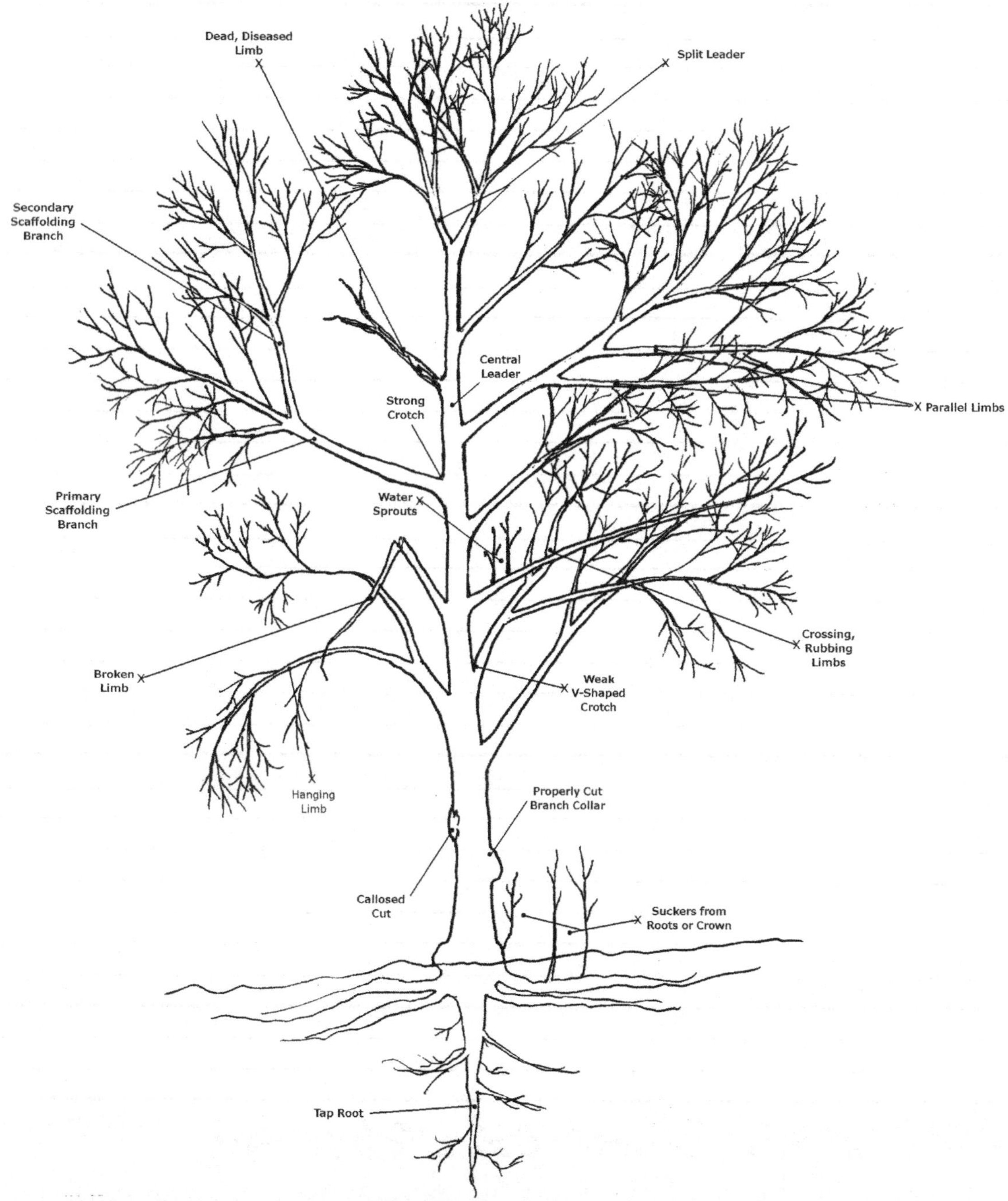

Dead, Diseased Limb

Split Leader

Secondary Scaffolding Branch

Central Leader

Strong Crotch

X Parallel Limbs

Primary Scaffolding Branch

Water Sprouts

Broken Limb

Crossing, Rubbing Limbs

Weak V-Shaped Crotch

Hanging Limb

Properly Cut Branch Collar

Callosed Cut

Suckers from Roots or Crown

Tap Root

Bud Pruning

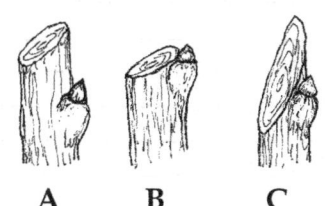

A   **B**   **C**

A. Too High
B. Too Close
C. Too Angled

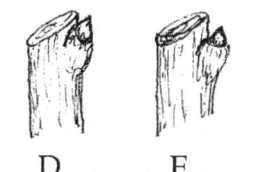

D   E

Distances for Seasons
D. Winter (Dormant)
E. Summer (Growing)

Tree Pruning

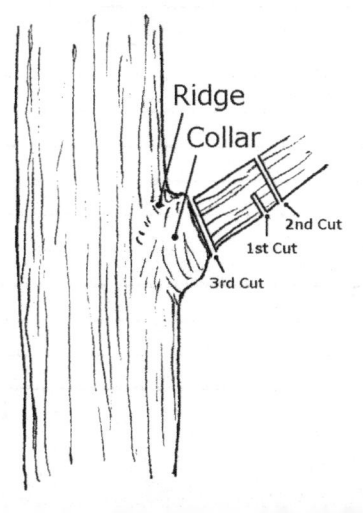

Ridge

Collar

2nd Cut

1st Cut

3rd Cut

Prune, Trim & Tidy Schedule

Early Winter

Late Winter

Early Spring

Mid-Spring

Prune, Trim & Tidy Schedule

Prune, Trim & Tidy Schedule ~ Early Winter ~ Mid-Spring

Mid-Spring

Early Spring

Prune, Trim & Tidy Schedule ~ Early Winter ~ Mid-Spring

Late Winter

Early Winter

Prune, Trim & Tidy Schedule

Early Winter   Late Winter

Early Spring   Mid-Spring

Prune, Trim & Tidy Schedule ~ Early Winter ~ Mid-Spring

Prune, Trim & Tidy Schedule

Late Spring

Early Summer

Mid-Summer

Later Summer

Prune, Trim & Tidy Schedule

Late Spring

Early Summer

Mid-Summer

Later Summer

Late Fall

Storage, Clean-up & Organizing

Prune, Trim & Tidy Schedule

Early Fall

Mid-Fall

Prune, Trim & Tidy Schedule

Early Fall

Mid-Fall

Late Fall

Storage, Clean-up & Organizing

Prune, Trim & Tidy Schedule ~ Early Fall~Clean-up

Plant Propagation

General Guidelines

In general, divide plants when they are not flowering, so that the plant's energy can go to root and leaf growth. Divide spring and summer blooming perennials in fall, and fall bloomers in spring.

If you divide in the spring, allow enough time for roots to settle in before hot weather. Spring division is ideally done in the early spring as soon as the growing tips of the plant have emerged. Spring divided perennials will bloom a little later than usual the first year.

Fall division should take place at least four to six weeks before the ground freezes for the plants to become established.

It's best not to divide perennials on hot, sunny days. Cloudy days are ideal, with several days of light rain in the forecast.

Water plants to be divided thoroughly a day or two before you plan to divide them, so that the ground is soft, but not heavy. Prepare the area that you plan to put your new divisions in before you begin to dig the parent plant.

It's often good to prune the stems and foliage to 6 inches from the ground in order to ease division and to force new growth.

Lift the Parent Plant

Use a sharp pointed spade or spading fork to dig down deep on all four sides of the plant, about 4 to 6 inches away from the plant. Pry underneath with your tool and lift the whole clump to be divided. If the plant is very large and heavy, you may need to cut it into several pieces in place with your shovel before lifting it.

Separate the Plant

Shake or hose off loose soil and remove dead leaves and stems. This will help loosen tangled root balls and make it easier to see what you are doing.

Perennials have several different types of root systems. Each of these needs to be treated a bit differently:

Spreading Root Systems

These spreading root systems have matted roots with no distinct pattern. These can crowd out their own centers. Some can be invasive unless divided frequently. They can usually be pulled apart by hand, or cut apart with shears or knife.

Large plants with thickly intertwined roots may need to be separated with digging forks. Put two forks back to back in the center of the plant and use them to pry the pieces apart.

Divide the plants into clumps of three to five vigorous shoots each. Small or weak and woody divisions should be discarded. Discard the center of the clump if it is weaker than the outside edges.

Clumping Root Systems

Clumping root systems originate from a central clump.

It is often necessary to cut through the thick fleshy crowns (the central growing area between the roots and the leaves and stems of the plant) with a heavy, sharp knife. You can also pry apart these roots with back to back digging forks.

Keep at least one developing eye or bud with each division. If larger plants are wanted, keep several eyes.

Rhizome Division

Rhizomes are stems that grow horizontally at or above the soil level. Bearded irises are the most common perennial with this type of root system. Divide irises any time between a month after flowering until early fall.

Cut and discard the rhizome sections that are one year or older. Also, inspect rhizomes for disease and insect damage. Damaged rhizomes should be trimmed and treated, or discarded if too badly damaged.

Iris divisions should retain a few inches of rhizome and one fan of leaves, trimmed back halfway. Replant with the top of the rhizome just showing above soil level.

Tuberous Roots

Tuberous roots are very similar to rhizomes, but shorter. The tubers should be cut apart with a sharp knife. Every division must have a piece of the original stem and a growth bud attached. After division they can either be replanted or stored for spring planting.

Dividing Large, Tough Roots

If the root mass is very large, or tight and tangled, you can raise the clump 1 to 2 feet off the ground and drop it. This should loosen the root mass, and you can pull the individual plants apart. This is not recommended for plants with brittle roots such as peonies.

Plants that have very tough, vigorous root systems such as ornamental grasses may have to be divided with a shovel, saw or ax. You can also vigorously hose off soil to make the root system easier to work with.

Plant the Divisions

Never allow divisions to dry out. Have plastic bags or pots ready to enclose cuttings as soon as you trim all broken roots and remove anything in surrounding soil that is not part of the plant.

Replant divisions at the same depth they were originally. Firm soil around the roots to eliminate air pockets. Water well after planting.

Perennials divided in the fall should be generously mulched the first winter to prevent heaving. The best winter mulch is loose and open, such as pine straw or leaves.

Cultivation and Propagation Log

Code	Plant Name	Location	Soil Prep	Start Date	1st Leaves	Plant, Graft Divide	Fertilized	Bloom	Fruit Harvest	Seed	Notes

Cultivation & Propagation Log

Cultivation and Propagation Log

Page:

Code	Plant Name	Location	Soil Prep	Start Date	1st Leaves	Plant, Graft Divide	Fertilized	Bloom	Fruit Harvest	Seed	Notes

Cultivation and Propagation Log

Page:

Code	Plant Name	Location	Soil Prep	Start Date	1st Leaves	Plant, Graft Divide	Fertilized	Bloom	Fruit Harvest	Seed	Notes

Cultivation & Propagation Log

Cultivation and Propagation Log

Code	Plant Name	Location	Soil Prep	Start Date	1st Leaves	Plant, Graft Divide	Fertilized	Bloom	Fruit Harvest	Seed	Notes

Cultivation & Propagation Log

Cultivation and Propagation Log

Page:

Code	Plant Name	Location	Soil Prep	Start Date	1st Leaves	Plant, Graft Divide	Fertilized	Bloom	Fruit Harvest	Seed	Notes

Cultivation & Propagation Log

~ Pests and Disease Prevention ~

~ Grow your plants in healthy soil ~

Healthy plants have the best chance of survival against disease and pests. Annual garden cleanup should be performed every fall and into winter. Garden pests and pathogens love to breed and multiply in leftover plant debris, and especially in areas kept moist and warm with matted leaves.

~ Remove and dispose of any . . .
~ diseased, infested or unwanted plants ~

Depending on the disease, either put these in the trash or burn them. Some things, such as poison ivy, and some plant diseases will become airborne if burned. The landfill is the healthier alternative in that case. Healthy plant debris should go into the compost pile or be turned under the soil to decompose.

~ Rotate vegetable crops ~

Many insects and disease-causing organisms overwinter in the soil near their host plants. If you grow the same plant (or a related one) in the same place the next year, you give those pests a head start. Crop rotation can reduce insect damage and minimize exposure to soilborne disease organisms. Wait at least two years before planting the same or related crops, such as onions and garlic, in the same spot. Potatoes, tomatoes, broccoli, cauliflower, brussel sprouts and onions are particularly vulnerable to disease problems when planted in the same location year after year.

Crop rotation also helps keep soil nutrients in balance. A first-year planting of heavy feeders, such as tomatoes and lettuce, can be followed the next year by legumes, which increase the nitrogen in the soil. In the third year, let the soil rest by planting light feeders, such as carrots or beets.

~ Diversify ~

If you place smaller groups of plants throughout the garden, rather than planting all of one plant in one place, it will be less likely that pests or disease will attack the various locations. Interplanting herbs and flowers is another effective way to protect your garden, especially with the use of companion plants. The list of companion plants is too long for inclusion in this book, but can be found online with a simple search.

~ Plant damage that may NOT be from pest and disease ~

~ Wilting ~
~ Is usually due to a lack of moisture. Don't assume plants have enough water if the soil is moist knuckle deep. Make sure the soil is moist to a depth of at least 6" for most vegetable plants and annuals.

~ On the flip side, soil that is too wet can also cause wilting, because the roots are suffocating.

~ Is also a normal response to extreme heat. Wait to see if the plants recover in the evening when temperatures cool. If not, more water or shade may be the answer.

~ Is common for newly transplanted seedlings and other plants that have recently been moved outdoors. Either give them shade or, if still in pots, move them throughout the day to gradually expose them to more time in the sun.

~ Sunburn ~
~ May look like bleached areas on the foliage of new transplants or plants that have been moved from indoors to outdoors. Discoloration will be most pronounced on the leaves most exposed to the sun.

To prevent sunburn, seedlings and other tender plants should be exposed to direct sunlight gradually, over a period of several days. Plants will usually outgrow minor sunburn.

~ Frost damage ~
~ Will appear as black areas on leaves. The outer leaves will usually show the most damage. Foliage that have been damaged by a late-spring frost will not recover, but the plants will usually recover. Allow damaged leaves to remain until the threat of frost has passed and the plant has begun to show new growth, then remove the affected leaves.

~ Weather damage ~
Torn foliage can be the result of heavy winds, rain or hail. This makes the plant more vulnerable to invasion by disease. It's usually best to remove damaged foliage. In most cases the leaves will be quickly replaced.

~ Off-color foliage ~
~ Is often caused by a nutrient deficiency. Symptom and possible nutrient deficiencies follow:
~ color paler than normal=nitrogen
~ leaf veins are green but the area between them is yellow=iron
~ reddish or purplish cast=phosphorus
~ stunted growth=overall shortage of essential nutrients.

~ Dried leaf margins ~
~ May indicate fertilizer burn or wind burn. Always apply fertilizers according to label directions to avoid over-fertilizing. Organic fertilizers rarely cause burning because the nutrients are released slowly over time.

~ Burned foliage ~
~ especially in one specific area on the plant ~
~ May indicate damage caused by animal urine or herbicide overspray. Spray with water and prune any damaged foliage.

Pest & Disease Treatment Log

Code	Date	Plant	Symptom	Treatment	Reapplied	Results	Notes

Pest & Disease Treatment Log

Page:

Code	Date	Plant	Symptom	Treatment	Reapplied	Results	Notes

Pest & Disease Treatment Log

Code	Date	Plant	Symptom	Treatment	Reapplied	Results	Notes

Pest & Disease Treatment Log

Code	Date	Plant	Symptom	Treatment	Reapplied	Results	Notes

Pest & Disease Treatment Log

Code	Date	Plant	Symptom	Treatment	Reapplied	Results	Notes

Pest & Disease Treatment Log

Soil Testing and Amendments

~ Soil Test #1:
The Squeeze Test

Soils are classified as clay, sandy or loamy soils. Clay is nutrient rich, but slow draining. Sand is quick draining, but can't retain nutrients and moisture. Loam is an ideal mixture of decomposed organic matter filled with nutrients.

To determine your soil type, take a handful of moist (but not wet) soil from your garden, and give it a firm squeeze. Then, open your hand.

One of three things will happen:

~ It will hold its shape, and it crumbles when you poke it. This means you have good loam.

~ It will hold its shape, and sits stubbornly in your hand when poked. This means you have clay.

~ It will fall apart as soon as you open your hand. This means it's sandy.

~ Soil Test #2:
The Percolation Test

It is important to determine whether you have drainage problems or not. Most plants will die if their roots stay wet.

To test your soil's drainage:

~ Dig a hole about six inches wide and one foot deep.

~ Fill the hole with water and let it drain completely.

~ Fill it with water again.

~ Keep track of how long it takes for the water to drain the second time.

If the water takes more than four hours to drain, you have poor drainage. You will need to add sand.

~ Soil Test #3:
The Worm Test

If you have earthworms, you should also have all of the beneficial microbes and bacteria that make healthy soil and therefore strong plants.

To do the worm test:

~ Be sure the soil has warmed to at least 55 degrees, and that it is at least somewhat moist, but not soaking wet.

~ Dig a hole one foot across and one foot deep. Place the soil on a tarp or piece of plastic.

~ Sift through the soil with your hands (gloves are okay) as you place it back into the hole, counting the earthworms as you go.

~ At least ten worms should be in this amount of soil. Less than that indicates that there may not be enough organic matter to support a healthy worm population, or that your soil is too acidic or alkaline. More worms means you have spares to go fishing or start a vermiculture farm.

~ Soil Test #4:
The PH Test

The Ph (acidity level) of your soil must be the correct balance. Ph is rated on a scale of zero to fourteen; zero is acidic and fourteen is alkaline. Most plants grow best in soil with a fairly neutral Ph, between six and seven. When the Ph level is lower than five or higher than eight, plants will not thrive.

Every home and garden center carries Ph test kits that can be mailed to a testing center. Make sure you follow the testing instructions precisely. Please note that the PH level of soil can be different within a few feet or yards, depending on things like overhanging trees, rocks and concrete which change the PH level nearby.

If your plants are still struggling after you've made the necessary amendments and checked for disease and insects, the next step is to contact your local cooperative extension service. They will tell you how to go about collecting a soil sample and sending it to their lab for a thorough analysis. They will return a report that will alert you to any mineral deficiencies in your soil, as well as steps to correct the issues.

~ Amending Soil

Bear in mind that different amendments take longer than others to break down. As far as organic amendments, manure takes weeks to break down, compost months and shredded bark and peat moss years. All are valuable and can be used at once or applied over time. If you live in an area where winters are cold, a spring application of faster materials is advised. Manure, compost and commercial additives should be thoroughly mixed prior to incorporating into the top 6" of soil. Mulches are spread on top of the soil for protection, weed prevention and to break down slowly into loam.

~ Soil Ratios

There are as many opinions about soil ratios and ingredients as there are gardeners. Some use a 50/50 combination of top soil and compost, some use 1/3 vermiculite, 1/3 compost and 1/3 peat moss. In the Giving Garden we've had great success with mushroom soil (which contains horse manure) and township mulch mixed with some topsoil and a little lime to reduce the acidity of the mulch.

If you want to make your own compost, it is important to pay attention to the carbon to nitrogen ratios of the ingredients you are adding. Too much of one or the other could be death to your plants, regardless of how good your compost appears to the naked eye.

~ Compost

Do an online search for "compost mix calculator." This makes it easy to know how to adjust the amount needed to maintain a healthy carbon/nitrogen balance. Not all calculators will list all ingredients, so search for one that does.

In case you have access to fresh manure or wood products, don't be tempted to use them directly in the garden until they have aged. Manure should not be used on plants until it is aged six months, and wood until it is aged a year. However, those time periods can best be spent in the compost bin, where they will help break down the compost more quickly. The fresher the manure, the hotter (literally hotter ~ i.e. contains more nitrogen) the compost pile. Not all manure is equal. Manure contains both poo and pee (high in nitrogen) and the bedding (high in carbon,) but different animals and bedding produce these at different nitrogen ratios. Bird manure is the hottest of all, so use sparingly.

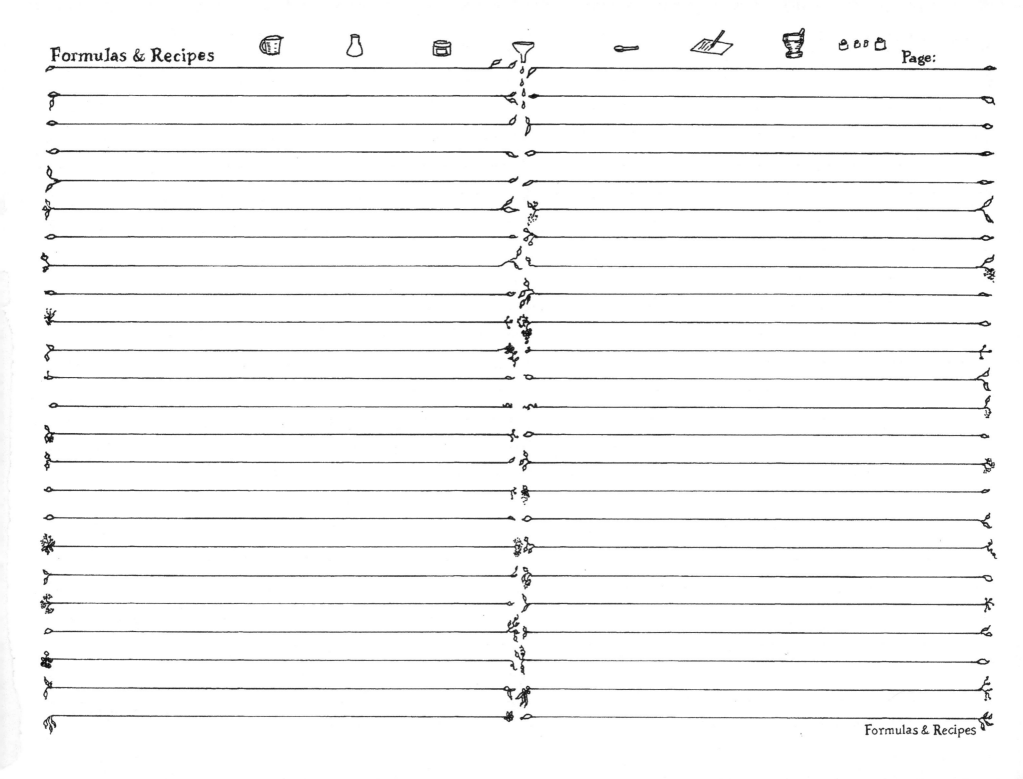

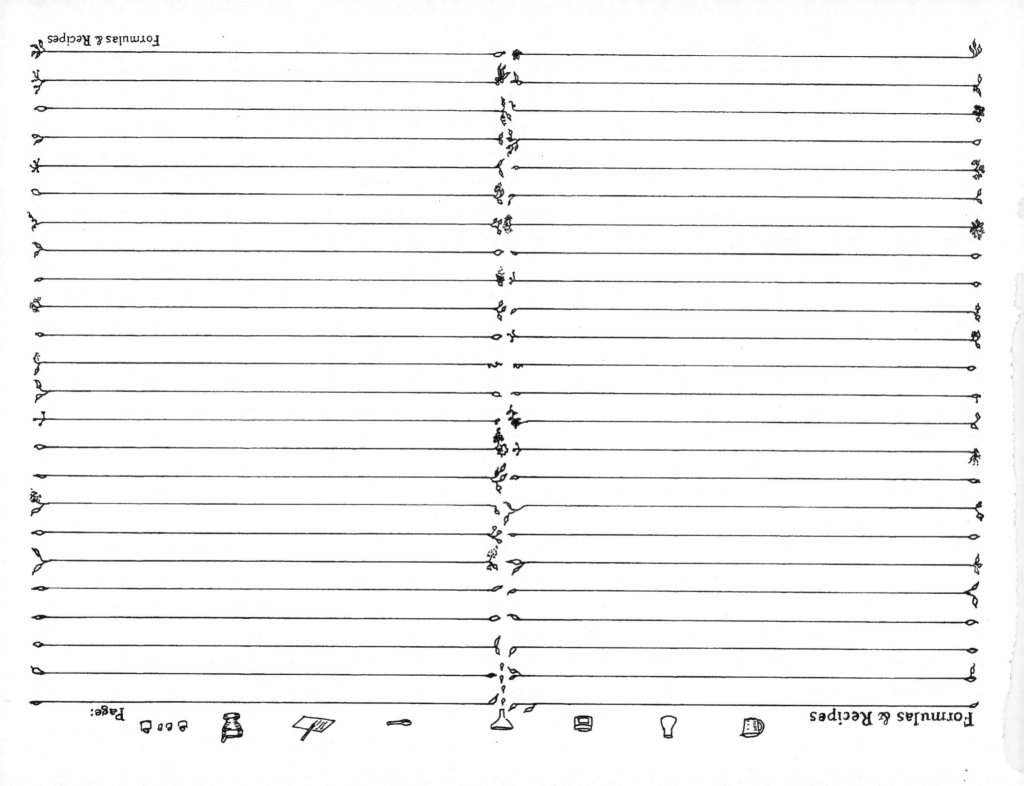

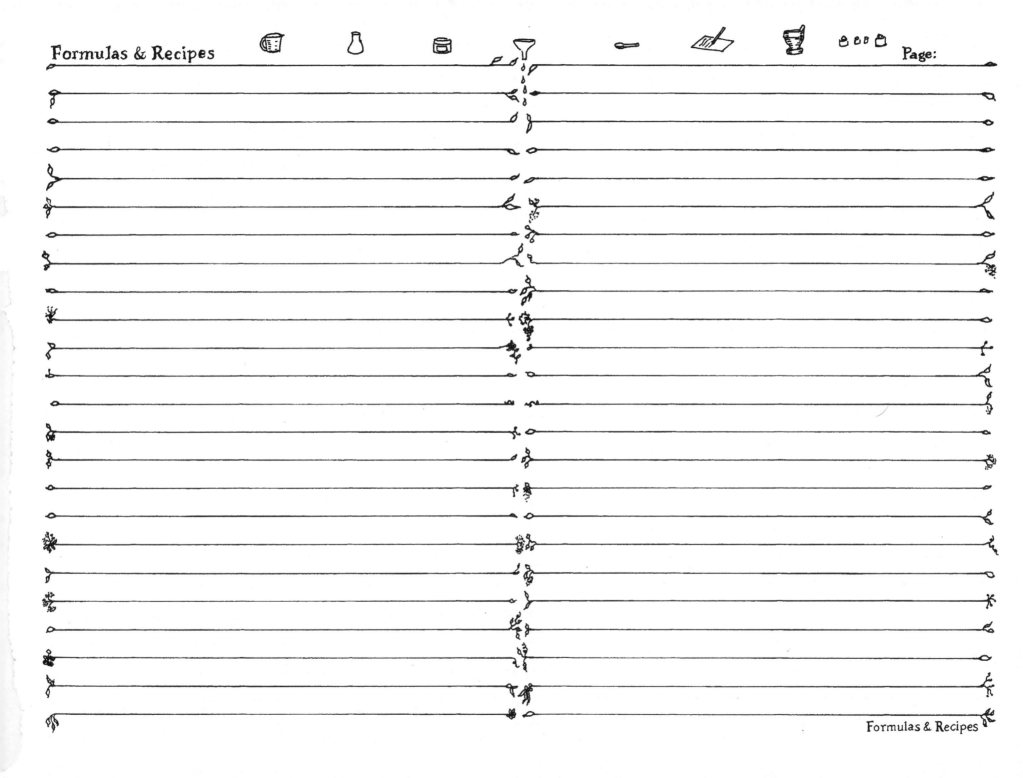

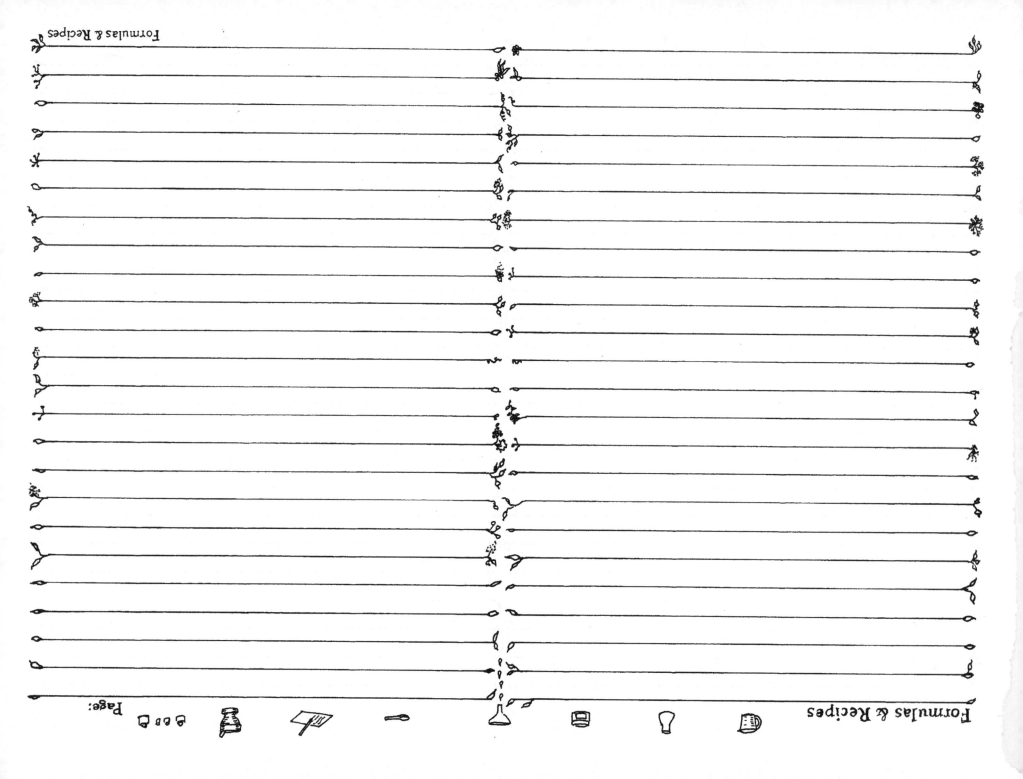

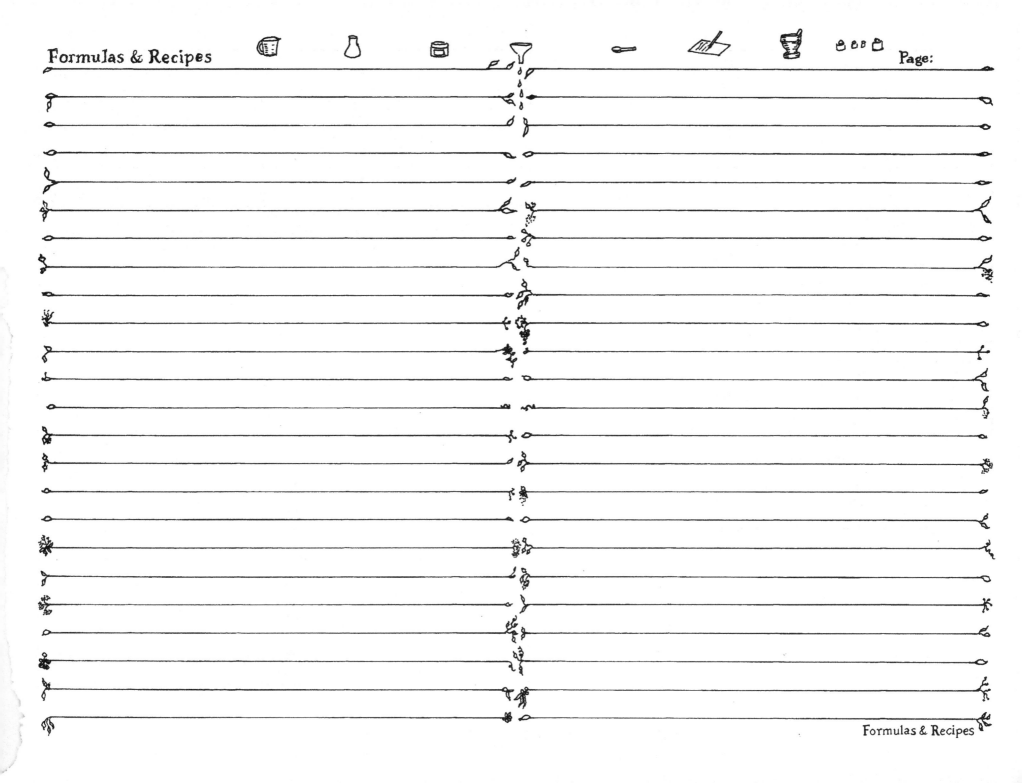

Conversion Charts and Tables

Dry material weight		
1 ounce (avoirdupois)	=	28.4 grams (g)
1 pound (lb)	=	453.6 g
1 kilogram (kg)	=	1,000 g = 2.2 lb
Volume		
1 cubic inch (in^3)	=	16.4 milliliters (ml)
1 cubic foot (ft^3)	=	7.48 gal = 28.3 liters (l)
1 bushel (bu)	=	1.24 ft^3 = 35.2 liters
1 cubic yard (yd^3)	=	21.7 bu = 765 liters
Linear		
1 inch (in)	=	2.54 centimeters (cm)
1 foot (ft)	=	30.48 cm
1 yard (yd)	=	91.44 cm
1 meter (m)	=	100 cm
Area		
1 square inch (in^2)	=	6.45 square centimeters (cm^2)
1 square foot (ft^2)	=	0.09 square meter (m^2)
1 square yard (yd^2)	=	0.84 square meter (m^2)
1 acre (a)	=	0.40 hectare (ha)
1 square mile (M^2)	=	2.59 square kilometer (km^2)

Equivalent quantities of dry materials (wettable powders) for various quantities of water based on recommended pounds per 100 gallons

Water	Recommended Rate					
100 gal	**1 lb**	**2 lb**	**3 lb**	**4 lb**	**5 lb**	**6 lb**
50 gal	½ lb	1 lb	1½ lb	2 lb	2½ lb	3 lb
25 gal	4 oz	8 oz	12 oz	1 lb	1¼ lb	1½ lb
12.5 gal	2 oz	4 oz	6 oz	8 oz	10 oz	¾ lb
5 gal	3 tbs	1½ oz	2½ oz	3¼ oz	4 oz	5 oz
1 gal	1 tsp	2 tsp	1 tbs	4 tsp	5 tsp	2 tbs

Example : The directions specify a rate of 4 lb per 100 gal. water. 1 gal of solution would require 4 tsp of material

Rate of application equivalent table		
Rate Per Acre	**Rate Per 1000 sq ft**	**Rate per 100 sq ft**
Liquid Materials		
1 pt	¾ tbs	¼ tsp
1 qt	1½ tbs	½ tsp
1 gal	6 tbs	2 tsp
25 gal	4^2/3 pt	½ pt
50 gal	4^2/3 qt	1 pt
100 gal	2^1/3 gal	1 qt
200 gal	4^2/3 gal	2 qt
300 gal	7 gal	3 qt
400 gal	9¼ gal	1 gal
500 gal	11½ gal	1¼ gal
Dry Materials		
1 lb	2½ tsp	¼ tsp
3 lb	2¼ tbs	¾ tsp
4 lb	3 tbs	1 tsp
5 lb	4 tbs	1¼ tsp
10 lb	½ cup	2 tsp
100 lb	2^1/3 lb	¼ lb
200 lb	4^2/3 lb	½ lb
300 lb	7 lb	¾ lb
400 lb	9¼ lb	1 lb
500 lb	11½ lb	1¼ lb

Dilution of liquid pesticides at various concentrations

Dilution	Amount Desired			
	1 Gal	3 Gal	5 Gal	15 Gal
1-100	2 tbs + 2 tsp	½ cup	¾ cup + 5 tsp	1 cup + 3 tbs
1-200	4 tsp	¼ cup	6½ tbs	½ cup + 2 tbs
1-400	2 tsp	2 tbs	3 tbs	4 tbs + 2½ tsp
1-800	1 tsp	1 tbs	1 tbs + 2 tsp	3 tbs + 2½ tsp
1-1000	¾ tsp	2¼ tsp	1 tbs + 1 tsp	1 pt +½ cup

Coverage estimates for perlite, peat, topsoil and straw

Thickness	4 cu ft	6 cu ft	1 cu yd*	1 Bale	
	Perlite	Canadian peat (compressed)	Peat mulches		
			Topsoil, etc.	Pinestraw	Wheatstraw
2 in	28 sq ft	72 sq ft	162 sq ft	90 sq ft	180 sq ft
1 in	48 sq ft	144 sq ft	324 sq ft	180 sq ft	360 sq ft
½ in	96 sq ft	288 sq ft	648 sq ft	360 sq ft	720 sq ft
¼ in	192 sq ft	576 sq ft	1296 sq ft	720 sq ft	1440 sq ft

Liquid Measurement Conversion Table

					Units of Measure:				
Gallons (gal)	Quarts (qt)	Pints (pt)	Fluid Ounces (fl oz)	Cups (C)	Tablespoons (tbs)	Teaspoons (tsp)	Milliliters (ml)	Cubic Centimeters (cc)	Liters (l)
1	4	8	128	16					
	1	2	32	4					
		1	16	2	32				
			1	1/8	2	6	30		
				1	16	48	240		
					1	3	15		
						1	5		
							1	1	
							1000	1000	1

Conversion Charts and Tables

About the Author

 Joy comes from a long line of farmers, but it wasn't until she worked for J. Franklin Styer Nurseries, a major contributor to the Philadelphia Flower Show, that she learned that not everything should be planted in rows. She and her father still laugh about his single line of tulips across the front yard. After his own stint working for a nursery he has developed his property into a miniature Longwood Gardens. The Garden Journal, Record and Log book is the result of knowledge gained from her father, the library and co-workers at Styer Nurseries, her experience running the Lifewerks Giving Garden ~ a food pantry garden ~ as well as maintenance of gardens at four properties.

Made in the USA
Monee, IL
22 September 2020